Thomas Edward

Irish Methodist reminiscences

Being mainly memorials of the life and labours of the Rev. S. Nicholson

Thomas Edward

Irish Methodist reminiscences
Being mainly memorials of the life and labours of the Rev. S. Nicholson

ISBN/EAN: 9783744726849

Printed in Europe, USA, Canada, Australia, Japan

Cover: Foto ©Thomas Meinert / pixelio.de

More available books at **www.hansebooks.com**

IRISH METHODIST

REMINISCENCES;

BEING MAINLY MEMORIALS OF THE LIFE AND LABOURS

OF THE

Rev. S. NICHOLSON.

BY

EDWARD THOMAS.

"The Holy Ghost was upon him."

LONDON:

J. C. WATTS, 30, FURNIVAL STREET, HOLBORN, E.C.

1889.

PREFACE.

THE reasons for the appearance of this volume are
various. It contains a wife's tribute of affection
to the memory of her sainted husband. He still
lives in her heart and every-day life, and she knows—

> "The touch of a vanished hand,
> And the sound of a voice that is still."

When asking us to undertake the compilation of the
memorial, Mrs. Nicholson said:—"My only motive in
desiring Mr. Nicholson's life to be given to the world is
that thereby God may be glorified and good done." This
wish agrees with the supreme aim of our departed brother's
life on earth, which was to glorify God and save men.
And surely even in the glorified state, it would be a great
joy to Mr. Nicholson to know that the aim of his life is
being promoted by the story of that life.

The issue of Christian biographies finds much of its
justification in the welcome they receive and the edification and comfort they confessedly bring to many devout
hearts.

a

The history contained in the fourth chapter is not intended to revive the controversy of a past age, but to supply what did not exist in connected form—an account of the origin, &c., of the Methodist New Connexion in Ireland. It seemed desirable to supply the friends of the Denomination with a reliable account of its inception and early labours. In the preparation of the memorial, we could not forbear casting side-glances at concurrent events and contemporaneous individuals. These glances, we hope, will prove, as they are designed to be, interesting and edifying to Methodist New Connexionists in general, and more particularly to the descendants of many of the good men and women whose names will be found scattered throughout the following pages. We have written under difficulties, inexperience in this kind of work being not the least of them, and our ordinary duties required unabated attention. If our narrative be the means, under God, of inspiring any mind with a devout thought, a holy purpose or aspiration; or if it incite any one to "attempt great things for God, and to expect great things from God;" or if it be the means of encouraging some souls under conscious guilt to look to Samuel Nicholson's Saviour, we shall be abundantly rewarded for our toil. It is but due to her to record the fact, that the work would have been impossible had it not been for the material supplied by Mrs. Nicholson, at the cost of much labour.

E. T.

BROOMHEDGE, LISBURN,
    Co. ANTRIM, *May*, 1889.

CONTENTS.

CHAPTER IV.

CHAPTER V.

CHAPTER VI.

CHAPTER VII.

viii.

CHAPTER X.

IRISH METHODIST REMINISCENCES.

CHAPTER I.

PARENTAGE.

"1 call to remembrance the unfeigned faith that is in thee, which dwelt first in thy grandmother Lois, and thy mother Eunice; and I am persuaded that in thee also."—*Paul.*

SAMUEL NICHOLSON was a descendant of a Huguenot family, who, in the days of dire persecution, found refuge in Scotland; whence they afterwards crossed to Ireland, and settled amongst other French refugees near Lisburn. Mr. Nicholson's paternal grandfather, Samuel Nicholson, was able to trace his descent from French ancestors. *The Burn,* a large farm near Dromara, Co. Down, was the property of Mr. Samuel Nicholson, and on it he had his residence. He likewise had a knowledge of the linen-trade, which industry he pursued with success. Miles says, "The settlement in the North of Ireland of many Huguenot families, expelled from France in 1685, exercised a most beneficial influence in this branch of industry (linen)." Popery cursed and expatriated them, but the curse fell upon France recoiling upon the Papacy, and it was changed into a blessing upon the exiled, and upon the peoples amongst whom they found sanctuary. In the days of the senior Samuel Nicholson, the linen-trade was but in its infancy. They were the days of the spinning-wheel and the hand-loom, scattered throughout the homes of a rural population. Mr. Nicholson bought the linen in its brown state, had it bleached, and conveyed it to Dublin for sale. Mr. John Richardson, father of the great manufacturers of Bessbrook & C., said that he had often stood beside Mr. Nicholson on the " cloth stands " in Dublin, when disposing of his linen ; and of the latter's character Mr. Richardson spoke in most favourable terms.

During Mr. Nicholson's trading visits to Dublin, he often heard the Methodist Itinerants preach; and their word was with power. They were savagely attacked by Papist mobs ; but the soldiers of the cross " stood like the brave with their face to the foe," and succeeded in planting their standard in the Irish metropolis. The linen merchant was counselled by the preachers in the words of the Apostle : " Buy of Me gold tried in the fire that thou mayest be rich ; and white raiment, that thou mayest be clothed, and that the shame of thy nakedness do not appear ; and anoint thine eyes with eyesalve, that thou mayest see." And the preaching had a peculiar adhesive quality about it which caused it to stick so fast to the devoted man's conscience that he found it well nigh impossible to shake it off. But the preachers of those days soon traversed the entire Kingdom. At length they reached the neighbourhood of *The Burn*, and Mr. Nicholson heard them near his own house. One of them named Barber (doubtless Thomas Barber), after preaching one evening, announced that on his next visit he would preach at Mr. Samuel Nicholson's of the *Burn*. This took Mr. Nicholson by surprise, as he had not been consulted. " However," he soliloquised, "it will do no harm for once." So Mr. Barber, in due course, returned to preach in the house of the staunch Presbyterian. More people attended than could be accommodated in-doors, and the service had to be held ontside, on the ample lawn in front of the dwelling. Mr. Nicholson was right, the preaching "did no harm for that once." But the preacher returned again and again, and at length harm was done, but it was to Satan's Kingdom: two sons and three daughters were converted to God; and a class of about forty members was formed. The good seed sown at the *Burn* bore ample fruit, which was carried to other parts where it was made a blessing. Mr. Nicholson's son, Samuel, was one of the converts. He proceeded to Edinburgh to study for the Presbyterian ministry, but when the time came, he found himself unable conscientiously to sign the Confession of Faith. He afterwards spent some time in the study of Medicine. Ultimately he settled at the *Burn*, where for over fifty years he lived a devoted Christian life, preaching the Gospel locally with much success. Two of his sisters were married to men named Carson, brothers, who resided at Rathmullen. The Methodist preachers of the Down-patrick Circuit found preaching places and homes in these good men's houses during their lives.

Mr. Nicholson, senior, had a remarkable and precise answer to prayer, which deeply impressed the minds of those who knew of it at the time. He was prostrated with a severe illness, and for a time his life seemed to tremble in the balance. In his extremity, the case of Hezekiah's sickness and restoration, came vividly before his mind. Like the king, he prayed to be spared; and an impresion was made upon his mind, that he would not then die, but would be spared a certain number of years. When the term

of years promised drew near to a close, he informed one of
the preachers, that the added years of his life were nearly
gone. Accordingly, in the year predicted, with but little
suffering, and, in "sure and certain hope," he "fell on
sleep."

This good man's son, John, one of the two sons who
were amongst the first converts at the *Burn*, was the father
of the subject of this memorial. John Nicholson, during his
father's lifetime, married Elizabeth Whitley, of Whitley's
Hill, Co. Armagh. Her forefathers crossed to Ireland
with the army of Oliver Cromwell, and remained in the
country, taking up farms in the Co., Armagh; and the
hill where they located came to be known as Whitley's Hill.
Elizabeth Whitley's parents held sittings in the Presbyterian Church, and were members of the Methodist
Society likewise, the preachers visiting and preaching in
their house regularly. Elizabeth was an earnest Christian
and met in class regularly before her marriage. John
Nicholson and his wife, Elizabeth, resided at the *Burn* for
some time after their marriage. It was here their eldest
child, the Samuel Nicholson of our narrative, was born, on
February 14th, 1811. Soon after this happy event, John
Nicholson with his wife and child removed to a farm
called Spring Valley, near Aghaloo, in the Co. Antrim,
the gift of his father. It was here that Samuel Nicholson
spent the first twenty-four years of his life, till he was
called of God to enter the Methodist ministry.

Mrs. Elizabeth Nicholson was stately and handsome in
person, and a woman of vigorous mind and of a strong
resolute will; and she had aquired much valuable knowledge from reading, for which she had a taste. The
Bible was her principal study; she loved it ardently, and
with its sacred contents was intelligently familiar. She

was governed by the highest principles of true Christian motherhood. Her sanctified maternal instincts and the impulses of the new nature within impelled her to aim supremely, and to pray continuously, and to strive earnestly for the salvation of her first-born, as also for that of all the children which God afterward gave her to train for Him.

The story of Hannah and her son, Samuel, was much upon her mind. Had not she, too, been "heard of God?" Had not the Lord given her a son whose appropriate name was Samuel? And had she not vowed to "give him unto the Lord all the days of his life?" Would not the Lord, therefore, accept the gift? She believed He would; and according to her faith it was done unto her. But to her faith and prayer, or rather because of them, she added appropriate works. In his diary, Mr. Nicholson wrote:—
"When very young, my mother taught me to pray. She used to take me with her into the parlour and make me kneel down beside her, before I understood what it meant. Often I wondered what she was whispering about, when her lips moved in prayer." She was careful to impress upon her little boy's mind, that he was not hers but the Lord's. "She often told me," wrote Mr. N——, "that she had solemnly promised to dedicate me to the Lord from my birth, and that I should be His for ever." Like Hannah, her holy ambition was that her boy should become a prophet of the Lord; and she succeded in causing him while yet a child to share fully in the interest which she herself felt in the Samuel of Bible story. Thus Samuel Nicholson's training for God *began with his life.* His mother did not wait to see what manner of child her son should be, but forthwith in prayerful dependence upon God, set about making him the manner

of child she meant him to be. Her influence antedated that of the great enemy of souls; and claiming by faith the Holy Spirit for her child, she succeeded in having holy principles planted in his mind before innate evil tendencies gained strength or full sway.

The Day School of sixty years ago was a very primitive affair indeed. The teacher's mental furniture, like his purse, was not very rich, and the teaching was emphatically rudimentary. Young Samuel, therefore, as a pupil, had to plod on under unfavourable conditions. To this fact he often referred with regret in after life. But in his earlier years his mother was his principal tutor; and there was at least one branch of knowledge in which she made her pupil proficient, and that was a knowledge of the Scriptures. The words addressed to Timothy applied to him—" From a child thou hast known the holy scriptures."

Samuel continued his attendance at school, and also, so soon as able, rendered what help he could upon his father's farm. It was intended at first, to send him to an academy at a distance, and to give him a superior education, but this was found impracticable. The lease of the farm expiring, the rent was raised to a figure so high, that every resource and effort were exhausted in the struggle to pay it. In this, however, was seen the Hand of Providence. Had Samuel gone from under his mother's care and training before he received the full assurance of the Divine favour, he might have lost the prayerful habits and godly principles in which he had been brought up, as the teaching and associations of the public school in those days were unfavourable, if not hostile, to spiritual religion. In our view, godly parents are wrong in giving over the training of their children into the hands of ungodly tutors.

When about eight years of age, Samuel was prostrated under a virulent fever, caught by contagion from a farm servant, who had brought the disease upon himself through gross negligence. Samuel suffered long and was highly delirious, the chief medicine administered aggravating rather than assuaging the disease. Seventy years ago, the idea prevailed in Ireland, that whiskey possessed a wonderful and varied potency as a medicine; even the Faculty shared in the pernicious delusion. But medical skill was not always thought necessary to determine the measure of the dose, or as to how often it should be taken. As a medicine whiskey had many attractions. It was thought to be good for the nurse as well as the patient; and the doctor and clergyman were thought to be strengthened and comforted by a drop of this wonderful medicine when pursuing their arduous duties. And so, under medical instruction, Samuel was severely dosed with whiskey, till he could hardly be detained in bed. One day he was left alone for a short time, and when his mother returned, she found him prostrate on the floor and insensible, he having risen, as he said, to dress himself. To the ill effects of the whiskey, given to him at this time, Mr. Nicholson always attributed the nervous weakness from which he suffered, often causing him great discomfort till the end of his life. During Samuel's illness, however, his parents made intercession for him continually; and the mercy of God in restoring him to health made a deep impression on the youth's susceptible mind.

Mr. Nicholson's parents continued to maintain their dual church-relationship by attending the Presbyterian Meeting house, and receiving the Methodist preacher's visits, till Samuel was about ten years of age, several additional children having been born to them in the interim from

their settlement at Spring Valley. But at this time a
change came, and the double church connection was given
up. Many of the Presbyterian ministers of those days
were Arian in doctrine, and by no means holy in life. The
one whom the Nicholsons called their minister came to
Spring Valley to baptize one of the children; but he was
unfit to perform the ceremony properly, he being under
the influence of drink. It should be remembered that this
occurred prior to the days of Dr. Edgar, and teetotalism.
Mrs. Nicholson, however, would never again enter the
meeting-house of that minister. At this early age Samuel
had an active enquiring mind, and was keenly observant of
all that was passing around him. Being her first-born and
specially beloved son, he was constantly under his mother's
maturer influence and made to share in all her deliberations,
and thus his mind was prematurely developed. Hearing
much upon the subject he took an active interest in the
comparative merits of the churches around him; and he
was not discouraged, but helped in his inquiries by his
mother.

Mr. Nicholson wrote :—

. " When about ten years old I had an inquiring mind for one so
young. I visited several churches in order to try and determine
for myself which was the best—the Moravian, Episcopal, and other
churches I visited in turn. But I found that the preaching of the
Methodists was plainer and more earnest than that of the others,
and I understood and enjoyed it best of all. But I did not at first
like the class-meetings or Lovefeasts, as they seemed to me like
the popish confessional. Yet I began to enjoy the services at the
Chapel and in my father's house."

Methodism in Ireland had experienced a great agitation
for and against the administration of the Sacraments. A
resolution in favour of their administration under certain
restrictions was passed by the Conference of 1814. As

the Connexion was divided upon the question, there followed, all over the country, great commotion and hot discussion. The Conference of 1816 declared again in favour of administering the Sacraments. But the question rent the Connexion in twain. The party against the administration of the Sacraments called themselves "Primitive Wesleyans," to signify that they were abiding by Mr. Wesley's express injunctions—that his followers should not leave the Church. They likewise decided that their Conference should be composed of preachers and laymen in equal numbers. Mr. John Nicholson and his family joined that division of Wesleyanism whose ministers now (1821) fully exercised their inalienable right to administer all the ordinances of the Gospel of Christ. Moira, where a chapel had recently been built, was head of the Circuit of which Spring Valley became a regular monthly preaching place. With the town of Moira is associated the name of a very remarkable maiden lady, Anne Lutton, born in 1791, and died, at Bristol, in 1881. This lady described the introduction of Methodism into Moira thus :—

"It was Sunday; a stranger rode up to the principal inn, dismounted, unstrapped a huge pair of saddle-bags, and flinging them over his arm, walked into the house. My father observed that the stranger was probably a Methodist preacher, 'My dear,' said he. addressing his wife, 'shall we ask him to come in and share our dinner ?' In half an hour the master and mistress of the mansion and eight children sat around the dinner table, with Mr. Jno. Grace, the Methodist preacher, occupying the most honourable place beside the lady. That Sabbath was the 'beginning of days' to a household which had hitherto 'sat in darkness.'"*

Anne Lutton was born a few months after the event just described; but she was not born of the Spirit till'

---

* Memorals of a Consecrated Life.

over twenty-four years thereafter. Here is, in part, her
own account of her conversion :—

"'O mother!' I exclaimed, 'if I do not get my sins pardoned, I shall
perish everlastingly!'—I went to my own room, knelt down at the
bedside, clasped my hands most imploringly, and with streaming
eyes said, ' O Lord God, I here most solemnly and heartily, with
all the faith I know how to use, cast my whole soul at Thy feet,
and take the Lord Jesus Christ as my Saviour from this moment,
and my Master and portion for time and for eternity, and will
henceforth believe I am forgiven for His sake.' As I abandoned
myself to Him so He gave Himself to me. There was an immediate
sense of acceptance.—Oh, such a love as never, never had I before
conceived !"

From this happy event onward, Miss Lutton's pathway
was one of increasing light, and her service in the Gospel
one of accumulating power. Her mental powers were of
the first order and surprisingly varied, and she cultured
them with rare diligence and amazing success. She
became an able metaphysician, an extraordinary linguist,
a mathematician, a musician, a poet of a high order, and
read innumerable volumes in nearly every department of
literature, and in fifteen different languages of which she
acquired an accurate knowledge. She made the Bible
her chief study, and many who heard her lucid and learn-
edly simple expositions of the Scriptures urged her to
write a commentary, but she modestly declined. She
preached the Gospel for years in and around Moira, and
throughout Ulster and elsewhere; but to women only.
She became a class-leader, having at times charge of three
and four classes. The latter half of her Christian life and
activities was spent in Bristol, twenty years of which she
was blind. Her name, and "the good works and alms-
deeds which she did " will not be forgotten in that City
for generations to come. Miss Lutton's refusal to allow

---

† Ibid.

males to hear her preach was most peremptory; and many
stories ludicrous enough are told of men dressed in women's
attire, seeking admission amongst her audiences, whose
curiosity received very humiliating rebuke. Mrs. Nicholson
was frequently one of the lady-preacher's most devout and
interested hearers; and her household was favoured with
very full reports of the discourses afterwards. Often did
her son Samuel tell of his having acted as door-keeper for
Miss Lutton. Most faithfully had he performed the Gospel
service. Not one of the proscribed gender escaped his
vigilant eye. It was a gospel to elect ladies only; and
even he refrained from bringing his masculine ears too
near the keyhole, through which some of the glad sounds
were passing. Probably at this time the germ was planted
in his mind of that predilection for female preachers which
he afterwards showed.

We have given the foregoing brief sketch of Miss Anne
Lutton, as we think it of great interest in itself, and because
it illustrates the high spiritual influences and agencies
which were in operation in the locality where Samuel
Nicholson's character was built up and his higher inspirations generated. In the Society at Moira, there were
men who were mighty in prayer and exhortation, and most
devoted and faithful as class leaders. In his notes, Mr.
Nicholson tells of remarkable meetings which he remembered, held at Moira, when he was a boy. He speaks of
prayer meetings of great " power," where " good, plain
men of God poured out their souls' desires to the Lord for
their families and the young," and of "the Holy Ghost,"
at such times, " falling upon old and young, mightily
convincing of sin, and making plain the path of duty. He
speaks also of numerous and striking conversions.

A friend named Mrs. Gibson came to reside near Spring

Valley, whom Mrs. Nicholson had known before either of them was married. They had been companions, and had met in class together in their maiden days; and now that they both had families, whom they were resolved by God's grace and help to train in His fear, they again became companions; and took sweet counsel together about the things of God, and they were mutually helpful to one another in their maternal anxieties and duties. Young Samuel heard these devoted mothers say—" We must take our children with us on the Sabbath Day. All the meetings are needed—public worship, class meeting, the Sabbath School, and the prayer meetings, to keep the children fully employed, leaving them no time to serve the devil." Excellent resolution, and it was fully and prayerfully carried out in the spirit in which it had been conceived. Samuel at this time, was nearly eleven years of age, and he mentally consented to his mother's resolution, except as regarded the class, which he disliked.

He was becoming increasingly sensible of the motions of the old nature within him ; often to his eye, the forbidden path seemed more pleasant than the path of duty ; and the struggle in his mind between inclination and a sense of duty was fierce at many times. This struggle is experienced by all the saved ere they enter the liberty of the Gospel. From his *memoranda* we learn, that Samuel had a severe struggle when passing through the seventh chapter of Romans to the eighth (many reverse the Divine order by placing the 7th after the 8th). He felt the motions within him of opposing principles and inclinations, which swayed him, now to the side of the good, and anon to the side of evil, but with greater force. He had been trained in good habits, his conscience was enlightened with Divine truth, and the Spirit of God was upon him reproving him of sin, and showing him that "the law is holy, and the commandment holy and just and good." His reason and will power fully inclined him towards obedience to the good law of God; but he lacked power to obey, and the principle of rebellion prevailed over the better principle. It was, he felt, a wretched state; and, though but a boy, he was painfully sensible of it, and groaned for deliverance. His whole outward life was without a stain from its beginning till its close. At any age he might truthfully have said, "All these have I kept from my youth up? But at the time about which we now speak (his eleventh year), he felt the rebel heart within. Class meeting severely tested him and made enquiries and demands, against which the carnal man rebelled. The atmosphere of the class seemed to aggravate the struggle within him. Hence he writes, "I did not like the class meeting. It seemed to me that if I attended it, I should have had to give up many of my little pleasures . . . The class and the Lovefeast I did detest. . . I trembled at the thought of being so closely united with the Methodists." His "precious" mother, however, as he designates her, reasoned the matter with her "darling" boy, showing him that the interchange of Christian experience was Scriptural and binding; and that the class would help him on in the ways of God. She went further and absolutely required him to remain with her for the class, after the morning service; and he never outwardly rebelled against her authority; and besides, his filial love was deep and strong. He writes, "This blessed mother compelled me to go to class, but it was greatly against my mind. Well, I had only attended it a short time till the Spirit of God came upon me showing me that I was a sinner."

Shortly after this, when Samuel was eleven years of
age, the Rev. John Armstrong came to labour upon the
Moira Circuit, of whom Mr. Nicholson writes, "He was a
holy, devoted man of God; not talented as a preacher,
but mighty in prayer." He was a Connaught man, born
in 1788, and he retained a rich trace of the brogue. He
was stout, round, low of stature, rough in features, homely
in dress, his hair was coarse and stood straight up in defiance
of all efforts to make it look sleek and clerical. The writer
has a vivid recollection of Mr. Armstrong. He was
familiarly known as " Johnny Armstrong;" and was
quite an "original character." In his early life as a
preacher he had travelled on the "General Mission,"
often preaching in fairs and markets, or elsewhere to
Romish mobs, and "enduring hardness as a good soldier
of Jesus Christ." Sixteen years ago he related the
"Story of his Life," as a lecture, for Mr. Nicholson, at
Newtownards. The writer heard the lecture, and he is sure
the reader will be pleased with an extract or two from it;
they are from memory. Mr. Armstrong said :—

"When I was called out on the General Mission, I was told to
go straight to Kilrea. When near that town I overtook a man,
and began to ask him some questions about Kilrea. I wanted to
know about the Methodists ; but I went round it a bit. 'Now, is
there a Church in Kilrea?' 'O yes,' replied the man, 'there's wan
not far aff.' 'Now, and is there a Chapel?' 'A Chapel!' said the
stranger, 'there is for sure.' Well, now [here the lecturer dropped
his voice to a rough whisper] and is there any Methodis' in the
town?' 'There is,' replied the man, 'two prachers—one is a tinker
and the other is a cooper. The tinker will be out through the
country with his budget; but the cooper will likely be at home
minding his work.' I soon found the cooper, Jack Mc. Dougall,
and told him I had been sent there to join Gideon Ouseley as a
preacher of the Gospel. Jack's wife was preparing dinner, down
in a kitchen cellar. 'Biddy,' shouted Jack, down the trap door

'here's the pracher, put another herin' on the fire.'" When the young preacher met his superintendent, he asked for his plan. "Plan, my son!" exclaimed Ouseley, "I have no plan to give you The whole country is before you; go into every house where you will get leave to preach, exhort, or pray."

Mr. Armstrong had a rich tinge of native humour in his nature; and in his lecture he also related the following incident; in most witty style. He had preached in the market at Castlebleyney, calming Popish anger by singing a verse of a hymn in Irish; and after some time, returned again to the same place, and proposed a third visit, if any person would give him accommodation. He returned and found a lodging at the house of a kind countryman, whose wife was a Romanist. During the night the tail of his horse was cut off. The hair, however, was found, and his hostess sewed it to the leg of a stocking, drew it up over the stump, and fastened it to the saddle. "This contrivance," said Mr. Armstrong, "did very well till the hair grew, and then I cast it away." Here the lecturer bent forward, and assuming a most comical expression, added, "When I came near a respectable town, I always looked behind to see if my tail was in its place."

Mr. Armstrong's earnest manner, short lively sermons, "mighty" prayers, and great revivalistic tact in conducting meetings, made him very popular in and around Moira, drawing crowds to hear him preach. To young Samuel Nicholson the new preacher was a great attraction, and continued ever after a special favourite. Indeed Mr. Armstrong evidently stamped his own impress upon the plastic mind of our young friend; as in after life, when a preacher himself, Mr. Nicholson's preaching and methods bore more than an incidental resemblance to those of the preacher of his special early admiration and love.

And now we reach that point in Samuel Nicholson's history known in Methodistic and Scriptural phraseology, as conversion—that great spiritual crisis in his history when the direct consciousness of the Divine favour was given him, and the filial spirit sensibly inspired his breast, and when he received full power over inbred sin. Hannah's lips "moved," and Eli grossly mistook the significance of their motion; Elizabeth Nicholson's lips moved in like manner, and her little son wondered what his mother's whispering meant; but God understood the motion of these mothers' lips, and to their importunate prayers lent an approving ear. Elizabeth Nicholson gave her child to God, at his birth, and even before his birth, and she prayed and waited on in faith, till she was assured that her first-born was an adopted child of God. We believe Samuel Nicholson was a subject of special grace from his birth; and that the struggle within him of the evil against the good, and the good against the evil, resembled that with which every child of grace is familiar. But not till the period of which we now write, was his understanding fully enlightened to perceive and receive Christ as his wisdom, righteousness, sanctification, and redemption—his Saviour and Redeemer, as well from sinning as from sin. Doubtless with his physical and mental growth, there likewise grew in his experience the sense of his need of a Saviour; and this prepared and qualified him, to receive the full revelation of his Redeemer, which was given him at the period we call conversion.

We have known several devoted Christians who had given them at their conversion, a very vivid conception of Christ upon the cross, bleeding, and agonizing and dying for them—indeed, a mental picture so distinct as to appear almost an actual visual manifestation of the awful scene of Calvary. Was not this experience in Bunyan's mind when he described his Pilgrim coming in sight of the Cross ?

" He ran thus," writes Bunyan, " till he came to a place somewhat ascending, and upon that place stood a *Cross*, and a little below, in the bottom, a sepulchre. So, I saw in my dream, that just as Christian came up with the Cross, his burden loosed from off his shoulders, and fell from off his back, and began to tumble, and so continued to do, till it came to the mouth of the sepulchre where it fell in, and I saw it no more. Then was Christian glad and lightsome, and said, with a merry heart, ' He hath given me rest by His sorrow, and life by His death.' . . . He looked, therefore, and looked again, even till the springs that were in his head sent the waters down his cheeks."

It will be seen from the following account of his conversion, left by Mr. Nicholson himself, that he experienced this vivid conception of the Sin-Bearer upon the Cross suffering for him. He wrote two accounts of the same event, which the writer combines and gives almost in Mr. Nicholson's own words.

" In a few Sabbaths after I began to attend class," he writes, "and when under conviction of sin, the lovefeast was announced to be held in the new Preaching House, at Moira. All prejudice against the class and lovefeast had vanished out of my mind ; and I looked forward to the coming meeting with pleasure and joy. I attended the lovefeast. Mr. Jno. Armstrong preached. He preached short and earnestly, and had great power in prayer. After the sermon, several old men witnessed for Christ first ; and then followed many others. In a short time, the speaking could not be continued. Men and women rushed forward to the communion rails, weeping and crying out for mercy. In a few minutes, the rails were crowded with penitents. I was in the gallery, and saw the people weeping below and heard their cries. Tears of penitence began to flow from my eyes. It was impressed upon my mind, that if I would go down to the rails and join the seekers, I

C

should find peace, all my sins should be forgiven me. I walked
down the stairs at once, and the burden of guilt upon my heart
seemed to get lighter at every step. I kneeled beside the others in
heart distress. The first thought that came to my mind was—
'You are too bad to be forgiven; you must go down to hell. The
earth may open and swallow you up.' I was but eleven years of
age, and had not entered into any open, wilful sin; but I was in
great distress. No doubt, temptation came from Satan to frighten
me from seeking pardon. Soon my mind was directed by the
Holy Spirit to the Saviour upon the *Cross*, nailed there, and dying
for me. I thought I saw Jesus in agony and blood transfixed to
the accursed tree. It was with my mind's eye. As I gazed, the
question arose in my mind—'What led Jesus to that cross to suffer
and to die?' The reply suggested was 'Not to send you to hell,
but bring you to heaven. He came there to die for your sin; and
in order to pardon your sin and prepare you for heaven.' In that
moment I believed on the Lord Jesus Christ; and that my sins
were pardoned, and I was reconciled to God. Instantly the words
of the hymn came to my mind,

> 'If all the world my Saviour knew,
> Sure all the world would love Him too. '

"Oh! how happy I was! I stood up and told the people what
God had done for my soul. Shame and fear alike forsook me.
Afterwards I felt as though all things were changed. Nature
itself seemed new; and I rejoiced with a joy unspeakable and full
of glory. The meeting that day lasted about seven hours. The
conversions of young and old numbered between forty and fifty.
The two preachers left the meeting so hoarse from talking to penitents, that they could not continue speaking. Several little boys,
who were converted on that occassion, became preachers of the
gospel in different Methodist Societies. I had two miles and a
half of a walk home. I was so happy all the way, that it seemed
as if the trees and hills, and universal nature were paising God."

Mr. Jno. Turtle (formerly of Megabbery), an aged
christian pilgrim, said to the writer, a short time ago,
with deep emotion—"I was in Moira Chapel when
Samuel Nicholson was converted to God, now over sixty
years ago."

"Excitement, all mere excitement!" exclaim certain pious people and others; but, of course, not excitedly, only in "becoming warmth." Excitement there certainly was, on the occasion described above; but excitement surely is not an evil in itself. The quality of the excitement is found in the cause that produces it. Many of the mighty beneficial revolutions in nature are attended with excitement—great upheavals and convulsions of the earth's crust. Mighty national revolutions—as when slaveries are abolished, or tyrannies overthrown—are attended with widespread excitement; and no one decrys it. Great mental revolutions are not easily suppressed, as when the mind is compelled, under pressure of fact, or argument, to surrender long cherished convictions, and forced to adopt new opinions. And no one complains if the mental disturbance finds excited expression. Now, the greatest mental and moral revolution possible takes place in the human soul when it is converted to God. It passes, in an instant, out of darkness into marvellous light; out of bondage into liberty; from under "condemnation" to a state of "no condemnation;" from grief and apprehension the most intense, to joy and hope of the brightest nature; from a condition of mind at enmity to God, to a state of reconciliation and love to the Redeemer. Surely, then, no wonder should be caused or dissent expressed if the ardent soul, when passing through this, the greatest transformation of all, should give vent to its emotion: first in tears and cries; and then in shouts of joy and triumph and praise. Against "quiet" conversions, we have no complaint. Temperament must be taken into the account. Lydia's temperament differed from that of the jailer; and their surroundings, at the time of their conversion, widely contrasted, yet were they

both equally and instantly transformed by the renewing
of their mind. Had the jailer been at the quiet prayer-
meeting by the sea-side, when Lydia's heart was opened,
his heart, we fear, would have remained as hard as a
stone. And if Lydia had been in the jailer's room, when
the earthquake shook the prison so alarmingly, she, perhaps
would have swooned away, or been rendered incapable
of rational thought. Yet when Lydia's heart was opened
to receive the truth as in Jesus, and was changed by it,
she was thrilled with the strongest emotions that ever
moved her ; and when she "constrained" the disciples to
abide at her house, no doubt, her beaming eyes, and
grateful voice, and the urgency of her hospitality betrayed
the strength of the emotions which swayed her mind. In
a mixed multitude, where many souls of varying temperament are anxious, and many are being born of the Spirit,
emotion is too strong to be prevented from outward expression. When a multitude are " pricked in their heart,"
many of them will exclaim aloud, "Men and brethren, what
shall we do ? " And when the Holy Ghost, in His plenary
power, falls upon the disciples of Christ, doubtless they
will appear to some like men under the excitement of
intoxicants, or fanaticism. It will be said of them, " These
men are full of new wine," or, that they are " mad."

"Mere excitement" is short-lived, but Samuel Nicholson's religious excitement remained with him for upwards of
sixty years, intensifying as his knowledge increased, and his
experience matured. Here is a phenomenon that demands a
place in our philosophy : the conviction comes in an instant
to a youth of eleven years of age, that God has pardoned
his sins and changed his heart, shedding His love abroad
in it, and that conviction never dies, but rather increases
as years advance. Verily, " This is the finger of God."

CHAPTER II.

ACTIVITY AND LIFE.

Life is "Organization in action."—*Béclard.*

"Through all the orders of intelligent beings, not excepting God himself, activity is a great normal law of intellect,"—*Trail.*

"The love of Christ constraineth us."—*Paul.*

WHATEVER may be the nature of life, motion is one of its attributes. When God created man, "He breathed into his nostrils the breath of life; and man became a living soul;" and immediately the Lord set him to work. So, in the "new creation," when God breathes into the soul spiritually dead, its spiritual faculties are quickened and come into natural exercise; and immediately the Lord sets him to work, saying, "Go *work.*" When Lazarus was made alive he began to exert his limbs; he came forth from the grave bound with the habiliments of death, and Jesus saith unto them, "Loose him and let him go." Yes, he was thereafter to *go,* exerting the functions of life. And the impulses of the new life prompt the soul to the very activities which the Lord enjoins.

So was it with our young convert; born again, the motions of the new life began to show forth themselves in him. He might have heard the Lord's command addressed to himself—"Go home to thy friends, and tell them how great things the Lord hath done for thee, and hath had compassion on thee." The following extracts from Mr. Nicholson's own pen will illustrate these remarks:—

"I was very happy, and I thought all would partake of what I enjoyed, if they only were told about it. We had a Roman Catholic servant girl; I thought when I would tell her of the love of Christ in pardoning my sins, she would be converted at once. But all I said to her did not move her. I was enabled to begin to pray with my brothers and sisters. We held prayer meetings together in our garden; and I prayed as I was drawn out by the Spirit. I have no doubt, that the Holy Spirit turned my mind to these blessed engagements to prepare me for greater work."

Many years afterwards, Mrs. Captain Benson, of New York, a sister of Mr. Nicholson's, referred in many of her letters to him, in very tender, grateful terms, to those early juvenile prayer meetings, which he conducted, and to his loving instructions, and earnest prayers for her and the other children of the family. Mr. Nicholson, in notes before us, says, "For some time after my conversion, I had rapture and song every day; and I thought that soon the whole world would be turned to God." But he soon discovered that in Christian experience there is something more than rapture and songs of joy; and that many a severe struggle and much persecution will be experienced before the world is turned to God. Our young friend was constitutionally nervous, impulsive and vehement; and when purified, inspired, and controlled by the grace of Jesus his natural disposition predisposed him to earnest activities in the cause of his Redeemer. His youth and fervour attracted pleased attention, and soon he was asked to lead in prayer in the class and other social meetings.

Mr. Armstrong and his colleague took special notice of

the lambs of the fold; and encouraged youths to use the talents which God had given them. A change of ministers, however, upon the circuit was soon followed by a decline in the general fervour and evangelistic earnestness which had prevailed. Now, a sanguine, excitable temperament is very sensitive to a chill; and our young friend felt the change, and his zeal began to cool. Besides, as his years and physical strength increased, he was called to increasing labours upon the farm. Out, toiling in the fields, he had for companions "ungodly men, and he had to go to market with them."

For a time, he experienced many trials and fierce temptations; yet he did not totally fall from grace. He did not abate his attendance upon any of the means of grace, all of which he much enjoyed; and his mother's prayers, loving counsels, and encouraging words were invaluable to the young disciple in the conflict. But he became timid, and was disposed to serve the Lord in comparative silence ; and might have succeeded in settling down into a quiet, easy-going "member" had conscience only slept. The enemy thrust sore at him, torturing him upon the subject of his ignorance and unfitness to pray or speak in meetings. He keenly felt his inability to speak correctly, and did not think he could "speak to edification." So for a time he declined to take any public part in meetings when called upon to do so. He ever afterwards looked back upon his experience at this time as an epoch of great trial. But the trial proved instructive; in it he acquired influential knowledge of Satan's "devices," and learned that the hand of the Lord was about his tried servant for good. He says, "I did not see through this snare of the evil one until afterwards."

It pleased God, about this time, to lay his young

servant upon a bed of affliction ; a bilious fever prostrated
him.   Doubtless great anxiety of mind contributed to the
attack.´   Soon   two medical   men   pronounced his   case
"hopeless."   Men who had " power with God," however,
visited him ;   and when they heard the report of the
doctors, they appointed a meeting for special intercession
on his behalf.   God heard prayer, and the fever fled.   Mr.
Nicholson says, " At the time of their meeting, a heavenly
whisper came to my soul—' If you be raised from this bed
of sickness, will you use your talents for God, and work
for His glory ?' I said, ' Yes, Lord, I will rush into every
open door and work for Thee according to my ability, and
the grace given to me.'   From that hour I began to
amend ; and in a short time I quite recovered."   During
this sickness and his convalescence, the impression, that
God designed him for a wide sphere of usefulness, arose
in our devoted young friend's mind.   His faith in the
power of prayer, too, was much increased at this time.
It formed a valuable epoch in his spiritual history.   He
kept his vows of full consecration to God's service, and
literally entered every door of usefulness which opened
before him.

Having been a diligent student of the Bible from childhood, and knowing "the truth as it is in Jesus" experimentally, he became an efficient teacher in the Sabbath
School.   Confidence in his ability, earnestness, and
steadiness grew ; and, ultimately, the superintendence of
the Aghalee Sabbath School was confided to him, though
still but a youth.   Very soon he was chosen as a prayer
leader, and his gifts of prayer and exhortation were fully exercised and developed in the many prayer meetings around
him.   He was also early appointed a class-leader, and a
very efficient one he became.   He likewise became a

diligent visitor of the sick, many of whom he had the joy of seeing brought to Christ.

Mrs. Nicholson steadily held to the conviction that her Samuel had been received by God, and that the Lord would eventually call him to the work of the ministry. This idea in her heart gave to young preachers a special interest in her eyes. When able, she took great delight in being present at the ordination of young ministers. On these occasions she took Samuel with her, hoping and praying that he might catch the spirit which had moved the young men to the work. Mr. Nicholson writes:—"Though our home was fifteen miles from Belfast, yet when the Methodist Conference held its deliberations in that town, my precious mother made preparations, and took lodgings in Belfast for a week, that I might be present at all the public meetings and hear and see all I could. Her aim was to increase my love for the high and holy calling of the ministry. Year after year, 1 had the privilege of attending the ordination and other public services of the Conference, which did my soul good, and increased my desire to work for God and win souls for Him."

Samuel Nicholson early acquired the conviction, that his every step and the course of his life were under the care and direction of a special Providence ; and as life advanced, the conviction strengthened. In the memoranda left by him, he refers to "incidents in his life which point out the watchful care of his Heavenly Father over him all his days." Amongst these incidents are three special inter-positions of Providence, which he mentions as having in early life deeply impressed him with a sense of the Divine nearness and care. His fraternal love was strong ; and he shared fully in the care of his brothers and sisters. When "in his teens," one day, after dinner, he strolled out into

the garden to procure some fruit, and left the garden gate
open as he passed. A brook ran down the side of the
garden. He had no idea that any of the little ones were
following him. But he had not gone far, when suddenly,
he heard a sound resembling the opening of the garden
gate, which he was sure he had left open. The impulse to
return along the side of the stream instantly seized him;
and soon he came upon his little brother, John Hall, whom
he found insensible in the water, his face downwards. He
quickly rescued the child from his perilous position, and
immediately used means for his resuscitation, which very
soon proved successful. "Thus," adds Mr. Nicholson,
"under God, I saved my brother's life. He became one
of the most loving brothers, and was very kind and useful
to me all his days."

Another incident we give almost in Mr. Nicholson's
own words :—

"One day when I was detained at home, my little sister came
running into the house greatly alarmed, and cried out, ' O mother,
there is a large black dog in the street. He looked at us, and his
big eyes are like a flame of fire.' The servant rushed towards the
door to see the dog; but from a sudden impulse, I ran before her,
and shut the door, making it fast. I had hardly done this, when
the dog dashed against the door, which he did several times as if
trying to break it in. Our own little dog lay crouched close to the
door outside; the mad dog tried to bite him, but seemed unable to
do so. When he went off, I followed him with a loaded pistol in
my hand; but he turned fiercely round and came towards me.
Providentially there was a tree near, which I quickly climbed;
and thus my Heavenly Father saved me. The dog bit one of the
beasts on a neighbour's farm, and the poor animal soon showed
terrible symptoms of hydrophobia, and had to be destroyed. I
could never forget such a deliverance of a whole family. Surely
the word of the Lord was fulfilled:—' The angel of the Lord
encampeth round about them that fear him, and delivereth
them.'"

The third incident occurred some time after the foregoing (about 1830), but as the three events were ever after united in Mr. Nicholson's mind, exerting upon it a combined influence, we introduce it here. But, before we do so, a word or two of explanation seems required. The distance between Belfast and Aghalee is over fourteen miles ; and in those days the means of travelling were few and slow; aud night journeys were avoided as much as possible. Also, it was usual for friends to detain visitors all night, who had come to them from a distance. Such hospitality was freely accorded at Spring Valley; and the breach of it in the following narrative was, according to the ideas of the time, considered a gross insult, as well as a flagrant breach of the commonest hospitality :—

"I was sent to Belfast by my father to settle some accounts with a business man. After tea with his family, I went to hear a sermon in Donegal Square Methodist Chapel. I was intimate with the family, and had spent the night with them before when on business visits. After the service, I returned to my friends, expecting to spend the night with them as a matter of course. Shortly after my return, a friend of the family asked me to speak with her at the door. She informed me that I could not be entertained there that night; and immediately I found myself alone in the street in that large town where I was almost a complete stranger. It was winter; the stars shone brightly in the sky. A feeling of great solemnity came over me. I looked up at the lonely stars, and up at Heaven; and my first thought was, 'I am now like my Master for the first time ; I know not where to lay my head.' I remembered that a servant who had lived with us resided not far off, but the street or house I knew not. Looking up to God, I entered a street in search of her, where I soon saw several girls standing at a door. As I drew near to them, the girl herself stepped forward from amongst them, and accosting me by name, enquired why I was on the street so late, or why I was in town. I related my circumstances, and said I had come in search of her, expecting her to direct me to a safe lodging. 'Come with me,' she said: 'the family are from home, and I am at liberty to entertain a friend, if I please.' Very soon I was seated at a comfortable supper-table; and I had the use of a splendid bedroom for the night. Gratitude and love to my Heavenly Father filled and overflowed my heart, for his kindness in preserving me, His simple child, from all danger, and guiding my steps."

Many years afterwards Mr. Nicholson met the "gentleman" of the foregoing narrative upon the streets of Belfast, in a state of abject poverty, and Mr. Nicholson was able to return good for evil. The inhospitable man had squandered, in his time, about £1400; and at length, died in the Poor's House. "The way of transgressors is hard."

The Methodist Ministry represents a spiritual and Divine succession of prophets, the mantle of the one, as he passes away, falling upon his successor. One is begotten of another, and they stand in the relation of fathers and sons in the Gospel; just as Paul was a father and Timothy and Titus his sons. If the Circuit has upon it a pious, devoted youth, having in him the making of a preacher, the minister soon finds him out and has him in training. The curriculum is highly practical: like the pupil-teacher, the embryo minister becomes a pupil-preacher, putting his knowledge into his addresses as it is acquired, and delivering his addresses as they are prepared. The Theological College now usually completes the training; but in Mr. Nicholson's day, Methodist colleges had not taken a distinctive form. In this mode of perpetuating "men of God" and "ambassadors for Christ," there is nothing arbitrary or artificial: the method is most natural, and God has hitherto favoured it with His blessing.

In agreement with this procedure, Samuel Nicholson became the subject of special notice and attention from successive ministers upon the Moira Circuit. But it was from the Rev. George Carter, resident about a mile and a half from Spring Valley, that he received the most efficient help and encouragement. He attended a class in Mr. Carter's house; and a very strong attachment grew up between them. Mr. Nicholson writes of Mr. Carter in terms of strong affection. He says, "We became united to one another like David and Jonathan." Mr. Carter encouraged our young friend to cherish the idea of becoming a preacher. He put him upon a suitable and systematic course of reading and study; helped him in the preparation of essays, addresses and the outlines of sermons; and heard him exhort at prayer meetings, that he might practically instruct and guide him in his juvenile efforts. Mr. Carter also lent his friend Theological works, and instructed him in Systematic Divinity. And the two young men mutually aided one another in their longings and strivings after a nearer walk with God; for though a few years younger, and inferior in knowledge, yet Samuel Nicholson was rich in Christian experience and able to help his minister in the cultivation of his heart and his strivings after all the mind that is in Christ. Under Mr. Carter's guidance, our embryo preacher greatly matured in his understanding of Christian truth, and his course towards the ministry became plain before him. No wonder that he ever after held Mr. Carter in grateful esteem and affection.

It should be added here, that our young friend by continuous application, greatly improved his general education. In his later years his penmanship was a puzzle. The compiler of these memorials became able to read it very well; but at first, the effort resembled his early attempts to read Greek. The Rev. W. McClure, himself a first-class penman, in a letter to Mr. and Mrs. Nicholson, from Canada, in 1867, says, "Dear Mrs.

Nicholson, write yourself, for I can't read some of Mr. Nicholson's writing; if he don't preach better than he writes, it must be awful." The surviving correspondents of his later years will be surprised when informed, that in his earlier years, Mr. Nicholson wrote a very small, clear, neat hand, quite easily read. In his manifold studies, and labours for God, our devoted young friend did not abate his care, and attention to the arduous duties to which he was called at home and upon the farm. He was always a most dutiful and affectionate son, and a tender, attentive brother. It will occupy but little space to insert here the names of his brothers and sisters, and the date upon which each was born :—Robert, born Oct. 8th, 1813 ; James, born Sept. 12th, 1815 ; Elizabeth, born Feb. 25th, 1817 ; John Hall, born Jan. 9th, 1820; Margaret, born April 19th 1822 ; Thomas, born Dec. 27th, 1825.

The family at Spring Valley was a very industrious and happy one. Love was the uniting, as it was the ruling, principle of the household. They had, in the fullest sense, chosen the Lord as their portion, and to His blessed will they tried to conform in all things. At the family altar, they offered up their thanksgivings and prayers together morning and evening, and the Bible was their daily study and guide. "It was arranged," says Mr. Nicholson, "that father and I should pray alternately at family worship." He adds, "I can well remember, when father would be about to start in the early morning for the Lisburn and Belfast markets, with farm produce, and when the horses stood yoked and ready, we would all gather at mother's bedside and commit ourselves in prayer to the care of our Heavenly Father." "The eyes of the Lord were over them," and "walking in all His ways they found their heaven on earth begun." The rent of the farm was exorbitant, and the expenses of the family were a growing item ; hence the most rigid economy and unremitting industry were found necessary.

The subject of these memorials was now an industrious, as well as a devoted young man, he was "not slothful in business, but he was fervent in spirit, serving the Lord." He "worked out upon the farm in all kinds of weather," at all kinds of labour, "side by side with the servants," and it was healthy employment for both body and mind. The student of sedentary habits, who reads so much by gaslight in a vitiated atmosphere, deteriorates rather than improves in physical energy, and in that brain power which comes of healthy blood. No wonder, that he cannot sustain an amount of preaching and physical toil equal to that which the early Methodist preacher found but an exhilaration. Samuel Nicholson's mind and body, being in a state nearly normal, he enjoyed life. and the God of his life, as he laboured on from day to day. He saw the finger of the beneficent Creator in Nature around him, and felt the power of his Redeemer's grace in the mind within him. The lark, that soared o'er his head and poured out its song at the portals of light, was not happier than the pious country youth, in whose heart the lark's song awoke responsive echoes of praise and gladness. He could think and pray as well as work; indeed, his physical exertion aroused the mind to activity at the same time, awoke thought and stirred the imagination.

Many a blessing reached his heart in the fields, and many a bright idea came to enrich his head. The address at the evening prayer meeting often grew in his heart and brain during the day, as the wild flowers grew around him, and came home to the hearts of the worshippers as fresh and natural and sweet as the scent of the flowers. He saw God in everything; and God spoke to his servant words of comfort, and inspiration, and direction; and, like another Samuel, our friend responded—"Speak; for thy servant heareth." God has anointed many young men whilst engaged in agrarian pursuits, and called them to be kings or prophets. As the prophet's mantle fell upon the shoulders of Elisha while he was ploughing in the field, so upon Samuel Nicholson the Divine clothing and endowment for the work of the ministry fell, as he, too, followed the plough.

Thus the subject of these memorials held on his happy useful way till his twenty-third year. His Sabbaths were days of high enjoyment and abundant labours. He was very observant of children, and heartily devoted to his duties in the Sabbath School. He refers to the portion of his life, from the sixteenth year of his age till his twenty-third, as one of great enjoyment and spiritual growth. He says, " I was happy in the love of God. God was with me. I had the sympathy and confidence of ministers and leaders. It was my privilege to unite with the older brethren in prayers and labours for the glory of God and the salvation of souls." During those years he does not seem to have had any extraordinary conflicts with the enemy—none at any rate, which he thought worthy of record. He is careful, however, to state that he had not attained "perfect love." He was concious, too, of inward defects which no outward observer could see. Roots of bitterness, and the remains of the carnal mind within, and the incompleteness of his spiritual stature troubled him, and marred his joy, and caused his spiritual power to be often intermittent. Yet his had been an exceptionally virtuous life. He had not to struggle against the remains of any former vicious habits. On the contrary, by a steady continuance in well doing, he had acquired habits of the best quality. This gave him a .position of special vantage against the evil forces within and without him.

It was his custom to retire to his own room daily, at stated hours, and there to read his Bible (often upon his knees) and to " pour out his soul " to God in earnest prayer. And to " pray without ceasing " was his constant habit. When in his twenty-fourth year our friend had attained a very high moral and spiritual stature; and having given himself to reading, he had acquired a very correct knowledge of sacred truth. It is not too much to say of him that in his own limited measure, he had "increased in wisdom and stature, and in favour with God and man." We admit that perhaps in mental equilibrium and force he was not perfect; and his artlessness and ingenuousness were extreme; yet " even his failings leaned to virtue's side." Jno. B. Gough's last words were, " Young men make a clean record"! Well, Samuel Nicholson's record was a clean one. It might have truthfully been said of him, " Behold, an Israelite indeed, in whom is no guile!" At the age of which we write, he was tall, straight, slender and lithe in person, ruddy in complexion, having "a single eye," "a conscience void of offence," and a heart which loved all truth and all goodness.

D

CHAPTER III.

PERFECT LOVE.

" In 1729, the late Mr. Wesley and his brother, upon reading the
Bible, saw they could not be saved without holiness; they followed
after it, and incited others to do the same. In 1737, they saw
holiness comes by faith. They saw likewise that men are justified
before they are sanctified; but still holiness was their point. God
then thrust them out, utterly against their will, *to raise a holy
people.*"

OUR earnest friend, being now about twenty-three
years of age, we reach another marked epoch in
his spiritual history.   Growth has marked his
experience hitherto, but now he reaches spiritual maturity,
becomes "sanctified wholly."   In this year of grace, 1888,
the subject of Holiness is receiving special attention in all
the Evangelical Churches.   Conventions for the promotion
of Scriptural holiness are being held in different places.
Distinct realizings are taking the place of distant longings
after "more holiness," in the experience of many Christians belonging to the different Christian Communities.
This is one of the most hopeful signs of our times.   God's
people are awaking at the bidding of their Lord, and
"putting on their beautiful garments."   The Head of
the Church, by increasing their holiness, is maturing
their strength, and thus preparing His sanctified people

for a mighty forward march upon the world of darkness, scepticism, sensuality and rebellion. This "holiness movement," seems to favour the hope, that soon the Church of Christ will answer to the prophetic and symbolic discription of Inspiration, when it says, "She that looketh forth as the morning *is* fair as the moon, :clear as the sun, and terrible as an army with banners." The literature of the auspicious movement is very rich, copious, and varied. The conviction is growing, that the Word of God sets forth a distinct blessing, much richer and higher than regeneration and conversion, which is immediately attainable, and hundreds profess that they have received it. We here yield to the impulse to give a scrap from *Divine Life* : ' " Brother Johnstone,' said the negress, ' I and the Lord had been working on the old heart for forty years and more, and we could make nothing of it, so He just threw it away altogether, and gave me a new one.' " The blessing is variously defined as "the higher Christian life," "a clean heart," "a second conversion," and "the baptism of the Spirit." By and by the terms "perfection," and "entire sanctification," will doubtless come into greater favour. When Mr. Nicholson was a young man, the subject of holiness excited but little interest outside Methodism. Indeed even the "knowledge of salvation in the remission of their sins," was a doctrine eschewed and decried. But one of the distinctive features of earlier Methodism was the prominence which it gave to the doctrine of entire sanctification. Within her borders there were not wanting those who enjoyed and exemplified the blessing, amongst whom were many notable characters.

At the time of which we now write, Mr. Nicholson had before his mind, the subject of holiness, not as a speculative question, but a practical one, which absorbed his whole thoughts and desires. It is worthy of special note here, that our friend did not study any article of faith as a merely abstract or speculative question, but as one in which his heart, and life, and hopes, as a fallen, but immortal, responsible, and redeemed being, were vitally concerned. He studied in the school of experience, rather than in the Hall of Divinity; and his creed was not written upon his memory merely, as a train of ideas in the head, but, under the Spirit of God, it was a living reality, enlightening his understanding, sanctifying his affections, and governing his whole life. Mr. Nicholson's view of holiness was that exemplified by the Fletchers, and by Mrs. H. A. Rodgers, and others of the same type; and that taught by Mr. Wesley. Being a Methodist divinity student, as a matter of course, Mr. Nicholson studied "Wesley's Notes," and Sermons, especially the first fifty-two. From these sources his views upon Christian perfection were derived. His favourite conception of the blessing was that of " perfect love." Under this idea he could understand, and intelligently enter into the experience of it, perfect love being but the fulness of that principle, which had all along possessed his heart, and governed his life. The doctrine is set forth in 1 John iv.

We offer the following summary of the Apostle's teaching :—
1. There is a love to God which is " perfect." The love of God shed abroad in the heart at conversion is *perfect* in itself, but is not perfect in degree or quantity. He, who is made perfect in love, has love in its fulness. Mr. Wesley describes it as *adult* love. He says, "A natural man has neither fear nor love; one that is awakened, fear without love ; a babe in Christ, love and fear ; a *father* in Christ, love without fear." 2. It brings the soul into full conformity to the image of Christ. As He is, so are we, in this world." Christ is all love, and so are fathers in Christ. 3. It is

an expulsive principle. "It casteth out fear." because it casteth out sin, in the absence of which fear is impossible. "There is no fear in love." Perfect love destroys all terror of *God*, or *judgment*, or *death*. 4. Its foundation is God's love to us. "We love Him because He first loved us. 5. It is derived from God, being a direct participation of the Divine nature, "God is love; and he that abideth in love, abideth in God, and God abideth in him." 6. From perfect love to God there necessarily flows pure love to man; to vicious men in the form of active pity; and towards the Christian brotherhood, that of complacence. "And this commandment have we from Him, that he who loveth God love his brother also." 7. It is meritoriously through the blood of Christ. "The blood of Jesus Christ his Son cleanseth us from all sin." 8. It is instrumentally by faith. "And we have known and believed the love that God hath to us." The reference is to the love of God, in sending His Son, to be the propitiation for our sins. The Holy Spirit enables the soul to discern and confide in the love thus exhibited.

> "Lord, I believe a rest remains,
>   To all Thy people known,
> A rest where pure enjoyment reigns,
>   And Thou art loved alone :
>
> A rest where all our soul's desire,
>   Is fixed on things above ;
> Where fear, and sin, and grief expire,
>   Cast out by perfect love."

For a long time Mr. Nicholson hungered and thirsted after this blessing of perfect love. He sought it by prayer and fasting, till at length he entered the Canaan of holy satisfaction and rest. The following account is from his own pen:—

"My heart yearned for more love to God; I longed to be more holy. I read much upon the subject, I read Wesley on Christian Perfection, and many other writers on the same subject. My desire for all the mind that is in Christ increased. I added fasting to prayer, omitting four meals in the week, which did me good. The Rev. Chas. Mayne was our minister at the time. He was a

holy Christ-like man. I often slept .n his house, in the absence of
his wife. His conversation was Heaven, and how to win souls for
Christ. I consulted him upon the subject of entire sanctification,
and sought his advice. All he said to me at that time was
simply—' Hold what grace you have, and get more.' One day
when I was out working as usual in the fields, the thought
suddenly came to my mind,—' Go home, and kneel before God, as
you are accustomed to do daily after dinner, and the Lord will
sanctify you wholly.' Instantly I laid aside my work and went
home, and prostrated myself before God. I had read my Bible
upon my knees, mostly in the Book of Psalms. This time I did
not select a place, but just opened the Bible and read the first
words which presented themselves, asking the Lord to direct my
eye to some passage that I could rest upon for the blessing. I
opened upon the words of Hezekiah,—"Behold, for peace I had
great bitterness; but thou hast in love to my soul delivered it from
the pit of corruption: for thou hast cast all my sins behind thy
back." As in the case of Hezekiah, I had great bitterness: but
the Lord in love to my soul, delivered it from the pit of corruption
[inbred sin], and cast all my sins behind His back. With the
application of this scripture to my heart by the Holy Spirit, there
came such a glorious light, and my soul was filled with love to
God, and love to all around me. I believed then that I was
sanctified wholly. In the class meeting, on the following Sabbath
morning, I told what God had done for my soul. On our way
home my brother, Robert, said to me, ' Samuel you have made a
fool of yourself, for who gets such a blessing as that now.' I did
not reason with him, but kept on rejoicing in God. It was our
love-feast day. I prayed earnestly to the Lord to show me by
the Holy Spirit, if what I had received was really the blessing of
perfect love. The minister's text on that day was :—' But ye
have an unction from the Holy One, and ye know all things.'
The words came with power to my heart, and again I received
the witness of the Holy Spirit that I had received the great
blessing I had sought so long; and I rejoiced with a joy unspeakable. When I related in the love-feast, what God had done for
my soul, the minister immediately announced the verse, beginning
with the words :—

' Praise God from whom all blessings flow,'

which was heartily sung. Thus, my God gave me my heart's desire; and showed me that my life and talents, for the future, were to be directed and used for His glory."

Mr. Nicholson ever after looked back upon this crisis in his Christian life, as the one when his Divine Master endued him with " power from on high" as a preparation for the work for which He had designated His servant. Now, the holy impulse and desire to give himself up, wholly and immediately, to the work of preaching Christ to perishing men seized him. The live coal from off the altar had touched his lips; and he heard the voice of the Lord, saying, " Whom shall I send, and who will go for us ? " To which, like the prophet, he responded, saying, " Here am I, send me." Deeply and painfully sensible of his own weakness and deficiency in knowledge and mental culture, he yet felt the call of God, to go forth, and publish what he had felt and seen of Christ and His salvation.

To Samuel Nicholson God was not an unknownable something, or an abstract idea, or even a mere cause; but a glórious Person, a loving Father, and a gracious Friend, who was ever near to His " simple child," guiding, guarding, directing, and even speaking directly to his heart by the Holy Spirit. Hence our friend, in memoranda under the writer's eye, speaks again and again of impressions having been made upon his mind by the Holy Spirit. The impressions resemble those by which the Friends profess to be moved in all their ministry. No doubt there is danger here of looking exclusively to the inward "voice" or " light," and thus neglecting that Word which is given as a "candle" unto the feet and a "light" unto the path—the ordinary guide of our views and every-day life. Nevertheless, the Holy Sprit is the immediate

source of certain ideas and purposes or inclinings which
arise in the mind; the idea or impression, however,
should invariably be tested by the written Word, that
the evils of fanaticism may be avoided.   In 1834, Mr.
Nicholson visited relatives at a distance, and held meetings.   He kept a diary at the time, from which we
transcribe the following :—

"It was impressed upon my mind, that I should visit an aunt
of mine, named Carson, who resided about twenty-five miles
distant, in Co. Down.   She and her husband entertained the
preachers on their rounds for upwards of fifty years.   They prepared their large barn for my meeting; and a large congregation
assembled.   I spoke upon Repentance.   We had a profitable time.
As advised by our minister, I kept to exhortation for some time.

January 20th.—My soul enjoys sweet peace in God.   During the
ast two weeks, I have enjoyed a great nearness to God in prayer
and when reading His word.   He is mine, and I am His.   I desire
to spend, and be spent for Him.   When I meditate upon God's
greatness, and think upon His compassion and love to me,
and a lost world, I am filled with gratitude and love to Him.   The
language of my soul is, 'I am thine, save me.'   I pant for more
love and faith, that I may glorify Thy great name.

26th.—Spoke from Prov. i. 24—26.   A blessed day to my soul.
I trust good was done.   Was much blessed while reading Wesley's
Sermons and Hymns.   31st.—Left Uncle Carson's, Lecale, for
Downpatrick.   Felt weak in body, but the Lord strengthened me
by the way.   Saw some of my dear friends, the Skillens' and
Cummins'.   Spent the evening with three of my cousins, Mrs.
Wilson, Mrs. James, and Miss Matilda Carson.   How sweet is
Christian communion.   O Lord, guide them and me, so that we
all may meet in heaven, for Jesus' sake.   Feb. 2nd.—Met the class
in cousin Charles Carson's: a blessed morning to my soul.   The
Master was with us.   While walking along the sea shore, before
dinner, and beholding the works of the great Creator—the vast
sea, the towering mountains, and the broad earth—my soul
was reverently impressed with a sense of the majesty and power of
God.   "'Twas great to speak a world from nought, but 'twas

greater to redeem. Spoke at three o'clock, in Uncle Carson's to a good company. Had liberty; felt refreshed in my own soul; and I trust all felt it good to wait upon God. Spent the evening at Minerstown, near Killough, with Mrs. Thos. Carson, a very pious lady, and her family. I told them what great things the Lord had done for me.

Here I met James Magorian, a convert from Popery, now an aged man. When he first heard the gospel, he was a rank Papist, being a member of the Order of the Holy Scapular. On a market day, in Downpatrick, he heard Mr. Bell preach in the street. The preacher held up his Bible, and cried out, "This is God's Word, given to lead us to Heaven. It tells of the love of Christ, in coming to die for us guilty sinners. Get it, and take it home with you!" Magorian had never heard of such things from the *Priest;* and his mind became greatly exercised. To his wife he said, ' I must find this wonderful Book.' He first borrowed a Bible, and afterwards purchased one for himself. The eyes of his understanding became savingly enlightened; he renounced Popery, joined the *Primitive Wesleyan Society,* and regularly attended the monthly preaching and other services at my uncle Carson's. Magorian was much persecuted, even by his own family. They hid his shoes to prevent him attending the meeting. He has walked barefoot to near my uncle's door; but the shoes were sent after him. The priest anathematized him, but he remained firm. He was a diligent reader of the Scriptures, and had a rich Christian experience. When I met this remarkable character, he said, ' Young man, you will be preaching the gospel when I am in my grave.' He held my hand for some time, and blessed me. So rich a fruit of street-preaching impressed me in its favour ever after.

February 4th.—Came home much strengthened; had great peace of mind and was happy in the Divine favour. Glory be to my God. 14th.—Twenty-three years of age this day. Have not lived as near to God as I might have done. I covenant with my God afresh, in the strength of His grace, to live to Him and for souls. May the year upon which I have entered be one of great blessing to my soul! A sweet promise given me—' Thou shalt compass me about with songs of deliverance.' Praise God! 16th.—Began a new class in Wm. McKown's, ten present, above all, the Master graciously near. 20th.—During the last few days I have sat in heavenly places with Christ Jesus. Met the class in J. Campbell's. Attended the quarterly meeting: a good time. Held a prayer meeting in the evening. Found it profitable to meditate upon the perfections of God—His power and love. Felt such a sensibility of His presence with me, and my nothingness before Him—He Almighty, and I a worm of earth.

My Uncle Carson, of Lecale's minister, at this time, was the Rev. Chas. Reed, Primitive Wesleyan. His father's residence was quite near to my home. Being at his father's upon a visit, in March, he told my father that my friends in Lecale wished me to visit them again. My parents being agreeable, I accompanied Mr. Reed upon his return to his circuit. March 10th.—Left home very happy in the Lord. Dined at Mr. Scandrett's, Kilwarlin. Had a conversation with Mr. Thos. Archer, who enjoys perfect love. Felt strengthened and confirmed. Read, that Mrs. Fletcher had lost the blessing for a time, because she had not confessed it. Resolved to tell what God had done for my soul, exercising prudence as to time and place. Spent a night with Uncle Samuel Nicholson, Dromara, on my way. April 4th.—Mr. Reed preached at Uncle Carson's, and I closed the meeting. He announced that I should preach to-morrow evening, near Downpatrick. 5th.— Took my first text, Rom. v. 1. A good congregation. Had great liberty: thank God! 6th.—I preached my second sermon in the Parish of Saul, near Downpatrick, from the words, 'Repent, and turn yourselves from your idols; and turn away your face from all your abominations.' Sabbath, 7th.—Mr. R. preached at 10 o'clock a.m. I held a prayer meeting in the afternoon, at Uncle Carson's. Mr. R. and I held the love-feast, at Killough, in the evening. Testified what God had done for my soul. Praise His name! Spent the night at Mr. Parkinson's. 8th.—Preached at cousin Mrs. Wilson's, of Ardglass: "Take unto you the whole armour of God." A blessed time we had. Am fully persuaded in my own mind, that I am called to preach the Gospel. 16th.—Mr. R. went home to visit his father. Left me to take up a few appointments for him. I preached at a place near Ballynahinch, also at Castlewellan. Had liberty. God was present. Mr. J. Simmons, a godly man, encouraged me greatly. 17th.—Preached in Mr. Kennedy's, Knocksticken, also at Seaford, in Mr. Beer's, a good man. When about to leave him, he held my hand and said, 'My dear young man, God has work for you to do; keep humble and prayerful, and He will exalt you in due time.' 20th.—Preached at Clara, in Mr. Brown's. Two of his daughters pray in public. [A grandson of Mrs. B.'s emigrated to New Zealand, where he entered the Wesleyan ministry]. 21st.—Lord's Day. Preached at 9.30 a.m. A blessed day. 22nd.—Held prayer meeting, in Downpatrick, for Mr. Skillen. Heard that father wished me to return home. 24th.—Returned home by way of Uncle S. Nicholson's. My mother greatly delighted to know I had been so fully engaged in the Lord's work, as were all the family. Was often greatly blessed when away. Sensibly feel the defects in my education; am resolved, according to my ability and opportunity, to read and pray, and prepare myself for usefulness."

Amongst the few notes made immediately after his itinerant labours in Co. Down, Mr. Nicholson refers to a sacramental service in Moira, at which he was much blessed, also to band and other meetings, which were times of unusual refreshing. He likewise speaks in laudatory and grateful terms of individuals who had shown him kindness. Amongst these, the most prominent name is that of Mrs. Turtle, of Aghalee, of whom he writes, " She is a pious, devoted woman, who seeks the highest good of all around her." It was this lady's custom to take her husband's young shopmen to class with her.

About this time (1834-5) our earnest brother was officially advanced from the position of an exhorter to that of a local preacher. The exhorter's labours are mainly confined to cottage meetings. He is not called to the pulpit, nor is he expected to take a text or attempt to preach a sermon. The chapter he reads or the hymn he announces at the prayer meeting usually supplies him with the subject of his exhortation; and his own personal experience is the commonest, as it is the most acceptable, source of his illustrations. "What ho hath felt and soon," is mostly the burden of his addresses, and his direct aim is to persuade his hearers to become partakers of "like precious faith" with himself. Not being confined to a text nor to a sermon "outline," he is free to range at will through the regions of saving truth, and to give expression to such thoughts and feelings as may stir his spirit at the moment. There have been many powerful exhorters who could not preach at all, to whom a sermonic outline would have been like a strait jacket. William Black (of whom more again) said to the Rev. Wm. McClure, "I tried to preach once after many people had been urging me to take out a text and preach from it. I chose my time one night when travelling alone from Ballinderry, where I had been holding meetings. I took out a text, divided, subdivided, and concluded; it occupied my whole attention for more than an hour,—and so fully satisfied was I with my success, that I resolved, then and there, never to attempt such a thing again." He kept his vow. But the exercises of the exhorter supply a practical training for the more exact and artistic efforts of the preacher. Sermons, stilted in style and tame in application and appeal, are not heard from the preacher who first graduated as an earnest exhorter. It was, we believe, when Mr. Nicholson was an exhorter he acquired that readiness, fluency, and directness of style which characterized his preaching. Now, however, the exhorter merges into the preacher, and our friend takes a text, and takes the pulpit as well, under official sanction.

His evangelistic tours amongst the Primitive Wesleyans were highly appreciated; and an invitation to become a preacher of that Society was given him. His very near kinsfolk were influential members of the

Primitives, and the sphere of usefulness offered him was extensive and inviting. The invitation, however, was not favoured by either of his parents or any of his brothers; and that the Methodist ministry had a Scriptural right to administer all the ordinances of the Gospel was, with our friend, a decided conviction. After much thought and prayer inclination yielded to conviction, and he writes: "When I gave up the thought of it, peace, sweet peace of mind followed." No doubt he was Scripturally as well as providentially and wisely guided in this decision. The ecclesiastical status of the Primitive Wesleyan preachers was very low and despised. They occupied an anomalous and untenable position; and they were ignored by most of the Episcopal clergy, at whose hands, nevertheless, they had to receive the sacraments.

Our brother had long felt called by the Holy Ghost to give himself up wholly to the one work of preaching the Gospel; now there came to him the call of the Church. Hands were not laid upon him suddenly, as he was now twenty-four years of age, and a tried man. There were, in his case, the evidences of gifts, graces, and fruit. He is a pitiable as well as a contemptible creature who obstrudes into the sacred office, not having been moved thereto by the Holy Ghost, but by some inferior impulse. Mental culture, literary taste and an eloquent tongue are miserable substitutes for "power from on high." He who has not the "tongue of fire," will never be the instrument of igniting the holy flame in the soul of another. The lamp may be a very plain affair indeed, but if it be burning, it is capable of lighting one which has gone out: but the lamp of costliest material and most artistic design, which is not lighted, is insufficient, either to give light or set another lamp afire. Oh! it is the holy fire which is the primary qualification for a preacher of Christ's Gospel. Samuel Nicholson deeply regretted that he had not learning; but he had the holy fire, and many souls. through his instrumentality caught the flame of love and zeal and holiness. He humbly ascribed all to God:— the irrepressible desire to preach which stirred his soul, the favour of God's ministers and people, the call of the Church, and his reception as a preacher on trial. Here is his own account:—

"God gave me favour in the eyes of ministers and people, and opened up my way. The Rev. J Carter was superintendent of the Moira circuit at the time : it was he recommended me. I was examined, in 1835, at the Portadown District Meeting, of which Rev. Thos. Waugh was chairman. One of the ministers present spoke very kindly to me, and his words cheered and encouraged me. He bade me have confidence in them, and said they had all passed a similiar examination themselves. I was enabled to answer all the questions upon Christian Doctrine put to me; and the ministers seemed satisfied. In a few weeks afterwards I received a letter from the Rev. Elijah Hool, dated from the Mission House, London, instructing me to proceed to the Co. Donegal to assist the Rev. William Cornwall on the Mission there."

Of course, that letter caused a stir, and excited strong emotions in the godly home at Spring Valley. If, as she read it, tears of gratitude started in the eyes of a certain mother, whose little son years before wondered what she was doing, when he saw her lips moving in prayer, none of the readers of our narrative will wonder. Yes, Elizabeth Nicholson, God hears prayer ! Your gift was accepted. Now, may you, too, like Hannah, praise the Lord, adapting her language to your own happy experience :—" My heart rejoiceth in the Lord, mine horn is exalted in the Lord : my mouth is enlarged over mine enemies : because I rejoice in thy salvation." " The Lord maketh

poor, and maketh rich; he bringeth low, and lifteth up.
He raiseth up the poor out of the dust." Yet, when the
hour came for the son and brother to bid good-bye to the
loved ones at home, the scene was touching in the
extreme. His father, a quiet, undemonstrative man, felt
it very keenly, as Samuel was very dear to him, and his
willing labour upon the farm had been most useful. The
younger members of the family felt, that they were parting with the best friend they had on earth next to their
parents. But most of all, the mother felt the pang of
parting with a son who had grown dearer to her, and
increasingly useful as the years passed by. She had
found it easy to vow, but now felt it hard to fulfil the
vow; easy to give her firstborn to God by promise, but
hard to give him to distant Donegal. When the moment
came for mother and son to part, she tenderly and closely
pressed him to her heart, and exclaimed, " How can I part
with you, my angel boy!" The young preacher entered
earnestly and hopefully upon his labours in Donegal, as
surviving letters and fragments of letters from his pen
abundantly testify. These fading and discoloured fragments are interesting in themselves, as showing the style
of epistolary correspondence fifty years ago. The following extracts will be read with interest, the first being to
his mother upon his arrival in Donegal.

Rathmullen, 1835.
"When I presented to Rev. W. Cornwall, [his superintendent], the
letters of introduction I had from Rev. C. Mayne, Mr. C. was much
pleased, and said, 'These are two of my best friends.' *Sabbath*,
preached at Letterkenny, at 7 p.m. *Monday*, assisted Mr. C. at a
meeting three miles off. *Wednesday*: At Mr. Ellison's, Loughs-
whilley. *Thursday*: At Rev. Francis Armstrong's, (a supernumerary). *Friday*: Held a meeting, at 7 a.m. *Saturday*: Preached
this evening a mile out of town. To-morrow, I am to hold forth

the Word of Life, in this place, (D.V). Mr. and Mrs. Cornwall are so humble and loving, and they have shown much kindness to me. I am very happy with them, and in my great work for God and souls. I have great peace of mind, and joy in the Holy Ghost. Donegal and its people are very different from Ulster; a great difference in houses, &c. Food very plain, but wholesome. But the hearts of the people are very kind."

Two of his younger brothers were now apprentices, one in Aghalee, and the other in Belfast. Robert assisted his father upon the farm, which did not succeed so well in the absence of the more experienced son. The subject of these memorials had to return home upon a brief visit, to assist in some family affairs and important business which required his attention as the senior son. This visit involved a second leave-taking, which seems to have been more keenly felt than the first. When about to mount his horse and be off, his mother could hardly allow him to leave. Her tenderness touched him deeply, and utterly overcome, he threw the reins upon the horse's neck, and said, "Mother, I will not leave you, if you wish me to remain." At this, the pious woman quickly recovered herself, and exclaimed, "Go, Samuel, go! I gave you to the Lord at your birth, and you are altogether His, go, and do the Lord's work." This proved the final parting; she never saw him in the flesh again, as will presently appear. The following are portions of letters which returned to comfort her:—

"Rathmullen, Dec., 1835.

"My dear Mother,—I arrived at your brother's in safety,......travelled from Portadown to Dungannon, where I arrived at eleven at night. On nine miles to Armagh, where I spent the night with Mr. Cather, who has a son, a preacher in Dublin. Spent the night at Strabane, with the Rev. Robinson Scott, who was our minister at Moira, not long ago. Dearest Mother, do not be uneasy about me; I am in God's hand, and I know He will be with me and direct me aright."

"Rathmullen, 29th Dec., 1835.

To the same. "When travelling by the sea-side, I was awed by a sense of the majesty and power of God as shown in the vast ocean. It was grand to see the great waves dashing against the rocks, and to listen to their roaring and to the roaring of the numerous seals all along the shore. All seemed very solemn and desolate, as for six miles I saw neither man nor tree. I have twenty-one appointments a month. The Lord bless the preaching of His Word for Christ's sake."

"January 5th, 1836. 11 p.m.

Dear Uncle,—Mr. and Mrs. Cornwall welcomed me with open arms. I have had great pleasure in this place since I came. Thanks be to God! I travel from 8 to 10 miles a day, visit from house to house and read the Scriptures; have met with no opposition.........Have visited Glenlonagh, Ramelton, Rathmullen, Stranolar, Standalane, Cormoy, Donoughmore, Cracknamana, Loughswilley, &c. Preached last Sabbath, near Stranolar; the house was well filled. As I proceeded, some wept and others praised God......Have been cast down a little but the Lord lifted me up......Have been inclined to return home—sought counsel from the Lord......from my heart I can say, 'Thy will be done.' Yet who is sufficient for these things. Dear Uncle, pray for me, that I may be kept humble, holy, and steadfast, unmovable, always abounding in the work of the Lord.'"

"January 5th, 1836. 12 p.m.

Dear Brother John,—I hope you are prospering in the Lord and waxing confident in your God. I feel greatly blessed in doing something for my God and Saviour. I have been employed every day since I came here, reading the Scriptures, preaching the Word of Life and holding prayer meetings. I have peace of conscience and joy in the Holy Ghost. 'Unto me, who am less than the least of all saints, is this grace given, that I should preach the unsearchable riches of Christ! Not unto me, but unto the name of the Lord be the praise and the glory.' The people in this country are kind and hospitable. The work of the Lord is prospering in my

E

hands. The harvest truly is great, but the labourers are few. John, dear, live near to God; read His Word constantly, and often upon your knees. Attend all the means of grace regularly. Be in earnest at the throne of grace, for devils are in earnest to turn you out of the way. You cannot fall while supported by that 'prop' which holds the world and all things up. I hope you were not offended because I did not wait to see you. 'The king's business required haste.'"

Hitherto Samuel Nicholson has not known suffering, not in its intenser forms. His sky has been bright, with but an occasional dark cloud, which hid the sun for a moment and then passed away. But now he was called to experience suffering deepening into anguish. A cloud arose which deepened, darkened, and spread till it covered the whole sky. Fever of a virulent form prostrated his brother, Robert (who had through carelessness been put to sleep in a bed in which a fever-patient had lain), and afterwards his dear mother. The family at Spring Valley seemed paralyzed. The distressing news threw our young friend into the deepest distress. He received letters from home urging him to return, as all the servants had fled from the stricken house. His first impulse was to rush to the rescue. But his superintendent and other Donegal friends induced him to wait and not to expose himself where his presence might not be of much service. Soon, however, the sad tidings reached him that his dear brother, Robert, was dead. It would appear that his mother, ere she became delirious, wrote her "angel-boy," telling him all her trouble. In the following there was a word direct to each distressed one at home :—

"Stranolar, May 31st, 1836.

Dear Mother,

      I hope you are better. I went to the Coach-Office yesterday to take a seat for home, but could not get one outside, and so spent the night at——, and preached from the words, ' O death, where is] thy sting?' &c. You perhaps think I have lost my love for you, but I have not. Dearest Mother, I love you better than ever before. Mr. Cornwall, and many of the people said that I might take the fever if I went home, and that I could do you no good. But I intend to start from Letterkenny for home upon the 6th June. If, however, you be better, write to me immediately, and I shall remain away a little longer till the infection has left the house. I know not how I could be wanted upon this Mission till Conference. The will of the Lord be done, amen. Dear Father, let me know if my mother received—— that I sent her as a token of my love; but you need not write after June 4th. Dear James, and John, and Eliza, and Margaret, and my little Thomas, I hope you all enjoy the pardon of sin, and the love of Jesus in your hearts. If not, you may never see dear Robert in heaven. 'Without holiness no man shall see the Lord,' but the blessed Jesus died for your sins upon Calvary. If you take the fever, you may soon become delirious and unable to seek salvation. Think of the blessed station to which Robert hath attained :—

'Our brother the haven hath gained,
  Outflying the tempest and wind ;
His rest he hath sooner obtained,
  And left his companions behind !'

Dear Children, live for this happy world. Do not rest till you have received a sense of pardon. If mother be unconscious, tell me if she mentioned my name from the time she took ill. Suffer not the children to go near mother....attend strictly to the doctor's advice. Dear Mother, it is impressed upon my mind that I should go home for a little, soon ; write, I have been praying for you. Last night I dreamed that you were up and getting better. I am glad that Father is well ; I trust he keeps up family prayer regularly. Dear Father, live very near to God. Does 'Mr. Carter say anything about me coming home ?   S. NICHOLSON."

P.S.—I feel my mind graciously supported by the grace of God. If I did wrong in leaving home, I aimed at doing the will of God, which the day of eternity will tell. The grace of our Lord Jesus Christ be with you all. Amen. S. N."

When he reached Portadown, on his way home, the
saddest news of all awaited him. Here he learned that his
mother had suddenly expired under the burning fever.
Now darkness encompassed him, and grief unutterable
overwhelmed his spirit. Surely affliction is one of the best
adapted instruments in the development, purification, and
ennoblement of gracious character. " Perfect through
sufferings " would seem to apply to the choicest spirits of
all the ages. They who have dared, endured, and done
great things for God and their fellows have generally been
" chosen in the furnace of affliction." The God of love
would surely select another instrument, rather than pain,
if one of equal efficiency existed. As he neared home, it
seemed no longer *Spring Valley* to our sorrowing brother,
but rather the *Valley of Baca*. He found his father
suffering from a slight attack of fever, which, however,
soon passed off. Now trying, perplexing questions arose.
Mr. Nicholson, sen., was not a capable farmer, not having
been trained to labour. Two of his sons, being apprentices,
were bound to complete their terms. His father besought
him, and relatives and friends urged Samuel to resign his
preaching appointment for a time. What was he to do?
He writes :—

" I loved the work of God and believed I was called to it, and
God had blessed my labours ; but Father was unable to work the
farm, none of the children could help him, but were themselves an
additional care upon him. I was prevailed upon to resign for the
family's sake, hoping that the way would again open for me to
resume the holy calling of preaching the Gospel." He adds, " My
superintendent was displeased with me for resigning, as were other
Wesleyan friends ; but the circumstances compelled me. Some
time after I had joined the Methodist New Connexion I met my dear
old friend, Rev. W. Cornwall. He got off his horse upon the high-
way, came forward, kissed me and wept. ' My dear Sam,' said he,' why
did you leave us, did you not know that we all loved you dearly?' "

His brother Robert, was twenty-two years of age when he died; his last words were, "Victory, victory, through the blood of the Lamb! I shall arise to everlasting life!"

The following is from the pages of *The Irish Christian Monitor* :—

"MEMOIR OF ELIZABETH NICHOLSON.
BY HER SON, REV. S. NICHOLSON.

ELIZABETH NICHOLSON, whose maiden name was Whitley, was born in the townland of Drumahanision, Co. Armagh, in 1784. Her early years were watched over by a kind Providence, amidst many dangers. Her parents were both religious, and belonged originally to the Church of Scotland, and her father was an elder of that church for many years. When the first Methodist Preacher visited the neighbourhood of Richhill, he went to hear them preach, and sat under their ministrations with great delight, and was constrained to say, 'these men are servants of the Most High God, which show unto us the way of salvation.' He united with the Society, and invited the preachers to his house, where they were hospitably entertained until his death. The Lord made him very useful as a class-leader, which office he held till old age. At the time of the division in the Methodist Connexion Mr. R. Whiteley received a printed circular from the leaders and stewards of the Lisburn Circuit. That letter pointed out many evils which existed in the Wesleyan form of church government; and also devised a remedy for those growing innovations upon the rights of the members. He believed that the time had come when some change should take place in order to guard the liberties of the people. The Methodist New Connexion had no station at Richhill at that time, and for the sake of peace he remained with the Old Connexion. He lived to fill up 84 years upon earth, and died rejoicing in the Redeemer. His last words were, 'The best of all is God is with us.' Before his death, E. W. had commenced to tread in the footsteps of her father, and now her surviving parent encouraged her on the pathway to heaven. She delighted in class and in the fellowship of saints; her only companions were the children of God. At an early age, E. W. had a perfect and experimental knowledge of the doctrines of justification by faith and of sanctification by the Holy Spirit; and though she could not mention the time or place of her conversion, yet she enjoyed a clear witness of her acceptance with God. She laid aside all vanity in dress, gave up vain amusements and foolish company, and gave all the time she possibly could to reading, meditation and prayer. In the year 1810, Elizabeth Whitley entered into the married state with John Nicholson. He enjoyed religion and helped her forward in the Divine life: they were both devoted to God, and lived in love and unity until death separated them. Mrs. Nicholson trained up her children in the nurture and admonition of the Lord. She taught them to search the Scriptures; to attend to secret prayer; and also made her sons take part in family worship. Upon the Sabbath she would call her little flock around her chair and speak to them about the love of God, the death and passion of Christ for their sins, and dwell upon the willingness of Christ to receive little children to His fond embrace. The writer of this memoir can distinctly recollect impressions made upon his mind, through the instrumentality of this parent, when he was but six years old. He used to wonder what Mother was doing, when at secret devotion and whispering below her breath, at that time praying for his conversion. He will have reason to bless God for such a mother through one eternal day. Mrs. N., through life up to this time, was saved from temporal distress—the sun of temporal prosperity had shone upon her path. But cares awaited her, of which she had no apprehension. She was now chosen in the furnace of affliction, but she could say, ' He knoweth the way that I take, and when he hath tried me I shall come forth as gold.' Among her severe trials was the derangement of family circumstances. But the good hand of God was with her through all this dark and cloudy day. When the temporal sun was thus obscured by a cloud, the spiritual Sun did not withdraw His light, so that she could always sing of mercy and of judgment. Three days after the interment of her second son she lay down under the burning fever. Her constitution fell a victim to the disorder. Medical aid was called in, but all in vain. Mr. Carter, the Wesleyan preacher, called to visit her, asked the state of her mind—if she could rely upon Christ for pardon and salvation,—she answered him with great satisfaction, and said she had no wish for life, but could say, ' Father, Thy will be done.' Her youngest daughter would read to her frequently from the book of Psalms, and other portions of the Word of God. She would say, 'O, how precious are the promises of my God! They comfort and rejoice my heart!, Mrs. Nicholson continued to rejoice in the Lord, and when not delirious, expressed her confidence in God, and said she looked for a city that hath foundations, and now desired a better country, even the heavenly. She continued in this peaceful state until within forty-eight hours of her death, during that time she suffered much, and was often delirious. On June 6th, 1836, the weary wheels of life stood still, and the immortal spirit left the shattered tabernacle, to dwell in the house not made with hands eternal in the heavens,—

'No sickness there, no shades of night
Profane those mansions blessed ;
There in the happy fields of light,
The weary are at rest.'

Thus departed Mrs. Nicholson, in the 52nd year of her age, leaving a husband and six children to mourn her loss. May her surviving family follow her, as she followed Christ Jesus."

This memoir was not written till after he was received as a preacher by the Methodist New Connexion.

Our devoted friend resumed his labours upon the farm, and entered again upon the work of a local preacher, exercising his gift far and near. A torn scrap before us testifies also that he had entered upon those benevolent labours which held so prominent a place in his exertions In this scrap he says, "The attendance of scholars at the Aghalee Sunday School is far smaller than it would be; but for the poverty of many of the parents. It is very desirable that a Committee should be formed and monies raised for the relief of the poor." Thus he continued to work for a year or two till a younger brother, whose apprenticeship then expired, came home and took our friend's place upon the farm, thus freeing him to enter

wholly again upon the work to which God had called
him.

In 1837, he paid a visit to pious friends, named Anderson, who resided at Lissue. He slept with a young man,
a member of the family, who was notedly pious and mighty
in prayer, but somewhat eccentric. Their conversation
was highly spiritual. This praying youth received a
remarkable answer to prayer, as to the future sphere
of his companion's labours as a preacher. Mr. Nicholson
says, "Young Anderson arose and went down stairs,
where he remained some time. When he returned to
bed, he said, "I have been asking the Lord if you
would ever travel as a preacher again. He impressed
it upon my mind, that you would, but not amongst the
people with whom you are connected at present, but with
another Denomination in the North." This occurred
before Mr. Nicholson had any knowledge of the Methodist
New Connexion.

A friend, who resided in Lurgan, and carried on a lucrative business, invited Mr. Nicholson to reside with him
and help him in the business, and he would make him his
heir. Our brother could not consent to give up the purpose of re-entering the ministry, but went to reside with
this friend for a time. Mr. Nicholson often alluded to a
dreadful storm, which destroyed the spire of Lurgan
Church and wrecked many houses, during his residence
there. The house, in which he spent that dreadful night,
was almost miraculously saved from the fury of the tempest. The deliverance lastingly impressed him, and increased his faith in the guardian care of the God of his
life. In Lurgan our friend came in contact with the
Methodist New Connexion, learned its history, examined
its polity, read its rules, and through Mr. McMillen, a

leader, was introduced to the people and minister at Lurgan, and ultimately became a member and preacher of the Body. We shall here break the continuity of the narrative, in order to make room for a brief account of the Irish Methodist New Connexion Mission.

CHAPTER IV.

ORIGIN AND EARLY HISTORY OF THE IRISH METHODIST NEW
CONNECTION MISSION.

A BRIEF account of the origin and development of
the Mission upon which the subject of this
memorial laboured for nearly half a century will
here be appropriate. The Methodist New Connexion in
Ireland was not an exotic, but a plant of indigenous and
spontaneous growth. We shall best perform this part of
our work by supplying facts from various authentic sources,
viz.,—

1. *Crookshank's History of Methodism in Ireland,*—1798.
In his excellent history, Mr. C. says :—

"Several Societies had been dissatisfied and agitated in regard
to the course adopted by the Conference as to the ordinances and
lay representation. These differences led to the expulsion from
the Society on the Lisburn circuit of thirty-two stewards and
leaders. Against these decision they appealed to the Conference,
which confirmed the resolution of expulsion, with the addendum,
' That they be not received again into the Society, until God give
them repentance.' Upwards of two hundred members in consequence left the Society, formed a separate body, and appointed
as their minister, John McClure, who had been recommended by
the Belfast quarterly and district meetings, to the Conference for

the itinerancy. Subsequently a correspondence was entered into with those who had seceded in England, which led to a union. This was the origin of the Methodist New Connexion in Ireland. The dissentients were, in general, devout and conscientious, and some of them, as old William Black of Lisburn, and George Carlisle, of the Maze, men eminent in piety and zeal."

2. "Address to the Methodist Societies," by the Thirty-two expelled Stewards, &c. "*Lisburn*, April 2nd, 1798."

A copy of this printed address, old, discoloured, and torn, lies upon the writer's desk. In brief, it complains that the Societies were governed exclusively by preachers, and advocates the adoption of the Methodist New Connexion's fundamental principle :—

" *That the Church itself is entitled, either collectively, in the persons of its members, or representatively, by persons chosen out of and by itself, to a voice and influence in all the acts of legislation and government.*"

To this address the names of the famous thirty-two are appended, and are as follow :—

DUNCAN LIVINGSTON, Local Pr. PHELIX CUNNINGHAM, Steward.
WILLIAM BLACK, Ldr. & Trustee. JNO. WHISTON, Leader.
JAMES RICHEY, Leader. NATHANIEL DICKEY, L. & Trustee.
WILLIAM BALMER, Leader. JAS. CARSON, Leader.
GEO. PIKE, L. P. & Trustee. DAVID PATTERSON, Leader.
WM. BOYCE, L.P. & Leader. WM. WOODS, Leader.
JNO. SCANDRETT, Leader. JOS. CHERRY, L. & Trustee.
FRANCIS HAMILTON, Leader. MOSES BUCHANNON, Leader.
PATRICK CUNNINGHAM, Leader. JNO. KELLY, Steward.
TIMOTHY RUSK, Trustee. JAS. WRIGHT, Leader.
HUGH MURRAY, Steward, etc. THOS. BRADSHAW, L. & Trustee.
ROBERT LILLEY, Leader. WM. JOHNSTON, Trustee.
JNO. PEARCE, Leader. JNO. MC CABREY, Leader.
ROBERT BAILLEY, Leader. THOS. McPHERSON, Leader.
WM. COBURNE, Leader. CHAS. HALL, Leader.
WM. M'DOWELL, Leader. JEREMIAH SMITH, Leader.

3. "Memoir of Mr. William Black, of Lisburn, by the Rev. James Argue."

This memoir appeared in the Methodist New Connexion Magazine for 1840. We much regret having to condense a narrative so touching and instructive.

William Black was born at Malone, near Belfast. His parents were members of the Church of England. In 1764, William first heard the Methodists. At this time they had no chapel in Belfast; but an old slaughter-house was fitted up as a temporary accommodation. To gratify curiosity, William went to the preaching, but under the Word, was deeply convinced of sin. On their way home his companions derided the meeting. He asked them, 'Are you not ashamed to mock, coming out of the house of God?' They replied, ' *that* is no house of God, but an old slaughter-house.' 'Be that as it may,' said William, 'it was the house of God to *me*.' His convictions subsided for a time. In 1766, he married the daughter of Hanse Cumberland, of Lisburn, at whose house the Methodist preachers were entertained; and under whose ministry Mr. Black was converted to God. In 1767, he had the honour of entertaining the great and good John Wesley. In describing the labours of this venerated man, on this occasion, Mr. B. observed, ' Mr. Wesley preached in the area of the Linen Hall, from To-day is salvation come to this house.' He afterwards administered the sacrament to about forty or fifty persons, nearly all the Methodists in the counties of Down and Antrim. Whilst I received the sacrament from his hands, I felt Christ precious to my soul, to such a degree as I had never before experienced.' Mr. B. met the class: he and thirteen females constituted the Society in Lisburn; and for two years he was the only man in fellowship with them. Soon he and another began prayer meetings in different parts, classes were formed and the cause prospered. Mr. B. was an early and warm advocate of missionary exertion, and could relate many instances of signal success. He said, ' We sent a missionary to Coleraine, from the Lisburn Society; we prayed fervently for his success; a flourishing society was raised up to serve the Lord, and the great Adam Clarke was given as the fruit of our labours.' In 1798, Mr. Black, and other worthies founded the Methodist New

Connexion in Ireland; the cause of separation was not difference in doctrine or politics. The people wished to have the Lord's Supper administered to them by their own preachers, and not by the hands of ungodly ministers. They had petitioned the Conference, held in Dublin, in 1795, and received the following answer:—

" Dublin, 13th July, 1795.

Very Dear Brethren,—The Conference desire us to inform you, that they took your affectionate letter into long and serious consideration. They assure you, that [it would give them great pleasure, as far as consistent with the glory of God, to serve you in, and indulge you with everything in their power. But when the sense of the Conference was taken by vote, it was the unanimous opinion that: 'It is not expedient to introduce the Administration of the Lord's Supper, by the preachers, into this Kingdom now.' The Conference wish you every blessing of the New Covenant.

Signed on behalf of the Conference,

THOS. COKE, President.

JOHN CROOK, Secretary.

To the Stewards and Leaders of the Lisburn Circuit, who desire to have the Lord's Supper administered to them by the Preachers."

Another cause of separation was church government. Mr. Gordon, then superintendent of Lisburn Circuit, expelled a steward from office. The stewards and leaders called a meeting, and protested. . . Mr. Gordon proved before a special District meeting that he had acted according to the rules. . . The stewards and leaders next prepared an appeal to the Conference, held in Dublin, 1798, of which the following is an abridged copy.

Lisburn, July 9th, 1798.

Dear Brethren,—We think it our duty to address you. . . . , As long as the sun and moon shall endure, we wish real Methodism to flourish and increase. . . . We think that there is not any complaint contained in our address that is not well founded, nor anything contained in the propositions, but what is reasonable and Scriptural. . . . We think that a few of those (brethren)

delegated from the whole body, to District Meetings and Conference, to help to make or revise any law or laws, would not, in the
least degree, militate against the dignity (or sanctity) of the
preachers . . . We are determined to presevere in God's good
cause until our grievances are redressed.

[Here follow the names of the thirty-two leaders.]
To the preachers assembled in Conference."

THE FOLLOWING IS A COPY OF THE ANSWER RECEIVED:—

"Dublin, July 19th, 1798.

Sirs,—Your letter has been read in Conference, and we are
desired to send you the following answer:—The Conference
consider the plan of electing, by the votes of the people, and sending to the Conference and District Meetings, and Committee,
delegates, is founded on the principles of Jacobinism, principles
which we abhor. Such principles have an immediate tendency to
bring into the Church of God, disorder and confusion, similar in
its way, to that which the same principles have brought into the
state. We are certain that our late father in the Gospel detested
these principles as much as any man on earth. The economy he
established among the Methodists, his writings and public declara-
tions from the pulpit, have borne witness of this. We are,
therefore, determined in the most resolved manner, and with the
most unanimous spirit, to reject the plan of delegates in whatever
shape or manner it may be proposed : we are ready to receive any
complaints from our people, to consider them duly, and redress
them as far as they appear to be real grievances; yea, to make
every sacrifice which we believe consistent with the prosperity of
the work of God, to the satisfaction of their minds. As to you,
gentlemen, we consider your late conduct so perfectly opposite to
what we believe to be the true spirit of Christianity, that we can,
on no account, have any further connexion with you, till God,
through His grace, has given you repentance.

Signed on behalf, and by order of the Conference,—

T. COKE, *President*,
A. HAMILTON, *Junr. Secretary.*

The Conference addressed the King; proclaimed their loyalty;
but denounced their late brethren as disaffected. There was one
circumstance connected with these times, to which I never heard

Mr. Black refer, without tears streaming down his furrowed cheeks; in referring to it, he said, "After our expulsion our old friends looked upon us with a jealous eye, because we met and held prayer-meetings. Indeed, they were bitter against us. A spirit of rebellion prevailed in the North; a camp of the King's army was placed at Blair's Moor, near Lisburn; any persons, convicted of disloyalty, were shot or hanged, and beheaded, as examples to others; and a list of our names, thirty-two leaders, stewards and trustees, was given by someone to the General of the King's army, stating that we were rebels against the state, Jacobites in principle, that we held secret meetings, and were unfit to live. The General, while riding with Lieutenant Coulson, of Lisburn, on the road to Belfast, showed him the letter, and inquired of him concerning us. The Lieutenant, on looking at the document, said he knew us all, and there were not more loyal men in the Kingdom, and that the letter arose from a religious quarrel. The General gave the letter to Lieutenant Coulson, who showed it to us. . . . Mr. Black was the only lessee, and trustee of the Lisburn Wesleyan Chapel. . . . The expelled leaders, &c., formed themselves into a separate Body; and shortly after joined the Methodist New Connexion."

In 1828, when a sufferer, William Black was visited, and after prayer, he said, "I have an intimacy, familiarity, and friendship with Jesus, so that I can converse with Him as a man with his friend. . . . I was once uneasy about the things of this life, but the words were impressed on my mind, 'Be content with such things as ye have,' 'I will never forsake you.' On one occasion trade was bad, and I could not support my family. On a Saturday night we had no money; our provisions were done, and the last candle was burned almost to the socket; my wife asked, 'what was to be done for the Sabbath?' 'All is dark,' I said, 'my dear, we'll go to prayer.' While we were praying a knock came to the door. When I opened it, a man gave me a parcel, sent by his master, in which I found ten guineas. The servant said his master bade him not to tell his name. I gave the money to my wife, who burst into tears; we went to our knees and returned thanks. While at prayer there came another knock, it was Lorenzo Dow, who came to lodge a night or two with me."

May, 1831. W. B., was now nearly 90 years of age. He said to me, " I now spend much of my time in my closet, crying for perfect holiness, and communing with my God. I rise every morning at four o'clock, and walk out for meditation. I enjoy much of the life of religion in my soul."

"January, 1835. I visited William Black ; he was sick unto death. He seemed to dwell in both worlds, to enjoy heaven on earth, his soul was filled with the fulness of God; he exhibited as much animation and joy as a Christian in his first love. His heavenly appearance, his sweet rejoicings, and his unshaken confidence were delightful. In rapture and holy triumph he exclaimed. ' O death, where is thy sting? O grave, where is thy victory? Thanks be to God, which giveth us the victory through our Lord Jesus Christ." 'A little before his death, he asked a friend to read John iii. 16. ' Then' he exclaimed, ' I believe ; yes, glory be to God, I do! Then Heaven is mine, angels beckon me away', and Jesus bids me come. I shall not perish but have *everlasting life*, EVERLASTING LIFE!" No fierce disease shook his frame, it seemed gradually to decay, till at length it was dissolved, on 4th Fcbrurary, 1835.   JAMES ARGUE."

The following from the pen of the Rev. W. McClure, appeared in *The Irish Christian Monitor :*

"Wm. Black's soul's feelings, as expressed in his religious experience and address to the Church, while he stood bent down over his staff with age, his limbs trembling with feebleness, his hair white as snow, his face ever and anon raised toward the Heaven for which he longed, while the eyes, lit up with the light of life, long a resident within him, were laved with floods of tears, left an impression on my memory and heart which time can never efface. For it was the last time he stood in our chapel in Lisburn. Not long after I was called to preach his funeral sermon. Shortly after, while conversing with a near relation of my own, she asked me about Mr. Black, and when informed of his happy end, she was deeply impressed and related the following fact to me :—

"In my early life I attended the Parish Church in Belfast, but had no particular impressions about sin; my first anxiety about my soul arose from reading my Bible and Hervey's Meditations, but I kept my feelings to myself, indeed, I had none to whom I

could confide my painful secret. When I got married and settled
in the world, my conviction of sin became more powerful, but still
I knew not what to do. At this time Mr. Wesley was making a
wonderful noise in the country. I became very curious to see and
hear the Methodists, but then to be laughed at, pointed out, or
nicknamed, as one of them, stood powerfully in my way. One
evening—it was the Sabbath—I heard the Methodists were to hold
a meeting within a mile of where I resided, and I resolved to go.
When the hour came, my struggle was most painful; pride, shame,
curiosity, each was master by turns, the latter, however, was victor-
ious, and to be as much as possible unknown and unsuspected, I threw
my cloak over my head, and set off unknown to my family. When
I got to the place, the service was commenced, and without many
noticing me, I slipped in behind the door. The person who held the
meeting was Mr. Black. I had often heard of him, and was glad
to find him. He prayed with amazing earnestness; many were in
evident distress, weeping or praying aloud for mercy, or sighing
very deeply. I was most strangely affected. At first I got some
relief in tears, but soon again my heart got hard, and I thought
my heart would burst. Mr. Black began speaking about God's
love in the gift of Jesus for man's salvation. While he spoke on
this delightful subject, my struggling heart was again relieved by
a flood of tears. He then passed on to point out the necessity
existing for such love ; but how was I terrified when he gave such
a true and vivid account of my own character—my conduct, state,
and feelings were so plainly told to all the people, that I was near
fainting several times with shame and terror. I concealed my face
with my cloak, and bitterly regretted my coming there, and when
the people rose to sing, I slipped quietly out, and half ran all the
way home. What a night of distress that was to me. I thought I
must now be the jest and scorn of the whole place, and for several
days dare not venture from my own house.

Being pleasingly disappointed in the silence of my neighbours,
my thoughts had leisure to take another turn, and Oh, what misery
I was now plunged into, at the thought of my real state before
God. I sought secret places to weep, and my only relief
was the remembrance of what Mr. Black said of a Saviour's love.
At first I dare hardly hope, but at length I ventured to pray, and
in this I found wonderful relief, so that I prayed more and more

F

At length one evening when alone in the byre, milking the cows, my soul got into sore trouble, which became more than I could endure. I feared my perdition was come, I wept aloud, ceased milking, and kneeling down there, poured out my heart in prayer to Jesus. It was now life or death with me. My agony was indescribable. My whole soul became concentrated upon obtaining that of which I had heard such glad tidings from Mr. Black, the knowledge of salvation by the remission of sins, I cried in my agony, ' O Lord, Thou hast promised me this salvation, and died for me rather than let me want it, and shall I after all this perish?" When a voice, as if from Heaven, 'said in my heart—I almost thought I heard it—' No, sinner, no, go in peace, and sin no more.' And, Oh, the peace and power, and praise that came with that word, I feel its sweetness yet, though fifty years and more have passed away since then.

A class was formed near her house. The preachers found her house a home; they do so still. My father (John McClure), then a a local preacher residing in Malone, was useful and much esteemed. In his visits to this place he became acquainted with her eldest daughter, whom he afterwards married. Her eldest son is to this day a steady, holy, useful man; and of the chapel before noticed, many a soul both on earth and in Heaven, can say, "I was born there."

On Feb. 6th, 1835, the remains of Wm. Black were borne to their last resting place on the shoulders of four preachers, viz., J. Lyons, Wm. Mc Clure, T. Seymour, and T. Haslam. John Murray, according to the request of Mr. Black, gave out solemn hymns, as the body was being borne along to Refuge Chapel, and thence to the churchyard, the people joining in the singing."

4. *Memoir of John McClure, by his son William.*

In the Life of the Rev. W. McClure, by Rev. D. Savage, is given a memorial sketch of the Rev. John McClure. This account of a noble sire by a worthy son is most pathetic and interesting. Glad should we be to give the whole of it, if space allowed. We must confine ourselves to a few facts in condensed form.

" So soon as it became known that Jno. McClure had espoused
the cause of the expelled, a host rose to change his mind and bring
him back again, most of whom sincerely loved him, and were
actuated by the very best motives; and every motive that could
be urged was urged. He was even offered an immediate appointment to a Circuit if he ¡would abandon his colleagues. Still he
remained inflexible, and their endeavours only served to make him
examine his position the more carefully, and the more he examined
the more firmly he maintained himself. Then slander, anathema,
poverty, shame, odious party names, and private or public opposition, all tried their powers; and although they caused deep
anguish of soul, considering the quarter whence they came, they
only confirmed him more and more in the righteousness
of his cause. No man would meet him (though frequently
solicited) to discuss the questions at issue, either on the platform or through the press. These annoyances were not allowed
to interrupt his diligence in the ministry; and his reputation as
an able minister of the Word, spread far and wide, while the Lord
gave him many seals to his ministry.

I find, on referring to my father's notes of plans and texts for
the years, 1799 and 1800, that he preached at that time in Bangor,
Ballywoolley, Newtownards, Belfast, Knockbracken, Lisburn, Milltown, Broomhedge, Balmer's Quarry, Kircreeny, Maze, Moorside,
Kilwarlin, Halftown, Magheragal, Moyrusk, Grove, Broughmore,
Ballymecash, Hugh Murray's or Cairnban and Priesthill. In all these
places the fruits of his labours remain till this day, while much has
been gathered home to the garner above. This was his regular
Circuit, but he went beyond it, where God was not savingly
known. He usually experienced kindness, but sometimes rude-
ness, an instance of which it may be well here to state.

On going to preach at Knockbracken, several young men gave
annoyance during the service, but my father's eye restrained them
a good deal till the service was over, but when he left the place to
go home, they commenced an attack upon him, and pelted him
heartily with turf, which they procured from the stack of the good
man in whose house my father had preached. Having met with
no resistance, they promised the next preacher who visited them a
similar compliment. The news of the whole affair was soon known
in Newtownbreda, in which place some persons resided who re-

spected, and resolved to protect, the preachers. At the time appointed the preacher passed through the village on his way to Knockbracken. On seeing him, a very strong, daring man—a nail. maker—quitted his work, called upon a number of his fellow tradesmen to accompany him, and, taking their hammers in their pockets, went to the place of meeting. During the sermon the rowdy party pinched a young woman who started up with a scream, at which a loud laugh was set up. Instantly the un-washed nailers stood up and drew their hammers, while their leader shouted, that if any person gave annoyance, he would bury his hammer in his skull. "Now, boys," said the preacher, "keep quiet and we'll do you no harm." And quiet as mice they did keep, and never afterwards offered any violence to the preaching of the Word in that place.

I find in a memorandum book of my father's the following entry—" On Sunday, 7th September, 1800, I opened the first meeting for worship, in the Weaver's Hall, Dublin (I mean the first meeting that was held there in the name of God, and the Methodist New Connexion.) My father had in 1801, to return to the North of Ireland; but the Society in Dublin kept together, amidst reproach and difficulty, when they had no preacher for years, except those whom God raised up among themselves. After labouring in the North many years, and struggling with financial difficulties, Mr. McClure was found again in Dublin, in 1814.

It was in the spring of 1815, that Mr. Thos. West decided to emigrate to America. The Dublin Society had been kept together mainly by his exertions, and they loved him dearly as a preacher and friend. The vessel in which he was to embark lay off in the bay of Dublin. About thirty members of the Society accompanied him as far as the Pigeon-house. They all knelt down on the sea-shore, to commend one another in prayer to God, before parting. While Mr. McClure was praying, a regiment of soldiers approached the place where the praying company knelt. The commanding officer in front of his men, seeing the worshippers, uncovered his head, and slackened his pace; and his example was followed by all the soldiers. It was an impressive sight: on the one side the solemn military procession, on the other the ocean, and before them the ramparts and fortifications of the Pigeon-house, with the sentinels passing to and fro, and in the centre, the little band, with faces turned to Heaven, in earnest prayer.*

In May, 1817, Mr. McClure was prostrated under a serious illness. For a time he suffered extreme pain, until at length the end approached. He had a severe conflict with the enemy, but gained the victory. When all considered him inacpable of speaking, Mr. Prince said, "John, if thou art still sensible, though no longer able to speak, tell us by a motion of the hand, if all is still well with thee." The dying saint's eyes immediately opened, and looking upwards, he raised his arm, saying very distinctly, "Yes, all is well. My heart is bound by the cords of love." His eyes closed, a placid smile rested on his countenance, and he ceased to breathe, May 14th, aged thirty-eight years."

5. PATRICK CUNNINGHAM, JAMES WRIGHT, and JAMES HALLIDAY,—three of the noted thirty-two.

Our narrative would not be complete without some reference, however brief, to these worthy men.

"*The Life of Patrick Cunningham, written by himself, revised and corrected by A. Scott.*

A large tract, eighty years old, bearing the foregoing title, lies before the writer, and from it the following particulars are culled:

"P. Cunningham was born in the parish of Lisburn, on 24th of June, 1742. His parents were Roman Catholics, and he was trained from childhood in the mysteries and idolatries of Popery. He says, 'Thus was my mind overspread with a cloud of superstition which darkened the glimmerings of reason, and excluded the light of Revelation. I was taught that none could be saved but Roman Catholics, and that the rest of mankind were heretics, not fit to live.' He was, however, the subject of early and oft-recurring convictions of sin. His father kept a race-horse, and Patrick, had to attend the races, and take part in the cruel and degrading

---

* "It has been ascertained that the Mr. West of this sketch became, and continued to be for many years, the minister of a large and flourishing Church in New York; also that he had a son who laboured in the Gospel ministry after his father, and may perhaps still be engaged in his calling within the bounds of the United States."—*Rev. D. Savage.*

sport. He tells of faction fights, during the races, in those days, between the Broomhedge and Hillsborough men, in which some lost their lives. He became openly wicked, indulging in drink and other vices. God afflicted him again and again, and he as often promised to amend, which, however, only meant attending mass, counting beads, and going occasionally to confession, &c.

He married, thinking it would steady him, but he soon found that he was the same man after marriage that he was before, perhaps worse. The death of a brother alarmed him for a time. In 1775, he went to Halftown, expecting to hear Mr. Wesley preach, but heard Mr. Perfect instead, the former having taken ill. Patrick says, 'I felt the preacher's word to be quick and powerful, and it made such an impression on me as I had never experienced before.' Soon after a terrific storm of thunder and lightning greatly alarmed him, increasing his convictions. The Priest, to whom he applied in his distress, gave him a priest-book, which was not to be opened, but suspended from the neck with a string. In addition he was to read over St. Bridget's prayers five times the next week, and then return to the priest for the sacrament. These exercises only increased his sense of guilt, and left him tormented with slavish fears. In the midst of his distress he paid a visit to a stepson, James Wright, of Moyrusk. Patrick's story was the means of awakening James's conscience, and driving him into secret places to plead for mercy. Soon James's convictions could not be hidden, and often he was seen prostrate, crying aloud for pardon. He made his case known to the despised Methodists, at Broomhedge; heard Mr. Bredin preach; and at length was filled with joy and peace through believing. Patrick now said, ' I will be as good a christian as young James, without joining the Methodists.' But Patrick's trouble deepening, he was induced by James to hear Mr. Bredin and other Methodists preach. After an interview with him, Mr. Bredin said, that Patrick would leave the Romans; but Patrick says, 'at that time, I could scarcely have been persuaded of it by an angel from Heaven.' He wished for the sake of his parents, to be saved in the Church of Rome, if possible. But his mind became gradually enlightened to see the errors, superstitions, and idolatries of Rome, and at length he abandoned the mass, and threw his priest-book and all other idols to the moles and the bats. Now the Romans abhorred him; his father and mother ceased to speak to him, and tried to injure their "apostate" son. Here is the account of his conversion as related by Patrick himself:—'I went to Lisburn, to hear the Rev. Edward Smith, who had left the Established Church, and come amongst the Methodists. He preached Christ Jesus the Lord, in the power of the Holy Ghost. He had a message from God unto me. Under the sermon, a ray of heavenly light broke through the cloud which had so long involved me in darkness. The Divine impression went home with me, and that night, at family prayer, God set my soul at liberty. I was enabled to believe with all my heart unto righteousness, my burden of guilt was removed, and I received the witness of the Spirit.' Soon he began to lead in prayer, in which he had 'uncommon liberty.' For some time he met in class with Hugh Murray and Joseph Cherry, till he was made a leader himself.

In 1784 Patrick began a prayer meeting at Priesthill. James Cherry, a burning as well as a shining light, united with Patrick in his labours. In 1786, the first Chapel was erected at Priesthill. The Marquis of Downshire said to the people, 'When Cunningham comes again, put him overhead in the canal, but do not drown him.' The Marquis had been prejudiced by enemies, but soon ceased his unfriendliness to the Methodists. From seeing the evils wrought by intoxicants, Patrick Cunningham became a total and determined abstainer at an early date. We shall close this narrative in Patrick's own words. ' Before my mother's death there was a change in her sentiments; she was very glad to have me praying with her, and appeared to give a hearty reception to all my instructions. During her last illness, which lasted six months, she never prayed to any saint or angel. 'Save, Lord Jesus,' was her constant cry.'

A few years ago a division took place amongst the Methodists, and I went with those who are called the New Connexion. The sole ground of dispute was the Government of the Church. The preachers claimed the right of governing the people. We thought the people should have some share in the formation of their own laws. We also requested to have the sacraments administered by our own preachers. . . Since the separation we have had all the privileges we sought. And now, after a trial of eight or nine years, we are fully persuaded of the propriety of the measures we adopted. . . Both my sons are class-leaders. My only daughter died in the Lord in October, 1803. I have now been in the Methodist Connexion for thirty years, and am thankful to God that ever my lot fell amongst them. . . No sin has dominion over me; I am crucified to the world, and the world unto me; and the life that I now live, I live by the faith of the Son of God, who loved me and gave Himself for me.' It should be added that Patrick Cunningham's father, a few days before his death, sent for his despised son, requesting him to come and pray with him. When Patrick went into the room, his father burst into tears, and asked 'was there any salvation for such a sinner as he.' But whether he was changed by Divine grace, Patrick never knew."

James Wright's memoir was written by Rev. W. McClure, and appeared in the *Irish Christian Monitor* for 1844. In this memoir is repeated the interviews between Patrick Cunningham and his stepson, and the happy result to both men. When the Lord opened Lydia's heart, she opened her house to the Apostles, so, after James Wright's conversion, his house became a "home" for Mr. Wesley's preachers, on their monthly rounds. The first sermon in *Moyrusk* was preached by Mr. Jno. Bredin, on Feb. 16, 1776, from the text, "God is love." On a pane of glass the preacher, with a diamond, wrote his text, his own name, and the date. The glass afterwards was taken out, and framed; and is at present kept as a precious relic by Mr. Jas. Crawfood, of Chlorine, Belfast. Mr. McClure says:

" Our friend J. Wright took a deep interest in those differences and struggles, both in England and Ireland, which led to the formation of the Methodist New Connection in 1797-8. Though he never regretted the part he had taken in the conflict, yet his sensitive mind, looking back, could perceive chaff among the wheat, and he fervently prayed for the healing of differences. While he continued from the first firmly attached to the principles of our Connexion, none had ever to complain of his preventing their usefulness, or of his envying their success in doing good. It pleased God to suffer him to be severely afflicted with rheumatic attacks when in the very vigour of life, which, after binding with the cords of agony almost every muscle of his body, ultimately confined him for the last twenty years of his life to the house. Towards the close of life his soul was subject to sudden changes, and to very opposite states of feeling, now depressed, now filled with peace and joy. On one occasion when I visited my suffering brother, I found him the prey of anxiety and fear. We talked freely on the subject of his great uneasiness ; he was soon blessed with a view of the bright side of the cloud, his heart was melted into love and joy, his lips were filled with praises to the Lord, and we prayed, and wept, and rejoiced together. [No doubt James Wright's variable experiences were mainly traceable to physical causes.] Friend Wright was three weeks confined to bed before the conflict terminated. . . . His soul gradually settled down with immovable confidence on the merits of his Redeemer, and the promises of his God, and he entered the Heaven for which he longed, in undisturbed peace, on the evening of Sabbath, 22nd December, 1833."

In the homestead at Moyrusk, there survived James Wright, a seed to serve the Lord. The writer was acquainted with his daughter, Isabella, for the last twenty years or so of her life. He prepared a memoir of her, which appeared in the *Methodist New Connexion Magazine*, for May, 1876. She was one of the Rev. S. Nicholson's most attached friends in Christ. Though this chapter is exceeding the limit intended, yet all who remember her, will approve of the insertion here of the

Memoir of Miss Isabella Wright.

It was just 100 years, on 16th of February last, since the first Methodist preacher entered the house at Moyrusk, then the residence of Mr. James Wright, the father of our deceased sister. In this house Isabella Wright was born twice—of the flesh and of the Spirit; and it was her only dwelling place during the entire eighty-seven years of her earthly pilgrimage. As she led a single life, there was little of stirring interest in her outward history. It was one of her great regrets, that so many as thirty-six years of her life had passed before she became a Christian. She heard the Gospel preached regularly from childhood, and it must be said that, notwithstanding the outward morality of her life, her resistance to the Holy Spirit so long is evidence of aggravated guilt. The death of a brother, to whom she was ardently attached, was the means of awakening her fears of coming death and judgment. For a whole year she carried about with her the most painful sense of guilt and fear of Divine wrath. During this period her religious exercises were varied, painful, and continuous, being often carried on in the night as well as during the day. In her early life, she was timid, and afraid to be alone in the dark, but during the period of her anxiety this disappeared, giving place to the greater fear of a justly angry God. She was known to start from her bed in the morning, while it was yet dark, and to go out into an empty house behind her father's that there, alone, she might give vent to her pent-up grief and call aloud upon God for mercy. Her parents often heard her during the night pleading in prayer. She searched the Scriptures, but for long, she could see nothing in them but the sentence of her own condemnation. She listened to the voice of the law until almost driven to despair. In the terrible roar of Sinai's thunders the answering voice of Calvary was oft completely drowned. She fasted frequently; one of her fasts, at this time, during part of each day, extended over seven weeks. These fasts reduced her so much, that it was thought she would fall into consumption.

At length the glad day of her deliverance arrived. The following are nearly her own words :—" I was sitting," she said, " by the fire, not thinking very much on the subject at the time, when suddenly the words, ' I am thy surety, I am thy salvation,' seemed to sound all around me." These words awoke in her heart emotions new and heavenly. They were the words of the truth of the Gospel attuned to heavenly music; and she believed them, and was saved. During her last illness, referring to the time of her conversion, a friend asked her, " Do you think that fasting and agonizing and striving of yours had anything to do with your salvation? "No," she replied. "Well," he continued, "what was the reason you worked so hard for the blessing, and tortured yourself so much?" "Just," she answered, "because I thought my conversion would be all the dearer, and that I would be made more joyous and happy than any other Christian." "Yes," her friend replied, "You had a path marked out for yourself, but it was all spoiled." To this she heartily assented. Her conversion took place at Easter, 1819. She ever after kept this season of the year as a solemn fast and time of special prayer and thanksgiving. Miss Wright's place in the class was never vacant; and she had a particular seat in the Chapel which was as regularly occupied as that in the class. For years she thought it no toil to walk three or four miles to be present at the quarterly love-feasts. At the death of her parents, whom she had tenderly nursed, the paternal mansion and farm passed into her hands. It was all her life a house of prayer. During prayer her responses were frequent, earnest, and most hopeful, proving the concurrence of her sympathy, desires, and faith. The Word of God, wherever she sat, was always within reach. Her favourite portions of Scripture were the 14th of John, and the 8th of Romans. The former was the last chapter we read to her, and she seemed to receive the words of comfort as from the lips of Jesus himself. She had her hour for private prayer, and when that hour arrived, she would leave any company in order to keep her tryst with the Beloved. For many years she was unable to walk or to kneel from pains in her limbs, and she was helped off her car into the chapel by willing hands, Ultimately her affliction compelled her to give up attendance upon the public means of grace. She was much cast down, "but," she added, "the Lord seemed to say to me, 'am not I with thee?'" This assurance hushed her complaint and filled her soul with gratitude. Sister Wright had no enemies, and the reason is not far to seek—she was nobody's enemy. There is a garment of heavenly texture which, from frequent use, she well knew how to adjust—we mean the garment of charity. On one occasion, when conversing about evil speaking, she said, "Let that mind be in you, which was also in Christ Jesus; I mean, if you do not think evil thoughts you will not speak evil words." She acted on the belief, that the garment of charity is specially designed to cover

not the faultless, but the faulty and erring. Hardly a day passed
on which she did not give money as well as food to the poor. She
was known to clothe people that they might be fitted to attend
the means of grace; even to the undeserving she gave, knowing
their character. And her benefactions were not such only as she
could easily spare. She has been known to take garments off
her own person to give to those who were poorly clad. She was
an earnest Christian worker. If St. James himself had known her
faith, he would not have pronounced it dead but living. She
visited the sick and erring; held female meetings in her own
house; taught children to read; gave her class an annual tea, and
was emphatically "given to hospitality." Space will not allow a
full portrait. Her piety was a joyous thing; Jesus made her, not
sad, but glad, and a subdued humour sparkled in her conversation.
Children loved her, and they are good judges of character. "I do
wish," said a child to her once, "you were my mamma." She was
undemonstrative, humble and unassuming, and the fact never
seemed to strike her, that she was highly esteemed by all classes
of the community around her. Her dress was the index of her
mind, being severely plain, of the early Methodist type, Her
words were few and well-chosen, and her silence itself was 'golden.'
A Christian lady, having heard much about our esteemed sister,
called to see her, expecting to hear *much* from herself, but Sister
Wright "said so little" our friend could see nothing in her but "a
plain, quiet, old woman."

Our sister had her "dark days." After one of those days, the
promise, "I will never leave thee," was applied to her heart.
"You see," she said, in her quiet humour, "what company I'm
to have." Chronic rheumatism (her father's complaint) began at
last to affect Sister Wright's brain, yet she was as clear in her
personal apprehension of Christ and His salvation as ever, and
her personal trust and confidence in her Redeemer continued
strong to the last. Towards the last, when confined to bed, and
her sufferings intense, she prayed earnestly for "more patience."
"Do you think Jesus loves *you*?" She seemed as if startled at
the doubt which the form of the question might have started,
and replied with energy, "To be sure He does, could I doubt
it?" She seemed never for a moment to debate the question of
her personal safety in Christ. She said, "It is fifty-seven years

since God pardoned my sins,"—"Christ is everything to me now."
To a young friend, "J—, give your heart to the Lord, I would
not for a thousand worlds I had not my sins pardoned now at
the last." "It will be all Heaven by-and-bye," remarked a friend.
"Ay! Ay!" she responded, "that it will, and I shall see Him
as He is." It was suggested, "Is there not even more than that?"
"Won't it be even more to be *like* him?" "Yes," she replied,
"that is many steps higher." This thought remained with her,
and ministered greatly to her comfort. Shortly before the end we
were led to try and describe for her the company of old friends
who would greet her on the "golden shore."—"They will say, as
you enter through the heavenly portals, 'Welcome! welcome!'
and the shout will run along among them there, 'She is come!
Sister Wright is come!' The old members and leaders will be
there.' "Ay," she put in, "and the old preachers too;" and she
literally laughed out with joy. At length her eyes became dim,
her voice almost left her, and her enchained spirit began to flutter
in its clay tenement to be gone. On the morning of Tuesday,
14th Dec., before day-dawn, the earthly scene closed, and the
spirit of Isabella Wright vacated the body, passed the angelic
sentinels at the gate of the Eternal City, and with adoring
wonder and joy, fell prostrate at the feet of her Saviour and
God, in the presence of the glorified throng before the Eternal
Throne.

In the *Methodist New Connexion Magazine*, for 1840, a
memoir of James Halliday appeared, having been written
by Rev. W. Cooke, D.D.

Jas. Halliday was born of Presbyterian parents, in Bangor, in
1769. When about fifteen years of age, he was awakened and
converted to God under the ministry of the Methodist Itinerants.
After earnestly seeking it, he received the assurance of his accept,
ance, while at work in one of his father's fields. Thereafter he
became "a burning and a shining light." Zeal, firmness, benevolence, and consistency were the acknowledged features of his character. "In the year 1814, he was the chief originator of the
Methodist Sunday School, in Bangor, which was the first in the
province of Ulster." The Hon. Col. Ward presented a site for the

school-house, and Mr. Crawford, of Crawford's Burn, gave Mr. Halliday a liberal subscription towards its erection. Afterwards the Hon. Col. Ward gave additional ground, and a subscription of £10 towards the school's enlargement. James Halliday was one of the thirty-two worthies who founded our cause in Ireland. His house became a home for our ministers. At a love-feast, in January, 1839, our brother said, "It is more than fifty years since God convinced me that I was a sinner and led me to the Saviour. I bless God, I am not tired of his service. I feel old age and infirmity pressing on me, but I know in Whom I have believed. I have a blessed hope of everlasting life beyond the grave." Our brother's happy death took place on March 14th, 1839. At his funeral, an immense concourse of people were present from the surrounding country, and never was a more general manifestation of esteem and regret exhibited than on that solemn occasion. On the following Sabbath, his death was improved to an overwhelming audience, in the large Presbyterian Church kindly lent for the occasion.

"'Other lips must praise,' else Jas. Halliday's deeds were forever hid; for 'Thine was by stealth to wipe away misery's tear.' His house was the home of the 'man of God' before the death of John Wesley, and the longed-for resting place of our preachers seven years before I was born. From the evening I was taken into his house my orphanage was ever, for James, and Mary his sainted wife, were father and mother to me. He died when I was stationed in Dublin. His end was more than peace, and many that day wept with me over our own and the Church's bereavement. His firm attachment to the New Connexion Church was well tested. He was for many years an elder in the Presbyterian Church. At a Society meeting, our rules and doctrines were read, and Mr. Halliday was requested to decide upon being only one of two things—Methodist or Presbyterian. He refused to change his relation to the latter; and the Society was compelled to declare him no longer a member. His class book was given up, and the meeting appointed me leader in his place, After a painful pause, Mr. Halliday said, 'So you have put me out, brethren? Well, thank God for Methodism, it keeps no sinner out. I won't stay out, but come back again *on trial!* Then turning round to me, he said ' William, put my name down as one *on trial*; It was done, and he was ours ever after, with thanks for strict discipline."*

Did space allow, there are other names which deserve special mention, but the foregoing are sufficient to show the kind of men who founded the New Itinerancy in Ireland.

The Methodist New Connexion in this country had exceptional difficulties in the way of its growth from the first. The principle of government by representatives of the people, freely chosen, was very unpopular ninety years ago. It is at present the principle which prevails in the larger number of Methodist bodies. For example, the government of the *United Methodist Church* of Canada and that of the Methodist New Connexion are identical in principle, and, we believe, in form also. But in 1797, &c., the principle of which we speak was "abhorred." We have already given the language of the then Methodist Conference, in reply to the famous thirty-two:—"The Conference consider the plan of electing, by the votes of the people, and sending to the Conference and District Meetings, Committees, etc., delegates, is founded on the principle of Jacobinism, principles which we abhor." Doubtless the spirit of rebellion which so widely prevailed in Ireland, made fearful the hearts of the preachers who comprised the Conference of 1798, and disordered their perceptions and judgment on questions of government. Be this as it may, the cause upon which the opprobrium was cast, suffered much in consequence. It toiled bravely on, however, witnessing for a popular Church polity, doing much good, but reaping in members but a small propor-

* Life and Labours of the Rev. Wm. McClure, pp. 49-50.

tion of the fruit of its own labours. "At the Conference of 1799, a number of friends in Ireland were recognised as members of the Methodist New Connexion, and the Rev. John McClure was stationed at Lisburn."* This was mere recognition, and very little help in money or agents was rendered for many years. "At the Conference of 1824, Ireland was selected by the New Connexion as its field of missionary enterprise. The Conference of 1825, developed the plan in its details, appointed a committee to conduct the business of the Mission, and resolved on sending an English preacher to superintend the labours of the missionaries."† After this considerable progress was soon recorded.

"In examining the denominational literature of the period covered by the earlier year of Mr. Mc. Clure's ministry," says his biographer, the Rev. D. Savage,‡ 'I have been struck with the honest, hearty, and untiring vigour with which the Missionary appliances of the Methodist New Connexion in Ireland were at this time worked. Nor less noticeable is the cheering success with which the Lord of the harvest in so many instances, blessed the labours of the missionaries. That the results do not now, after many days, appear, in those forms of denominational consolidation and establishment, is true.—To communities as well as to individuals, the principle sometimes has application that 'one soweth and another reapeth'; and in many parts of

---

* The Jubilee of the Methodist New Connexion, p. 156.

†   ,,   ,,   ,, Id.   p.169.

‡ Mr. Savage was a minister of the Methodist New Connexion in Canada, when the different sections of Methodism in the Dominion amalgamated. We take the following from the *I.C. Advocate:* " Speaking of the wonderful progress of the Church in Canada, Rev. B. Sherlock said that much of it was due to the efforts of the Rev. D. Savage (and his Mission Band). Mr. Savage is the Thomas Champness of Canada."

Ireland the Methodist New Connexion has laboured, and others have entered into their labours.'

We have examined the letters of the Superintendents and those of the Missionaries which appeared in the *New Methodist Magazine*, from 1825 till 1840, and have collected the following list of preaching places, with the view of giving some idea of the extent of the Society's operations during those years. The names were transcribed as they occurred, without reference to geographical situation or connection. Some names may have escaped our notice :

Belfast	Bangor	Newtownards
Ballinahinch	Lisburn	Smithboro'
Newtownbreda	Priesthill	Downpatrick
Newcastle	Broomhedge	Selchin
Antrim	Moira	Blackwater
Ballymuldery	Lurgan	Tonnycoogin
Cornearney	Richill	Largey
Ballymena	Gracehill	Carnlea
Randalstown	Tubbermore	Cullybackey
Gloonen	Seaford	Lanehill
Drumnall	Bryansford	Killough
Ring-Woody	Armagh	Lismore
Ardglass	Quintin Bay	Magerhafelt
Scotchtown	Cohan	Monaghan
Drumnail	Anna Cramp	Derry Corr
Portadown	Ballyhaise	Dumnall
Woodburn	Nockranagan	Innisrush
Derrehalla	Tullyserran	Loughgall
Stradone	Slash	Charlemount
Glasslough	Crossforth	Ballyhay
Clones	Bailieborough	Ballyhorneu
Ballyhulbert	Crewe	Stonyford
Ballinderry	Moyrusk	Milltown

A few extracts from the forementioned letters will help to show the zeal, fidelity, and courage with which the missionaries prosecuted their arduous labours.

Letter from the Rev. H. Hunter, dated Lisburn, Aug. 4th, 1825.

Smithborough Station is not less than 120 miles once round it; here I travelled 18 months, and passed through a part of six counties. In Ballinahinch twenty persons meet regularly in class. In Moira we have a tolerable class. I have not a single night as a rest from preaching except one in twenty-one days. In Downpatrick we have a large chapel.

From the same, dated Belfast, Oct. 18th, 1825.

A revival on the Lisburn Station. Upwards of twenty souls have been added to our society. At Ballinahinch there is a special outpouring of the Spirit. In Belfast two Roman Catholics have joined our society.

From the Rev. Jno. Lyons, dated Downpatrick, Nov. 15th, 1827.

In the neighbourhood of Lismoor I obtained liberty to preach in a blacksmith's house; and, though it was a rainy day, the place was crowded to excess. We had a young priest and his father, who seemed to pay every attention. Ballyhornen may properly be called new ground, as the Gospel was never known to be preached here before. I took my stand at the door. There were about three hundred persons inside, and about half as many outside. More than two-thirds of the congregation were Romanists. As I endeavoured to show what sin had done upon them, they seemed quite surprised; but I went on to show Christ's willingness to receive them, after all they had done, the tears trickled down the withered cheeks of the aged. I had the pleasure of meeting a young man who was educated for a priest, but refused to become one. He stopped all night with me, and took great pains to recommend my sermon to the people.

From the same, dated Lisburn, March 17th, 1829.

At Stonyford and Ballinderry we have large congregations. Our society at Moyrusk has to lament the death of Mr. Nathaniel Dickey, one of the persons who commenced the Methodist New Connection in this country. I have no doubt but he lived and died a Christian. A Mr. Bradbury, who lives near the race-course, has opened his house to us. Here we have large congregations We have to lament the death of two of our leaders, G. Carlisle and W. Watson. The former kept a class in his house for forty years; the latter was a decided Christian.

From the Journal of J. G. Duff, dated Sept. 17th, 1829.

This day I read in the parish of Saul, where most of the inhabitants are Papists, ten chapters from the Renish Testament. When the name of His Holiness is affixed, all is well, and the people hear as for eternity.—Interview at Bryansford, between a Priest and a woman of the Presbyterian persuasion, who is unfortunately married to a papist. The husband had been repeatedly and publicly reproved for allowing his children to go to meeting with their mother. The Priest, finding his threats of no avail, resolved to try what speaking to the mother would do. He came and told his errand, not knowing that a Bible-reader was present. The woman was much provoked on hearing him declare that the children were not *hers*, but *his*. She replied it was the first time she ever heard of a *priest* having children; at the same time declaring they were *Neddy's* (that being her husband's name) and not "Father" H——'s. He drove off uttering threats: turning round he said he wanted the three eldest, but he cared not where the devil the *Methodist* fellow went, meaning the youngest, who was piously disposed. Brother Bartley and I held a meeting in Loughgant. Such were the blessed effects of the sermons, that the congregation fell down upon their knees in the street. An old woman was brought to God. One woman, on our going away, said, "Oh, sir, when will you be back converting again?" I smiled and said, "None can convert sinners, but God alone." Messrs. Burke, Bartley, and I held a meeting in Monaghan. The Papists surrounded us on all sides so that our lives seemed in imminent danger. The yelling and shouting were dreadful, The Protestants came to our help, several ascended the cart, saying they would die for us, rather than see us ill-treated. A schoolmaster cried out, "Order, order! Here is a man who says he is going to pray to the Lord Jesus on your behalf." They were immediately silent. We sung and prayed, and addressed them thirty minutes. The magistrates sent their police, who guarded us out of the town, as a mob had determined to waylay us.

From the Rev. Thos. Robinson, (Superintendent) Belfast,
Dec. 8th, 1829.

" I requested Mr. Hunter to visit Armagh, and if practicable, to
take a room and commence preaching. He did so, and twice
delivered the Gospel message to large congregations. Papists
opposed; but the police guarded him.—On Sabbath morning, I
repaired to the preaching-room, when I found the top part of the
door nailed up! Stooping under to gain an entrance, I saw
several of our friends within arguing with the Catholics, who
appeared determined to drive us from the place. I addressed
myself to the ringleader, who insisted that the place was
improper, and that if we persevered, we should have cause to
repent of it. At the request of one of our friends, the sergeant of
the police, with two of his men, came into the place before we
commenced worship. Our enemies, finding we were determined
to proceed, endeavoured to disturb the order of the service by
singing, shouting, etc., during the whole of it. At 5 o'clock p. m.,
we again repaired to the room, when we found the door nailed up
as in the morning; but Mr. Thompson, the occupier, burst it open,
and in a few minutes it was very well filled. The police were
again in attendance; but so soon as we commenced singing, the
Papists set up such a yell, as I never before heard. They procured
long pieces of wood, and beat against the floor, until I several
times thought the boards would spring from their fastenings.
Another party stationed themselves behind the partition-wall in
front of me, thumping desparately with their fists, hooting, and
crying, ' No surrender, no surrender.' It was with difficulty I
could speak so as to be heard. The next evening they were, if
possible, more outrageous than ever. We agreed to accept Mr.
Blair's kind offer of his parlour, which we have occupied ever
since. The man who was our principal opposer, soon after this
affair, was found dead in his bed. A woman of the same party
has also exchanged worlds."

From the Rev. Thos. Seymour, dated Armagh, Dec. 9th, 1829.

" Nearly two hundred persons assembled (in the market-house,
Loughgall). I preached to them a present salvation. Mr. Duff

gave an address; and truly God was present. The silent tear that stole down the cheeks of many, testified their inward feeling. In *Portadown* also, a town nine miles aside of this city, we held a meeting in the street. The people invited us to come again. In *Armagh* Mr. Duff and I went into the street and preached, published for the room, which in the evening was crowded to excess. The power of God fell upon the people. Our congregations have continued large ever since."

From the Rev. J. Seymour, dated Ballymena, July 6th, 1830.

"In some parts they assure me they never heard of Methodism till I visited them. Travelling over a mountain in this (Cullybackey) district, I saw a large, white house, and knelt down to pray near it. I thought I should be glad to have that house to preach in. Soon after I was called upon to visit the mistress of that house, who had taken ill. It is now one of my lodging-places on this station. New Ferry: The servant, a Papist, took a large iron sledge from the corner, and unnecessarily and unaccountably carried it to the loft above me. As I sat by the fire, a board of the loft was disturbed, and an opening effected above my head. In a few minutes the great iron sledge fell, within two or three inches of me. It shattered a dog's leg, and almost killed him. The girl was questioned, but no satisfactory answer obtained."

From the Rev. T. Seymour, dated Ballimore, Aug. 6th, 1831.

"Our prospects are daily opening before us. I have preached in two new places; and have invitations to three more. The wife and part of the family of a drunken Papist attended preaching among the Methodists, which his soul abhorred.—He called his eldest daughter to him, and told her that if she ever again durst go to hear those fellows, the Methodist preachers, might some judgment overtake him, if he would not break, I know not exactly, whether her legs or her neck. He then set off to the public-house—tippled till he became insensible, when, laying down his head upon a table, he slept to wake no more!"

From the Rev. Wm. McClure, April 5th, 1833.

"On Monday, to Saintfield, nine miles; on Tuesday, to Ballynahinch, four miles; on Wednesday, to Mr. Kearns', three miles; and
on Thursday, to Belfast, ten miles. One day I was led by a man,
over a high hill, to a hovel, the dimensions of which were about
9 feet wide, by 12 feet long, and the side wall about 4 feet high.
The smoke from the burning turf was so thick and sharp, I could
hardly see or breathe. The inmates assured me I should be better
if I sat down, and so I found, as my head was now lower than the
top of the door, whence the smoke escaped over our heads. The
floor was filthy, the walls and roof were like the inside of an old
chimney, and behind the door some large stones were piled to the
height of one's knee. Over this was spread a covering of sods, cut
off the surface of a grass field, a double row at one end serving the
purpose of a bolster; over this was thrown some loose straw, kept
from scattering by a ragged, filthy cloth. On this wretched pallet
lay an old man seventy years of age—a very long figure—his head
was very gray, and his whole body filled with a loathsome complaint. His anguish from sickness and thirst seemed dreadful,
and the complicated maladies of the body appeared to have
deadened every feeling of the soul, except anger, malice, hatred,
revenge, and impatience. To such a pitch did his bad feelings
lead him, that he ground his teeth with rage, and continued to
repeat injuries he had received more than thirty years before.
Expostulation and prayer seemed to make him worse. I had to
leave him."

The letters, from which the foregoing extracts are
taken, abound with records not less interesting than those
transcribed. But we must now hasten to notice the work
accomplished during the superintendence of the Rev. Wm.
Cooke, (afterwards the celebrated Dr. Cooke) which began
in 1836, and extended till 1840.

"In the following years,* the earnest co-operation infused into
the mission by the intrepid enterprise of the superintendent began
to show itself in substantial results. New chapels were built at

---

* Memoir of the Rev. Wm. Cooke, D.D. p. 39.

Belfast, Newtonards, Priesthill, and Dromore. He made an extensive tour through the South and West of the Island, inquiring laboriously into the moral and religious condition of the people, gathering information from every available source, with the view to erect the standard of the cross in the darkest and most neglected districts. Hence missionaries were stationed at Cork, Limerick, Waterford, and the Isles of Arran, where the Gospel was preached in the Irish language. Industrial schools were also established in connection with some of these missions. In addition to the above places, missions were opened in Dublin, Dromore, Galway, Ballyclare, and Lurgan. The number of missionaries employed was increased from nine to eighteen, and the membership rose from 971 to 1401; but the numerical increase, tabulated in the reports, was constantly kept down, by the large number of members and hearers who emigrated to Canada and the United States."

The Providence which supplied the mission with an agent who could speak the Irish language is remarkable:

" On my return from Ireland,* I was accompanied by Mr. Price, our missionary in the Irish language. This brother was brought up in the church of Rome, and when a boy, was one who attended the priest at the altar. He continued a dupe to Papal delusion until grown up to manhood; but the Lord enlightened his understanding, and delivered him from bondage in an extraordinary manner. A penance was imposed, which rendered it necessary for him to travel from London to the West of Ireland, a distance by land and sea of about 500 miles, to perform ' stations ' at the Virgin's Well, near Castlebar, his native place. On his way he stopped for a few days at Stone, in Staffordshire, and on the Sabbath, being desirous of attending a Catholic chapel, he was directed by mistake to our little chapel, where he learned, for the first time, that the blood of Christ alone cleanseth from all sin, and that the Saviour was then present waiting to save the worst of sinners. The word was spoken with plainness and affection, and the Spirit of God applied it to his heart. Such was the blessed effect that he at once relied upon the Saviour, and found that

---

* Letter from the Rev. Wm. Cooke to the Mission Secretary, Belfast, Oct. 8th, 1839. *Methodist New Connexion Magazine*, 1840, p. 38.

mercy in the humble Methodist chapel, which he was vainly travelling a journey of 500 miles to obtain. Of course, he then abandoned his journey, renounced his connection with the church of Rome, and became a Methodist. After labouring for a number of years as a local preacher, he was called by the Committee to go as a missionary to preach the Gospel in the Irish language to his poor benighted fellow-countrymen."

The blessed rate of progress which the mission attained under the superintendence of the Rev. W. Cooke, was maintained for a long time; but migration and emigration were, as they continue to be, a constant drain upon the membership, keeping the numbers down. Young people cannot find suitable or sufficient employment in the small or rural districts in Ireland, in which most of the mission Stations are situated. All over the Island, the population has been steadily going down. The Methodist N.C. Canadian Mission proved a great success, and it is noticeable from the denominational records, that the interest of English friends in the Irish Mission in a great degree gave place to the greater attractions of the more successful enterprise beyond the seas. Some of the Irish missionaries were early induced to leave for Canada, and their reports and letters from the " goodly land " attracted many of the Irish members to the Dominion, and these, in their turn, induced others to follow : so that there continued a constant exodus of Irish Methodist New Connexionists to Canada. The Rev. Dr. J. C. Watts, (editor of the " *Methodist New Connexion Magazine* ") who spent twelve years of his early ministry in the Dominion, in a letter to the writer says: —

" In one of the latter years of my Missionary life in Canada, 33 out of 90 ministers forming our missionary staff were Irishmen, many of them born in the North of Ireland, and some of them converted on our Irish Mission Stations. In all parts of Canada I met with Local Preachers, Leaders, Stewards, &c. who had either themselves been brought to God by our preachers in Ireland, or were the sons or nephews of men who had thus found salvation. Some of the best Christian workers, male and female, in connection with our Societies in Canada had previously been members with us in ' the dear old country.' Their sons and daughters across the seas are at this day active and earnest in the cause of the Lord Jesus. So that for any one to say that our Irish Mission has been a failure is contrary to blessed facts. Many an Irish missionary will be astonished into unspeakable joy when his spiritual offspring in Canada shall be made known."

CHAPTER V.

EVANGELISM.

"And they went forth, and preached everywhere, the Lord working with them, and confirming the word with signs following."

WHILE resident in Lurgan, Mr. Nicholson examined the principles upon which the polity of the Methodist New Connexion is based, and cordially adopted them, as harmonizing with the dictates of reason and the teaching of the New Testament; and his fidelity to these principles continued till death, though he never made them the subject of disputation. He was a man of peace, and of the broadest catholicity of spirit. It was in Lurgan he first met Dr. Cooke (then the Rev. Wm. Cooke), and to Mr. Nicholson the meeting was highly important and lasting in its issues; a friendship was formed and a correspondence began which only ended with the great and good Dr. Cooke's life. Mr. Nicholson says, "I heard Mr. Cooke preach in Dromore first, on *The Lamb in the midst of the Throne.* The sermon was one of great clearness, eloquence, and force, and delivered with remarkable power, under the influence of the Divine Spirit. The next time I heard Mr. Cooke was in Lurgan, when he preached on *The General Judgment.* The sermon was blessed to many." Mr. Nicholson adds, "Mr. Cooke lectured in Lurgan on Astronomy, using a Magic-Lantern to illustrate his subject. Never have I heard or read as sublime a description of the heavenly bodies. Mr. H., a solicitor, said, ' I would not have missed that Lecture for ten pounds.'" In 1839, during Mr. Nicholson's residence in Lurgan, the erection of *Providence* Chapel was commenced. The foundation-stone was laid by Lord Lurgan ; seven Methodist New Connexion ministers were present, including Mr. Cooke, who delivered a very lucid and catholic address on the doctrines and polity of the Denomination. About the time the chapel was opened, Mr. Nicholson held a field-meeting, and preached, as he says, "with great liberty under the felt presence and power of the Holy Ghost." Some time afterwards, a man whom he met said to Mr. Nicholson, " Do you know me ? " "No," Mr. N. replied, "I do not." " Well," continued the man, " You remember preaching in ——field? To that meeting I went in a careless state, but the Lord there and then, convinced me of sin, and converted my soul. Blessed be His name ! " Mr. Cooke became warmly interested in the young, fresh-looking, guileless local preacher, and invited him to his house, in Belfast. Mr. Nicholson ever after spoke in grateful terms of the counsel Mr. C. gave him, and the kindness he showed him during this visit.

Mr. Nicholson's name appears in the Minutes of the Irish Methodist New Connexion Conference for 1839, as lay-representative form Lurgan, the Rev. J. Ogden being ministerial representative. He was after that conference succeeded at Lurgan by Rev. T. Ogden. Mr. Ogden, in a report before us, of a remarkable love-feast, held in October, says, " Brother Nicholson had been under a cloud through severe and protracted temptation, and while he spoke the tears could not be restrained; but soon the cloud was dissipated, and his soul filled with God." When in Lurgan, the evils of intoxicating drink came painfully under Mr. Nicholson's notice, and the advocates of temperance were beginning to excite attention. Father Matthew's crusade against drink was in full force ; and Dr. Edgar's labours in the North were yielding good results and exciting general attention. .Our friend, always ready to obey the truth so soon as discovered, prepared and signed a pledge of his own formation. The very document itself, written forty-nine years ago, lies before the writer :—" I make the re-olution, in the strength of Almighty God and by His help, not to enter a public-house, nor treat any one in the same, except in case of extreme necessity. I am resolved to avoid drink, in the name of the Father, and of the Son, and of the Holy Ghost. Amen. Samuel Nicholson. Lurgan, May 30th, 1839."

Mr. Nicholson was invited to visit Mr. McClune, and to help him for a time upon the Smithboro' Mission. Mr. Nicholson cheerfully consented. There is just one private record extant, made during this visit, but it is sufficent to show that our devoted friend's constant aim was to " walk with God," and to be used in saving men :—" Smithborough, Meditations for the last day of the year, 1839.—My soul, devoutly consider the blessings of thy past life." After enumerating the experiences and blessings of his life up till this time, he adds, " Oh! my soul, what have I been doing all my past life ! When I think of the active zeal and holiness of such men as Wesley, and Whitfield, and Clarke, and others who moved the world, I feel that I have done nothing. Oh! Jesus, do give me something of their spirit. I am an unworthy worm. Pardon my failings, sanctify me afresh, and help me to do Thy holy will always. Amen, Amen, Amen."

A supply was required on the Mission, and Mr. Nicholson received a letter from Mr. Cooke on the subject. The identical letter of over 48 years ago, in Dr. Cooke's familiar hand writing, is now before us:

"February 27th, 1840.

"Dear Brother,

If you are agreeable, you may be appointed to labour as a hired local preacher until Conference, at the rate of 10s. per week, under the direction of Mr. Ogden. This engagement is only until Conference, but, if your services and your diligence be generally approved, I shall have no objection to advocate your admission to a more permanent situation at the next Conference. But in this I speak only as an individual in a private capacity. You will please to attend punctually to Mr. Ogden's directions.

Wishing you every blessing, I am, dear Bro.,

"Yours affectionately,

"WILLIAM COOKE."

Our devoted friend willingly entered the door thus opened, and very soon Mr. Ogden sent him to assist the Rev. W. McClune on the Smithboro' Mission, which, " embraced three counties." From this station Mr. Nicholson wrote to Miss Moore, (of whom more anon), and fragments of the letter still survive :—

"Coghan, Smithborough, 1840.

"My Dear Margaret,

"Through the mercy of God I am still well, Yesterday I met the class at Mr. Gordon's, and preached at 11 a.m. and 5 in the evening—two excellent congregations, the place was crowded in the evening. I have had a hearty welcome from all the friends. . . . May we be kept as in the hollow of Jehovah's hand. 'I am Thine, save me,' is the cry of my heart. Let us pray to God and trust in Him and He will direct all our concerns for His glory and our good. . . . The country is looking lovely just now, very different from what it did in the depth of winter when I last was here. . . . Journeys long—walked 15 miles—I am sensible of my own weakness and insufficiency, but the Lord is my strength and my tower, and I wish to give all my days and all my powers up to Him. I wonder that I have not more power from on high. . . . I have now preached four times in each of the places; and the Lord has greatly blessed His own word. The unction of the Holy One rests upon me. Ere this reaches you, I shall have been over my longest journey. . . . Sorry I have not helped you more on the heavenly road. May the Lord enable you and me to live only for the salvation of souls. . . . I have done nothing for God, compared with what I might have done.

. . Your last letter was most welcome. May the Lord lay around and about you His everlasting arms.

"I am, my dear love,

"Yours till death,

"SAMUEL NICHOLSON."

Mr. Nicholson, with Rev. W. McClune, represented the Smithboro' Station at the Irish Conference of 1840. They reported an increase of nearly fifty per cent. upon the returns of the former year. At this Conference, Mr. Nicholson was received as a supply, and stationed at Bellaghey on the Portglenone Mission, under the superintendence of the Rev. Jno. Lyons, whose "fatherly sympathy and counsels" were much valued by the young preacher. Mr. Lyons was every way a big man—tall in stature, strong in limb, having a massive head, and a big heart. When brother James L—, was "out of work," and sorely tried, Mr. Lyons called to see him. Holding out his big, open hand the preacher said, "James, God has a great big hand." Very many years after James said to the writer, "I never forgot Mr. Lyons's words, and his big open hand." At this time, the preachers kept a journal of their labours, which was regularly forwarded, through the Superintendent of the mission, to the Missionary Committee. In his own reserved copy, Mr. Nicholson added matter for his own private use. The following extracts from his journal at once show the humble, earnest, conscientious spirit of the preacher, and illustrate the kind and extent of the labour prosecuted by the heroic missionaries of those days:—

April 23rd.—The Conference of 1840, just ended, was a very happy one, all its deliberations were conducted in the spirit of brotherly love. President and deputation: The Rev. T. Berry, from Liverpool. On the first day of Conference the Rev. Jas. Seymour preached at 7 o'clock, a.m.; the power of God attended the word. My character was approved, and after examination according to rule, I was received as a Supply. O, my God, the spirit is willing but the flesh is weak. I feel insufficient for these things. The Conference missionary meeting was well attended. Messrs. Berry, Argue, and others spoke. Glory be to God, for Christian missions! Mr. Lyons gave the closing address of Conference. He spoke with power and in tears of the hope of glory in the soul, and of the prospect of the brethren meeting above, should they never again meet on earth.

———

Bellaghey, Co. Derry,
May, 1840.

To Rev. Wm. Cooke,

I sit down with much pleasure to give you an account of my labours upon this Station from Conference til the present time. Came by Randalstown over Toome Bridge to this place. Was received in a Christian manner by Bro. McNeal. In prayer with the family the Lord warmed our hearts with His love. Had a cordial reception from the friends at Gow. Sabbath, May 3rd.—Met the class of 7 members. Attended the Presbyterian Meeting House in the forenoon, and preached in Kelly's in the evening to about 50 persons, on Christ all and in all. 4th.—Mr. Lyons preached in Bellaghey fair to about 150 people; many Romanists. Tears rolled down the faces of many and some praised the Lord aloud for the good news of forgiveness through faith in Christ. The people were unwilling to leave. Visited a sick man a mile out in the country, ignorant of his state and of the way of salvation. May I be made the humble instrument of his enlightenment. 6th.—To Stathybogus, over three miles. Visited six families and preached at Dixons. Walked home, 9

miles. Find it difficult to get suitable lodgings. May God direct
me in this and in all things. May 8th.—Gullyduff: offered a new
preaching place. Preached at Mr. Atkinson's on, "This day is
salvation come to this house." A blessed time, the Lord was in
our midst. May 9th.—Study and preparation for the Sabbath.
May 10th.—Met the class of 9 members—held a prayer meeting—
preached at six in the evening to a goodly company. May 12th.—
Preached at New Ferry; a miserable bed. May 13th.—Arranged
to preach at Mr. Cammon's once a month. Mr. Cammon is Rev.
J. Dogherty's father-in-law. Had a most profitable conversation
with Mr. Lyons, whom I met at Portglenone. May 17th.—Class
in the country at 8 o'clock morning—prayer-meeting in forenoon,
and again at 3 o'clock. Preached in the evening. A good day to
my soul. May 19th.—To Croggie, but sickness in the family prevented me preaching: went three miles further, but did not find a
preaching place. 20—22nd.—Study—visitation of the sick—a
prayer meeting. 24th.—While Brother H. Hegan met the class
we felt the unction from above. Preached to a respectable congregation, on Rev. xvii., 14. I have seldom enjoyed so much of the
hallowing presence of God. Blessed be the name of the Lord!
May 27—29th.—Three miles and preached at Griggs; three miles
to Dixon's. Strangers at preaching.

S. N.

From Mr. Nicholson's journal:

June 1st.—Preached in the fair at Bellaghey; a magistate was
present; about 100 people. September 26th.—When I came to
Bellaghey the cause was very low. The ·———— had prejudiced
the Rev. G. Ash (Church clergyman) against us. They said we
were trying to break down the Established Church—were a refrac-
tory handful broke off from—I called upon Mr. Ash, showed him
our rules and explained our position and work. I said it was true
we were dissenters, but that the others were Dissenters as well.
Mr. Ash shook me warmly by the hand, and told me to preach
anywhere, and as often as I wished. He opened my way and
encouraged me. October 1st.—Mr. Cooke visited us, and preached
in Portglenone and Bellaghey. I informed him of the kindness
the Rev. G. Ash had shown me. As we had no service in the fore-

noon of Sabbath, Mr. Cooke accompanied me to hear Mr. Ash preach. The text was, "Blessed are the peacemakers." Mr. Cooke expressed himself as much pleased with the sermon. Our large preaching room was full in the evening and a holy fervour rested on the people while Mr. Cooke preached. October 4th.— We had the offer from Mr. K-— of ground upon which to erect a chapel, on favourable terms. October (Sabbath).—Held the love-feast at Portglenone; text, "Casting all your care upon Him." A blessed day to us all. Two penitents at the close. Glory be to God! 11-14th.—Preached in Bellaghey, on "Follow me"; a good time. Preached at Gow on, *Peter and the Rock.* Had a good collection for a poor woman. Had great liberty while speaking from "Behold the Lamb of God." 15th.—Called to see Colonel K—— about an empty house of his, which, we think, would suit for a preaching and dwelling-house. Was shown over his beautiful garden, and saw his splendid drawing-room. But time will consume all. Direct us, O Lord! in the matter of the house. October 16th.—Had a conversation with a Roman Catholic woman. She wept, and invited me to call again. O Lord, give her true conviction for sin. October 17-19th.—Preached at Logan's on, "Many be called, but few chosen." Walked eight miles to Dixon's: a good congregation. Preached at Kelly's. O my Lord, show the people their need of a Saviour.

Amongst the written miscellanea left by him, Mr. Nicholson often refers to one of Ireland's greatest curses—whisky. The following incident occurred about this time :—

"Two young men volunteered to accompany me to Longlerg, near Bellaghey, one of my preaching appointments. After preaching to a large congregation, I stood prepared to start for home, but the people informed me that supper was being prepared. It transpired, however, that there was *poteen* in the house, just new from a private still, down the water side. I firmly refused to wait for supper. There was snow upon the ground, and we had a journey before us by water, in an open boat. The young men were disappointed, and displeased with me, because I refused to

H

remain for supper (and poteen). When my companions had rowed for a long time, they said that they could not tell where we were. I grasped one of the oars and tried my skill for a time. God guided us. Soon we reached a place where we could safely land. I saw God's hand in this deliverance. Had my companions got the poteen we likely would have been drowned. It was midnight when we reached the shore; and we had to remain at a friend's house till morning.

Journal continued:

Oct. 24—26th. Accompanied Mr. Lyons to Ballyhey: reviewed our work, all satisfactory. Preached in Mullen's from, "One thing is needful." A blessed time it was. When looking over map of Ireland, was glad to find I could point to so many places in which it had been my privilege to preach the Gospel. May the seed sown bring forth much fruit to the praise of the Redeemer. Oct. 17th.—Received a letter from father informing me that sister Margaret lies ill of fever. O Lord, undertake for us, and spare my dear sister for Thy mercy's sake. O Lord, I see my deficiency, enable me to gain more knowledge; give me wisdom from above; fill me with the Spirit, and all the fulness of love, to fit me for this great work. Oct. 28th.—A letter from home; sister much better; bless the Lord! Visited twelve families and prayed with most of them. Called upon Rev. G. Ash, and had a very kind reception. I pray to be made a missionary like the one described in the letter from Spring Valley. Oct 30th.—I am carefully reading *Clarke's Commentary*, also *Finney on Revivals*. Lord help me to keep up my study, and bless to me what I read. Nov. 1st.—Walked seven miles and preached; was wet to the skin; tormented all night with f——. Nov. 4th.—Rev. Mr. Wilson, Presbyterian, called to see me; we had a friendly conversation. Methodism is the best *ism* of all. Nov. 6th.—Visited Spring Valley, spent a happy day. Saw some of the old friends with whom I used to take sweet counsel. Mrs. T. is a kind, happy Christian. Nov. 7th—11th.—Met the class at Gow, not many present. Preached in a room of a vacant house, a blessed time to my soul. Read *Clarke*, in many things, I think, I am like him. Preached in my own room, Mr. H. prayed, a blessed time to all our souls. Visited the G's, the L's, McB's, and K's: was grieved to see poverty so extreme. Lord relieve them, Amen. Am reading the "*Life of Lanktree.* Lord, make it a great blessing to my soul. Held the Quarterly Meeting at Gullyduff, the people soon gathered; I had liberty in preaching from, "He which hath begun a good work in you," &c.: the people spoke freely: H—. exhorted with good effect. The Lord blessed me and II—., as we journeyed by the way and conversed about the things of God. We had a good time at evening preaching. Mr. H—. wishes to join our Society. November 12-20th.—Clarke's Notes greatly refreshed and stimulated my mind. Visited the house of a friend just deceased; gave an address, &c.; returned much fatigued and was poorly all the day following. Preached at Dowdel's on, "Ye must be born again;" surely I felt much of God. Spent day making plan for future work upon the mission. O Lord, give me wisdom and understanding and enable me to conduct all to Thy glory and the good of the people. Attended Mr. Stafford's funeral: felt much at the grave, thinking of my mother and brother, Robert: the Lord blessed me richly in the evening whilst I preached upon victory over death and the grave through Christ.

The foregoing extracts from Mr. Nicholson's journal are given in detail, that a full idea of the nature and extent of his labours at this time, might appear. We now alter our plan and give selections only:—

November.—Went to the fair; took our stand in the street; about 150 people gathered; Mr. Lyons preached and I assisted. May the good seed spring up a thousand-fold, for Christ's sake. Glory be to God for street-preaching! After my visit to Mr. C——'s I came home strong and animated in both body and mind. I see, my duty is, not to heed any evil or foolish reports, but to bear the cross, and shun all appearance of evil. I bless and praise the Lord for the honour put upon me, in my call to declare His truth. Assisted Mr. Lyons at a field-meeting, held at Gullyduff: walked back to town and preached in the evening to a large congregation.

December.—We have rented K——'s big house and are about to remove to it. We will put up a pulpit in one of the large rooms and preach in it regularly. I am much pleased with Lanktree. He says, "How foolish is it for Methodists to divide about the sacraments." I believe it is right for us to have them. Began a meeting on Sabbath for the reading and study of the Scriptures.

I was greatly alarmed during a gale on the lough. The boat was leaky and took in much water. The wind was very high. A man accustomed to sailing and the management of boats, said that it took all his skill to keep our boat from foundering. Had he not been with us we must have perished. O Lord, I thank Thee for this deliverance. Preached in the street in Randalstown to a goodly company of Romanists. The Lord is opening up my way to this town.

I was so busy and happy in the work of the Lord, that I forgot all about quarter-day. Two souls were made happy at the love-feast. The number of our members is going steadily up; and in finance we are improving.

K—.'s large house which we have taken was called the "Haunted House." It had been a long time without a tenant; and there was a story of a wife having been poisoned in it many, many years ago, which, it was said, accounted for the strange sights which had been seen and the strange sounds heard, about the dismal dwelling. We let a part of the house to a man and his wife. A young man slept with me the first night I spent in it. Some time after retiring, and when my companion was fast asleep, something knocked loudly at our bedroom door, then seemed to enter and sit down on a large trunk in the room, which seemed to break down under the weight. The noise awoke my bedfellow. I began to sing, "Jesus the name high over all—devils fear and fly." Judging from the sound it made the creature left the room and proceeded down the stairs, every step of which seemed to break under its heavy tread. In a short time my tenant's wife came rushing into my room, exclaiming that some heavy weight had just fallen upon her in bed. For some nights after her husband kept a candle burning all night in their room. But they said, that there was not a seat they had or pot or pan that was not tossed about every night. They gave up their tenancy and left me alone. I did not hear any unusual noises after the first night. If Satan had anything to do with the strange sounds, his device failed to hurt us ; and the Lord blesses our labours in the house from time to time. Major Hill was present when I preached in the room, on .the *New Birth*. It was a blessed time to my own soul.

Mr. Nicholson, actuated from the first by the true missionary spirit, did not confine his labours within prescribed limits, but sought to extend the Kingdom of Christ in every direction. And it always afforded him great delight " to build an house unto the name of the Lord," or even to repair one :—

"Belfast, December 20th, 1840.

" My dear Brother,—

" Thanks for your interesting report of your visit to Randalstown. I hope you will be able to succeed in effecting an opening. I think it is not at all unlikely but a little assistance might be rendered to encourage your exertions in reference to the intended chapel at Bellaghey, at the next Conference. But very much will depend upon the state of our Society there and its prospects of usefulness.

" I am, dear brother, yours affectionately,

WILLIAM COOKE.'

To Rev. S. Nicholson.

To return to the Journal :

1841, Feb.—The Tea Party was a great success. Mr. Lyons, Mr. Atkinson and I spoke ; the people were well pleased, thank the Lord ! Read in *Clarke*, and *Coke*, and *Finney*. Visited Uncle Nicholson, and attended a service at the Presbyterian Meeting House, Clough. The minister failing to appear, I was asked to preach, which I did, and the Lord gave me great liberty. The Rev. Mr. Stuart said afterwards that he was much pleased I had preached for him. He told Miss M.—— that I was the only Methodist preacher to whom he would give his pulpit. I was informed that most of his people had been pleased with my humble sermon.— April.—The Portglenone Quarterly Meeting has recommended me to the approaching Conference as a preacher on trial, and the resolution contains the recommendation that the present year be counted the first of my probation. Mr. Lyons was well pleased with this result. I felt humbled before God and very grateful. My precious Jesus, keep me near to Thee, that I may be a partaker of Thy loving spirit and qualified for Thy service. My one desire is to live to glorify Thy name and save precious souls.

———

Rev. W. Cooke.   " Bellaghey, 1841."
    " Rev. and dear Sir,—
                "I have held field-meetings, and visited from house to house, and thus obtained liberty to preach in houses, in which before I would not be allowed to pray. At the love-feast a young woman, of a very superior mind, found peace with God, and many others, who had never been in a place of the kind before, wept, and prayed aloud for mercy. We have kept up preaching at every fair here. A respectable Roman Catholic woman heard preaching, and was convinced of sin. She afterwards invited Mr. Lyons to lodge in her house, and preach the Word of life to herself and her neighbours. She said that she did not care for the anger of the priest. Romanists attended family worship every morning in the house where I lodged. The priest has ordered 500 Testaments for his people; whereas his predecessor compelled one of his flock to put away a Testament which he had obtained. I believe God is working upon the minds of the Romish clergy. I took the house, towards the rent of which you promised me £4 a year. During the last four months our congregations have much improved, thank the Lord! We opened the Sabbath School with 26 children; last Sabbath we had 80, with a good staff of teachers. Mr. Lyons has written to Dublin for books. Several respectable persons have joined us lately, amongst whom is a Mr. T. Evans, a young man of talent and influence. . Last Sabbath at the renewal of tickets, tears started to his eyes while he expressed his thanks for Methodism. We have appointed him superintendent of the Sunday School.
                                    "S. NICHOLSON."

In his last journal record for the year, Mr. Nicholson refers again to Randalstown :

"Mr. Cook wrote to Lord O'Neill's agent, asking liberty for me to preach in the market-house, Randalstown, but the request was denied. I then took to the street. I was permitted to close the first time without any interruption. But on my next visit, as soon as I stood up, a noisy mob surrounded me; and a fellow had engaged to knock me down. A policeman heard the plot arranged, and when the man made to strike me, the policeman pulled him to the ground. This only enraged the mob the more. I was composed, and felt no fear. I asked them to give me a hearing, and I would relate to them many interesting things respecting Jesus Christ, the Son of the Virgin Mary. At this, they all cried out, 'Hear him! hear him!' and I was allowed to continue to the end without any further interruption. Thank God!

And now we are about to attend the Conference at Belfast. Mr. Lyons and I have had a blessed year. We proclaimed the glorious tidings of salvation in the street, in fairs and markets, and wherever we could find hearers. It is in my mind to build a house unto the Lord, if I be sent back to labour on this circuit for another year. A plot of ground has been offered me, and subscriptions have been promised."

There lie upon the writer's desk the "Minutes of the Annual Conference of the Methodist New Connexion Irish Mission, held in Belfast, on the 17th day of May, &c., &c., 1841. A brief extract or two from this record of nearly fifty years ago, will be read with interest by the friends of the Mission to-day:—

Question 1.—Who compose the present Conference?
Answer.—*English Deputation*—The Rev. T. Scattergood, and Mr. John Backwell.

Superintendent.—The Rev. William Cooke.

Belfast—S. Barton, Wm. Gater, Joseph Lee, Alexander McCurdy.

Bangor—William McClure.

Downpatrick—William Sorsby, Hugh McClinchy.

Dromore—William Barker.

Dublin—James Argue, James Banks.

Hyde Park & Ballyclare—John Sage, Andrew Blair.
Limerick—Edward Morris.
Lisburn—Thomas Seymour, Samuel Sayce.
————Joshua McKnight, James Boyd.
————John Carlisle.
Lurgan--Thomas Ogden, George McMillen.
Newtownards—James Seymour, William Wilson.
Portglenone—John Lyons, Samuel Nicholson.
Armagh and Smithboro'—William McClune, T. Mollart.
Waterford—Henry Harrison.
Galway, and the Isles of Arran—H. Price.

Address of the Irish Conference to the English Conference, Assembled at Halifax, Yorkshire, 1841.

Very Dear Brethren,—By the good providence of God, we have been brought together from our respective fields of labour, and from our Annual Conference we address you. There is an aggregate increase of one hundred and fifty members, and a considerable number who remain on probation.—Priesthill has followed the example of Belfast, by undertaking to support itself, independent of any further aid from the general fund. The stations recently formed in the South and West of this country, especially Cork, Limerick, and Waterford, present a very cheering prospect of good being effected. Mr. Stewart has commenced his labours in Galway. Mr. Price, in the Isles of Arran, has met with severe persecution.

Signed on behalf of the Conference:—
THOMAS SCATTERGOOD, President.

In Mr. Nicholson's journal occurs the record of a presentation which was made to Mr. Cooke, on the eve of his removal to England. During the period of his superintendence of the Irish Mission, Mr. Cooke won the confidence, esteem and love of the people, and more especially of the missionaries, to whom he was like a father, sympathizing with them in their trials and encouraging and helping them in their arduous labours. In their annual addresses to the English Conference, during his term of office, they speak of his zeal and brotherliness in the highest terms, Mr. Nicholson says, "The English Conference of 1841 appointed Mr. Cooke to an English circuit, and the Rev. G. Goodall was appointed as his successor in Ireland. I attended a soiree in Belfast, which was got up by the Salem congregation and other friends, for Mr. Cooke, ere he left for England. The ministers and his numerous friends presented Mr. Cooke with an address, and a copy of Bagster's Polyglot Bible in ten languages, bearing a suitable inscription. The speeches made on the occasion were excellent, and the tone of the meeting most enthusiastic. High hopes were expressed of the continued success of the Mission."

By the Conference of 1841, Mr. Nicholson was continued as a supply, and appointed to labour in Belfast, that here, in his studies, he might have the guidance and help of the Superintendent. The records made in his journal daily show, that he entered upon his labours in Belfast, with diligence, energy, zeal and faith :—

1841, July 4th (Sabbath).—Met a class in *Salem* in the morning; preached at Milltown at 3 p.m., and again at Richey's Dock at 5.30. Assisted at Salem prayer-meeting at night. 5th.—Visited six families, held two classes, and assisted at the Missionary prayer meeting at *Salem*. 6th.—Visited a few families, met a class, but did not fulfil my preaching appointment, on account of the riots in the town over an election. 8th and 9th.—Visited in company with Mr. McClure, distributed tracts; a man named Kennedy offered me his house for preaching.

In all my visiting during the past week I have been well received, except by a few Romanists. Poor people, who cannot attend a place of worship for want of proper clothing, received me gladly. Many with whom I read and prayed seemed grateful, and asked me to call again. Sabbath, 11th.—Met the class at Milltown

for *tickets*, preached at 3 p.m., at Turnpike-road. 12th.—Visited
eight families, met two classes, and attended Salem prayer-meeting. 13th.—Visited twelve families, prayed with a poor man, who
seems on the brink of eternity; he appeared much in earnest about
the salvation of his soul. Felt the presence of the Lord while
preaching at Mr. Collin's in the evening. 14th.—Visited twelve
families and read and prayed with most of them. A poor old
couple in Cromac-street were much affected during prayer, and
urged me to call again. 15th.—Called to see fourteen families
and had great liberty while praying with them, and exhorting
them to seek the Lord. 16th.—A family in E- -—— Street, wish a
prayer-meeting in their house. Husband and wife were once
happy in the Lord, and the husband was a leader: they are now
cut off from all public means of grace. 17th.—Spent some hours
in study and preparation for the Sabbath; called with a Roman
Catholic and gave him a tract, he wants a New Testament, and
will pay for it, he had had one but it was stolen from him. 18th,
(Sabbath).—Class, Salem prayer meeting, preached at Milltown at
3 p.m., and at Lindsay's at 5 p.m. Felt the presence of God with
me. 19th.—Visited ten families, met a class in Townsend Street,
and one in Salem vestry at 8 p.m. two penitents present, a blessed
meeting. Prayed with a sick woman who has led a very wicked
life; also with a dying man who is earnestly seeking salvation.
20th.—Visited six families: preached at Newtonbreda to an attentive congregation, a brother assisted in prayer at the close, all felt
it good to wait upon the Lord. 21st.—Was told by many that
they could not attend God's house for want of clothing; they were
glad of my visits. I trust that the Lord will bless the Word read
and hear the prayers offered, and that many precious souls may
be saved as the fruit of my humble labours. 22nd.—All day after
collectors, inviting them to the quarterly tea-meeting. 23rd.—
Visited several families and preached at Milltown in the evening
Oh, may the Lord bless His own word to the good of the people!
24th.—Reading and study. 25th (Sabbath).—Met two classes
preached at Milltown, and held a prayer-meeting at the Planting
26th.—Visited amongst others, a woman, in Pinkerton's-row, who
was dying, and delirious. O that sinners would seek the Lord
while He may be found! Attended a fellowship meeting of two

classes in the evening. May the labours of the day be owned of God! Amen.

27th.—Visited ten families, and held a prayer meeting at 8 p.m. 28th.—Called upon eight families, and preached in *Salem*, at 7 p.m. 29th.—House to house most of the day, praying, reading the Scriptures and exhorting the people to repent and believe in Jesus, and prepare for Heaven. 30th.—Was pleased to find that the people expected my visits; held a prayer-meeting in the evening; a happy day. Went to Dromore, on the 31st to supply for Mr. Sayce Called on Saturday to invite the people out for the Sabbath. Spent the week in Dromore, taking up six preaching appointments, and meeting two classes, &c. August 8th (Sabbath).—Met two classes, held two prayer-meetings, and preached twice in and near Dromore. 9th.—Visited nine families; attended Mr. J. Mc Dade's *wake*, exhorted the people to prepare for death. 10th.—Returned to Belfast, visited a few families, and preached at Mr. Collins's. My own soul was blessed, and I trust the people were profited. 11th.—Visited ten families, and preached in *Salem*. 12th.—Called to see a man who is in distress about his soul. Oh! that people would see that "*Now* is the accepted time." 13th-17th.—Held three prayer-meetings, met three classes, preached three times, visited, distributed tracts, &c. 18th-21st.—Was called to Bellaghey on important business; preached twice, and saw many of the friends. Attended a Leaders' Meeting with Mr. Gordon, and assisted the brethren to form plans for the extension of the work of God on that mission. Returned to Belfast on the Saturday, and spent the evening in reading and study. Sabbath, 22nd.—Met two classes, attended the prayer-meeting in Salem, &c. Mr. Nicholson here adds, "Since I came to Belfast I might have visited more, but, I find, that I must read and study, and, by God's help, qualify myself for future and more extensive usefulness. I am studying grammar, logic, and theology, and reading *Mosheim's Ecclesiastical History*." From an entry in a note book before us, made a little earlier, than this, we learn that Mr. N—— was giving attention to the study and practice of logic, maps, elocution, singing, and sermon writing.

Through the resignation of Mr. Sayce, Dromore was ow left without a Preacher, and the Missionary Committee requested Mr. Nicholson to proceed to Dromore immediately, and take charge of the Station. August 25th, found him in Dromore earnestly at work. We give, from his journal, a summary of his labours till September 13th.

"Found comfortable lodgings in Mr. McDade's. Visited Black-scull, &c., stopped at Mr. Spratt's, and felt happy with this Christian family. Heard Mr. Sayce deliver a good sermon in the Preaching House. Preached to the people assembled at Mr. Gray's *wake*. I lay in a damp bed in County Derry, and have been unwell ever since. Thank the Lord for a few days rest. I needed it much. Paid a visit to Mr. Goodall; saw Mr. Barton. Preached at Nelson's, Crockban, and Dromore, and met classes, was powerfully blessed at all these meetings. Preached at G—, for Mr. T. Seymour; here I met a man who had found mercy at a meeting I held at J. Watson's several years ago. Felt the Lord's presence with me on Sabbath all day.

Here Mr. Nicholson's labours at Dromore are arrested, and he is called to supply the Priesthill station, whose young preacher had resigned. The English Conference of 1841 expelled Joseph Barker;* but the heresy he had taught found favour in many places, and spread like evil leaven, causing disaffection and schism. Happily the pernicious leaven did not reach the Irish Mission, except in the case of one individual, a ministerial probationer named Samuel B , a young man of ardent, impulsive

---

* Soon after his expulsion, Joseph Barker dropped the mask and avowed himself a Unitarian. The Rev. W. Cooke, when stationed in Newcastle, accepted a challenge to a public discussion with Barker. Mr. Cooke triumphantly exposed the Unitarian's sophistries, and left Barker prostrate in shame. After devious wanderings, many years afterwards, the wanderer "came to himself," and he wrote Dr. Cooke avowing his repentance, and faith in Christ. Rev. S. Hulme, Dr. Cooke's biographer, says:—"These doubts (concerning the sincerity of Barker's repentance) have melted away, and I now rejoice in the belief that Joseph Barker 'found mercy of the Lord.'"

temperament, and thoroughly conscientious, who was led away by Barker's subtle sophistry and apparent disinterestedness and sincerity. The late Mr. S. Jones informed the writer, that Mr. B. said, when resigning his charge at Priesthill, " I go forth to assist Mr. Barker to convert the world." It is gratifying to find, that this earnest young man was soon undeceived. And not long since, his name appeared as President of the United Methodist Free Churches. In a letter from Rev. G Good_all to the Leaders, &c., of Priesthill, dated Belfast, Sept. 15th, 1841, he says, " It was deemed the most prudent course to place Priesthill and Dromore under the experienced superintendence of Mr. T. Seymour until Conference, that Mr. Nicholson should remove from Dromore and take up his residence at Priesthill. Mr. Nicholson is a pious, serious young man, and I hope will be a great blessing among you,—receive him kindly and encourage him." Mr. Nicholson, being "in the Lord's hands," felt "quite satisfied" with this change. Now, he enters upon his labours in that rich and beautiful district, the Maze, to which in after years, he was appointed again and again. In his Journal he accounts for every day from September till Conference. In his turn he occupied the pulpits of the four Chapels,—Lisburn, Priesthill, Broomhedge, and Dromore, and his weekly preaching appointments in all numbered five and six. It will interest many friends in different places, to glance over the names of the people at whose hospitable dwellings Mr. Nicholson at this time, preached from month to month – Jones, Carlisle, Currie, Miss Wright, Dalton, Topping, Catney, McConnell, Kennedy, Jno. Watson (with whom he lodged), Dugan, Dickey, Faulkner, Gracey, Shaw, Kidd, Menight, McClure, and Nelson. His journal tells of glorious conversions, gracious revivals, happy quarterly-meetings, successful soirees in different places, and zealous efforts in the Sabbath School. For his superintendent, Mr. T. Seymour, Mr. Nicholson expresses the strongest regard and affection, and he recounts many seasons of happy Christian inter-course with brethren beloved in the Lord. Here is one instance, " While visiting at Mr. Seymour's, his baby was baptized by Mr. Harrison. I felt the power of God abundantly resting upon us." Being now but a few miles from his father's, his three brothers visited Mr. Nicholson often, and he found time occasionally to spend a few hours in the dear old homestead. He says, " Found father well, I trust he is living for eternity," and again, " slept at father's, Lord, do keep my brothers in the right way, Amen." " Sister Elizabeth is ill. O Lord, spare her, if it be Thy will, and if not, prepare her for Heaven." Thus his heart retained all the warmth of filial and fraternal affection enriched by grace.

No one will blame us with divulging secrets if we add, that our bachelor friend likewise found time to visit a family where there was an unmarried daughter, a young woman of true piety, but the visits were not strictly pastoral. As a preacher of the Gospel, he read the Epistles to Timothy with care, and endeavoured to yield obedience to their teaching. He read these words, "A bishop must be the husband of one wife." Now who dare find fault if he felt willing to yield a cheerful obedience to this injunc-tion as well as to the others. But he felt that the posses-sion of "one" wife was necessary to obedience, and he wrote his friend Dr. Cooke upon the subject; but ultimately saw it to be prudent to postpone the question. A Method-ist preacher's life is full of contrasts, and so we pass on to a rather prosy subject. Mr. Nicholson tells of an " effort " to remove a small debt which remained on Priesthill Chapel. After making an extended domiciliary canvass for subscriptions, he says, " The people upon whom 1 called were not over liberal. But the gold and silver are the Lord's, and I have found ' He is faithful who hath promised.' I travelled many miles, and returned to my lodgings wet and weary in body, but, to my joy, I found money waiting for me, left in my absence." Our devoted friend also makes touching reference to death-bed scenes, some happy and others doubtful. Take the following : " I was painfully astonished to find Mr. Evans on a dying bed. I felt greater grief at parting from him than I ever did at leaving any man on earth. O may he be fully prepared for eternal glory. I had a letter from Mr. Hamilton informing me that after I had prayed with his father (during a visit), the Lord revealed His mercy to the dying man, and he passed away in great peace. Praise the Lord for another soul ! " None of Mr N.'s labours were gone through in a perfunctory manner ; whatsoever his hand found to do, he did it with his might. The joyful tidings upon his lips gladdened his own heart. We come again and again upon notes like this, " This was a grand day to my soul. I was so happy that, when night came, I could hardly sleep." Upon every page of his diary are sighs, and cries, and pleadings for blessing upon his labours. " We have the droppings, but, O Lord ! do send the mighty shower upon the parched ground that souls may be saved, and Thy name glorified." The journal, too, gives clear glimpses into the inner life of God's servant. His walk was close with God. He was ever on the stretch for more holiness and power and love. He searched the Scriptures daily for the food his own soul required. Christian biographies helped him much :—" Read in the

Life of the Rev. Mr. Roberts. O Lord, I thank Thee for sending such holy men upon the earth. Such a life instructs and stimulates me to be more faithful." His diary abounds with ejaculations for more of the life of God in his soul, and also with notes of praise for rich blessings received :—" I see more and more the necessity of a full dedication to God. Oh! for more love, faith, zeal, courage, self-denial, and power from on high!'' " My gracious Lord, I am Thine ; I make a fresh dedication of myself to Thee. Though I have done but little for Thee during the past year, yet Thou hast been with me O grant me fresh supplies out of Thy fulness, and enable me to be humble and to lie at Thy feet, and to Thy name I will ascribe all the glory. Through Thy grace I now promise to pray three times daily for a revival of Thy work upon the mission." " My gracious Father, I thank Thee for the power and love which rested upon me and the people. May the influence spread throughout the country!'' " The Spirit of God came down upon me in the fullest measure, and I had the clear evidence of entire sanctification. Bless the Lord, O my soul!" It was not, however, nearly all sunshine with our brother. He had his dark days, trials and temptations. He says, " I have been painfully exercised in mind for many days, but the Lord graciously sustained me, and in prayer I received the assurance that all will be well." " I felt much hurt at certain people indulging in evil speaking. O for more of the mind of Christ."

The Priesthill Circuit Quarterly Meeting was held on March 20th, 184!, commencing at 10 o'clock, a.m., the Rev. T. Seymour presiding. Mr. Nicholson says, " My Certificate was filled up satisfactorily, every question being answered in the affirmative without one dissenting voice.

My salary was fully paid, and there was left a small balance. Oh how shall I sufficiently thank Thee, my gracious, loving God!"

The Irish Conference of 1842 held its sittings in Belfast, on April 18th, &c. The Rev. William Cooke (General Secretary of Missions) was the English Deputation, and was chosen as President by the Irish brethren. The Rev. T. Seymour was selected as Secretary. Mr. Nicholson was allowed a seat in Conference though not legally entitled to one. In his diary he says, "I had great pleasure in meeting Mr. Cooke and dear old Mr. Lyons. Mr. Goodall was very kind, and most considerate and obliging. I was entertained at Mr. Crawford's—a good Methodist family, with whom I felt at home. Salem pulpit was occupied by Mr. Argue on Sabbath morning, and by Mr. Cooke in the evening; I preached on the street, at the Dock in the afternoon. I was received by Conference as a minister on probation. O may I be a faithful labourer in the Lord's Vineyard, and made the instrument of bringing many sinners to the feet of Jesus, and glorifying the name of the Redeemer. The Conference proved a trying, sifting time, but, bless the Lord! I felt His presence through it all." Priesthill had engaged to pay a young minister's full stipend; and Mr. Nicholson was given the pastoral oversight of the station.

Upon his return from Conference, Mr. Nicholson made a special and unreserved dedication of himself and his all to God, covenanting to be a good minister of Jesus Christ, and earnestly soliciting grace and wisdom, and strength for the work. He again lodged at Mr. J. Watson's, of whom he speaks in terms of affection. At Lisburn was stationed the Rev. Wm. McClure, a man of amiable and cheerful disposition, sterling piety, possessing a vigorous

I

mind well stored with a great wealth of varied knowledge,
which he most willingly communicated. From him Mr·
Nicholson received valuable aid in his studies and work ;
and many letters amongst his papers, in the clear neat
hand of Mr. McClure, attest, that between these two men
of God, though widely contrasting in many respects, there
arose an attachment which continued till the close of Mr.
McClure's life.

The writer has before him the *Plan of Lisburn, Priesthill
and Dromore Stations* for parts of the years 1841-2. It
shows that much work was crowded into each week. The
names upon this " plan " will be interestingly familiar to
many now living :—

Names of Preachers.	*Exhorters.*	
T. Seymour,	E. McClune,	W. Shields,
W. Gater,	J. Menight,	J. Boyd,
S. Nicholson,	J. Cunningham,	J. Breathwight,
R. Bailie,	T. Hall,	H. Dickey,
W. Sorsby,	J. Dickey,	S. McConnell,
A. M.,	A. Johnston,	J. McDade,
	J. Carlisle,	H. Price,
	S. Jones,	W. Boyd,
	F. Martin,	W. Arlow.
	G. Bradshaw,	

We have already divulged the fact, that other thoughts
than those immediately connected with this work shared
the attention of our friend during his residence at Bellaghey, &c., and we have given part of a letter to a Miss
Moore, whom he addressed as, " My dear Margaret," and
" My dear love." Margaret was the second daughter of a
respectable farmer named James Moore, of Knockstiken,
Co. Down. On a memorable occasion she went on a visit
to a friend at Killough, where the Methodist New Connection ministers preached monthly. Here she heard the

Rev. W. Haslam preach a sermon, which came with power
to her conscience. As the sermon proceeded, she said,
inwardly, "If this be all true, I am still on the broad way,
and I must decide about it now." That night Miss Moore
asked the preacher if he would visit her father's and
preach there. He said that he had once preached in the
neighbourhood of her father's, but that the only one to
offer him a bed was a policeman, and it proved a very hard
one, and he had to retire supperless. "Oh," said the
young lady, "if you come to father's you will have supper,
and a good, soft bed. Knockstiken thereafter became a
regular preaching place and home for the Itinerants on
their rounds. Miss Moore received the witness of the Spirit
in the Methodist New Connexion Chapel, Downpatrick, at a
love-feast, in 1837. A class of about ten young people
met regularly in her father's for some time ; and a distin-
guished Professor, who occupies a high position at the
present moment, met in that class in those days. About
the year 1839, Mr. Nicholson visited Knockstiken, in
quest of Rev. J. Dogherty. The friend who pointed out
Mr. Moore's to Mr. Nicholson, added: "There is a good
girl lives at that house ; it was she brought the preachers
to it." The house was soon found, but not Mr. Dogherty.
The young, fresh-looking preacher was invited to remain
all night ; and though on his way to his favourite Aunt
Carson's, yet the surroundings at Knockstiken were so
congenial and the society so agreeable, that he gladly
accepted the proffered hospitality. He afterwards paid
many other visits to the same cheerful home, but not to
see Mr. Dogherty. To young Mr. Nicholson, four years
imposed celibacy, under the circumstances, was felt to be
almost intolerable. And in truth, the young lady did not
think that *men* had any right to make such laws. Many

preachers, during the first four years of their career at any
rate, are able to prove to a demonstration that it is a frag-
ment of popery for the Church to impose celibacy, even for
a time, on any *man*.   But, these first years over, somehow
their views completely change, and they come to defend
the law as good and wise and *kind*.   However, no one will
blame our young friend for applying to have the law
relaxed in his case, as he was of "full age."   There lie
before the narrator several letters which were written at
the time on this subject of perennial interest.   A sentence
from one of these, from the Rev. T. Ogden to Mr. Nicholson, written on 22nd January, 1841, we quote, as it makes
favourable mention of the lady :—"I introduced Mr.
Cooke to Miss Moore, and he is highly pleased with her ;
but he advises you both to defer marriage for at least
another year."   In a letter from Rev. W. Sorsby to Miss
Moore, dated 21st May, 1841, Mr. Nicholson is spoken of
in terms of esteem :—"As to Mr. Nicholson's case (at
Conference), I may say the resolution is just to my mind,
and is, I think, right in itself, but I will (again) explain it
to you more particularly.   I never heard a young man
better spoken of, or more respected than he, and, I am
sure, there is a disposition to promote him as fully as his
improvement will warrant."   The union was accordingly
postponed.   It was expected that the Conference of 1842
would give Mr. Nicholson permission to marry, and preparations were made for the event ; but, it would appear,
Conference did not favour the idea.   What was he to do ?
He proceeded to Knockstiken, and on his way spent a
night at Clougher with Mr. Jos. Catney, who long ago,
described to the writer, Mr. Nicholson's perplexed state of
mind all that night.   It was on a bright day, on 12th May,

that Mr. Nicholson reached his intended. All the con-
veniences for a wedding were ready; and Margaret
Moore and Samuel Nicholson were there and then united
in holy wedlock; and God smiled upon the union. The
Rev. E. Stuart officiated on the happy occasion.

CHAPTER VI.

THE WORK OF THE MINISTRY.

"Thus to relieve the wretched was his pride,
And even his failings lean'd to virtue's side;
But in his duty prompt at every call,
He watch'd and wept, he pray'd and felt for all:
And as a bird each fond endearment tries,
To tempt its new-fledged offspring to the skies,
He tried each art, reproved each dull delay,
Allured to brighter worlds, and led the way."

"THOU hast found me, O mine enemy!" exclaimed
our Bridegroom when, with his Bride, he met
the Rev. W. McClure, who had strongly
advised the postponement of the marriage, and who now
was of the number of those who had power to censure the
law-breaker. Mr. McClure did not meet the "foolish
couple" with a frown, but with a smile. As Mrs. Nicholson says, "Father McClure received us to his heart and
home, gave us much wise counsel, helped us in every way,
and his friendship continued till the end of his life." A
probationer's stipend, in those days, afforded the reverse
of a "fat living," but from memoranda before us covering
this period, we learn that the Priesthill friends were most
kind and attentive to their young minister and his wife.

Mrs. Carlisle (a mother in Israel, who had been converted at nine years of age), her son, Mr. Jas. Carlisle, and Mr. A. Stansfield are mentioned in grateful terms, as also the Misses Bradbury, Mrs. Topping, and Mrs. William Hunter, with Messrs. J. Watson, S. Jones, P. Gorman, and many others. The material comfort of our young friends was also practically remembered by the relatives at Knockstiken and Spring Valley, and it continued for years. Jno. Hall Nicholson, who when a child had been rescued from drowning, was tenderly attached and abundantly kind to his senior brot he. Thus were drawn out and richly displayed some of the best feelings and principles of the human mind. All the year, however, there hung a cloud in the sky of the newly wedded couple. What would Conference say or do? In the interest of law and order, that supreme court was bound to say something, and so, in 1843, it passed this resolution : "That, in reference to the marriage of probationers, this Conference resolves to adopt the rule of the English Connexion on the subject, which states, that any preacher marrying during his probation, without the consent of Conference, shall be discontinued." Now, Brother Nicholson, do not attempt to do the like again. And ye probationers, marry if you dare! Yet notwithstanding all that has been said on the subject of imposed celibacy, Methodist Ministers marry at an earlier age than do other ministers.

In memoranda before us, other names occur of persons to whose history special interest attaches. One of these is James Richey, one of the notable Thirty-two. " He used to take up the collection in Broomhedge Chapel, and as he passed round the plate, it was his custom to repeat some suitable portions of Scripture—'God loveth a cheerful

giver,' &c. Another memorable name is that of Margaret
Carlisle. Turning to the pages of *The New Methodist Mag-*
azine, for 1831, we find an obituary notice of this estimable
young woman, from the pen of the Rev. J. Argue, but it
is chiefly an autobiography : She says,

"My father, Geo. Carlisle, was a man of exemplary piety.
He was convinced of Sin in his youth, under the preaching
of Mr. Wesley, and soon after was truly converted to God.
He then joined the Methodists, and continued a member of
the Old Society till the formation of the New Connexion,
when he joined it from principle, and continued with it
till taken from earth to heaven. My mother was convinced
of sin in the ninth year of her age, and shortly after was
changed in heart and life, and became a steady member of
the Methodist New Connection." When about 19 years
of age Margaret came under powerful conviction of sin,
and began to read and fast and weep and pray. She
continued in a state bordering on despair for three months.
She says, "When I was about to give up all hope, my
spiritual Joseph made Himself known to me and spoke
peace and joy to my troubled breast." For a time, she
continued a happy, growing Christian, rebuking sin,
visiting the sick, praying with and for the unsaved around
her. But alas! she began to shun the cross, and to think
she was not required to reprove sin, &c., and she lost her
"peace and power." At the bedside of her dying father
she was fully restored, and her backsliding healed. Now
she became an earnest Christian worker and one of the
most exemplary of her sex. Many still living, who were
members of her "Juvenile Band," bear grateful testimony
to the value of her earnest, loving instruction; and not a
few are themselves on the way to heaven and leading others
to accompany them, who were in youth induced to start on

the heavenly way by Margaret Carlisle. In May, 1829, her brother William, was seized with a fever; and afterwards Thomas, George, and James caught the infection. Thomas died, Alas! Margaret was likewise seized with the dire complaint, under which she too sank and died, on the 16th July, 1829. Her last words, in reply to a question of her dear mother's were, "I am very happy." The precious memory of Margaret Carlisle is still sacredly cherished by those surviving kindred and friends who knew her worth.

It was in 1842, the year under review, that the *Irish Christian Monitor* was commenced. Two volumes of this unpretending serial lie upon the writer's desk. The glimpses which they give into the Connexional life and work of over forty years ago are pleasing and instructive. The articles show that the missionaries of those days were men of considerable mental force and intelligence. Those from the pens of the Revs. Wm. McClure, and James and Thomas Seymour are of a superior order of literary merit. In one of these volumes, over the signature of Mr. Nicholson, appears the Memoir of Samuel Hinds, dated *Priesthill, 25th November*, 1842. This touching account we here reproduce; it serves to exhibit the piety and diligence and faith of its author. Besides, the name of Hinds has all along held an honourable place in connection with Zion Priesthill:—

"Samuel Hinds was born in the parish of Blaris, County Down. He joined the Methodist Society at the age of eighteen, and at that time enjoyed a clear sense of the Divine favour; but at a more advanced age he lost the enjoyment of religion, though he retained the form. During the autumn of 1841, he caught cold, which terminated in consumption. When seriously ill he became alarmed about his immortal concerns, and cried to God for mercy, with all his heart. He attended class-meeting as long as he was able. He urged me to visit him as often as possible, which request

I attended to, and always found him much in earnest for salvation. I pointed him to the Lamb of God who taketh away the sin of the world, and told him that Christ had immense riches laid up in store for all who ask, seek, and knock at mercy's door. After I prayed with him, he said that his soul was much comforted, and that he would not rest until he could read his title clear to a mansion in the skies. I called to see him a few days before his decease, he told me he was much harassed with worldly cares, that to leave his wife and little ones on the rough sea of time without a guide or (human) provider was worse to him than death itself. He said that the enemy of souls had tried him much with fiery temptations during the past night, but thanked the Lord, he had left him now. The next time I visited him I found him changed in expression and in heart; he told me that he had found the pearl of great price, that his sins were all removed, and that he could commend his wife and children to the care of that God who had said, that he will be a father to the fatherless, and a husband to the widow. As our brother came nearer the Jordan of death, his confidence in God increased greatly, and when on the verge of the river which separates the wilderness from the heavenly Canaan, he longed to cross the flood to be with Christ. I visited him on the morning of that day on which he changed time for eternity, and earth for heaven. I said, 'Brother Hind, you will soon be with Jesus,' to which he replied, ' O, yes ! I shall soon be at home in my Father's house, the palace of angels and God;' and added, ' I have no doubt of my acceptance with God, I can trust in God my Saviour.' A few minutes before his departure he told his friends that Jesus was with him ; and said, ' *There*, there is my Saviour to take my soul to the kingdom of glory.' After he had uttered these words the weary wheels of life stood still, and his redeemed spirit quitted the tabernacle of clay. and took its flight to join the celestial throng who have washed their robes and made them white in the blood of the Lamb. He died on the 1st September, 1842, aged 28 years.   S. NICHOLSON."

It is a gratifying fact, that two nephews (cousins) of the foregoing deceased brother are at present engaged in important spheres of work for the Master. One, the Rev. Samuel Hinds is pastor of a Congregational Church ; the other, the Rev. John Hinds, is one of the staff of Me'hodist New Connexion missionaries labouring in China.

The details of Mr. Nicholson's work during this, his second year, at Priesthill, very much resembled those of the first ; but now he had a helpmate, who in sympathy and prayer and effort entered heartily with him into his manifold labours for God and souls. She was no hindrance but a help to the diligent man in the prosecution of his studies; often when he returned home weary, she read to him for hours from th se works which required his attention. To this day, she cherishes very pleasing reminiscences of this, the first year, of her experience as a missionary's wife. In notes carefully prepared for this memorial, she tells of very pleasant and profitable journeys to preaching-appointments with her dear husband. The kind entertainment of the friends and the happy meeting in the farmer's kitchen have left sunny traces in her memory. For example, she says, "I remember us going to Ballinderry, to a Mr. Kennedy's, where my husband preached monthly. It was six miles distant from Priesthill ; but we were hospitably entertained for the night, in a home where there was ample means. After the preaching service, a class was held, to which about twenty persons remained. Mr. Kennedy had a niece, named Mrs. Neill, who was long a member of our church at Bangor." At the close of the year Mr. Nicholson's certificate was affirmatively filled up at the Priesthill Quarterly Meeting, and he was commended to the favourable consideration of Conference as a probationer. Mr. James Carlisle, as lay delegate, accompanied Mr. Nicholson to Conference. In the *Irish Christian Monitor*, vol. II, we find a report of the Conference of 1843, which we here transcribe slightly abridged.

THE METHODIST NEW CONNEXION IRISH CONFERENCE, 1843.

The services connected with our Annual Assembly, commenced on Sabbath morning, April 16th, 1843, in Salem Chapel, Belfast. At six o'clock a.m. a prayer meeting was held, and at seven, a luminous and profitable discourse was delivered, on Matt. xvi. 18, by the Rev. Thomas Seymour. At 11 and 7 o'clock the Rev. Wm. Ford (deputation from England) preached two admirable discourses. Ten sermons were preached in the open air, to crowds, by several ministers, well supported by our friends in the singing. On Monday, at five a.m., a sermon was preached by the Rev. W. Barker, and in the evening the Rev. H. Harrison preached. Sermons were also preached on Tuesday and Wednesday mornings, by Rev. McClune and M. On Tuesday evening, the public missionary meeting was held. On Wednesday evening an Ordination Service was held, when Messrs. McClune, Barker and Sorsby were solemnly devoted to the work of the ministry, by prayer and the imposition of hands. The questions were asked by Rev. G. Goodall, the ordination prayer was offered by Rev. Thos. Seymour, and the charge was delivered by the Rev. Wm. Ford. The answers of the brethren were satisfactory, and those relating to their early religious impressions very affecting. Conference requested the publication of Mr. Ford's charge in the pages of the *Monitor*. The business of Conference commenced on Monday morning, in *Salem*, at six o'clock, when the Rev. Wm. Ford was chosen President, and Mr. Joseph Lee, Secretary. The sittings closed about noon, on the 20th. It was by unanimous consent the best Conference remembered. Everything was done in the spirit of perfect brotherly kindness. The spirit of prayer was richly poured out; and there was perfect unanimity; and, we trust, God directed all.

At this Conference Mr. Nicholson was duly examined according to rule, and continued on probation; and he was appointed to the Ballyclare Station, which had been commenced but a year or two before. Wm. Connolly and his cousin, John Connolly, were the principal agents in originating the interest at Ballyclare. We knew the former brother intimately. He had held an important situation as bleacher at Hyde Park, where, from principle, he had united with the Methodist New Connexion; and, having acquired sufficient means, he retired from business, and settled down at Ballyclare, his native place, where as leader and local preacher, he stood by our cause till the end of his life. There are some invertebrate creatures who are the sport of the strongest prevailing current, but Wm. Connolly was not one of these, having a backbone of principle, he remained "faithful among the faithless." The Rev. Wm. Cooke, in a letter to the Mission Secretary, in 1840, says. "It will afford you pleasure to learn that the Marquis of Donegal has freely granted us a site of land, for the erection of a new chapel, in Ballyclare." Accordingly the *Monitor* for July, 1842, gives an account of the stone-laying: "On Tuesday, the 31st May, the first stone of a new Chapel was laid at Ballyclare, Co. Antrim. A hymn was sung, and prayer offered by the Rev. Wm· Barker, when Samuel Archibald Esq., of Clareview, laid the stone in the name of the Holy Trinity. Our friends have hitherto worshipped in an incommodious house, and for some time, have contemplated the erection of a chapel." The *Monitor* for February, 1813, tells of the opening services: "On Sabbath, January 15th, our new Chapel, in Ballyclare, was opened for Divine service. In the afternoon the Rev. G. Goodall preached; and in the evening the Rev. H. Harrison—Collections, about seven pounds. Wm. Smith, Esq., Whitepark, Dr. Agnew, and Messrs. S. Archbold, and James Walmsley acted as collectors. More than £70 have already been raised by subscriptions."

With hot tears of parting in their eyes, our friends bade adieu to Priesthill, and after a few days at Knockstiken, proceeded to their new sphere of labour. Here they were for a time uncomfortable in the lodgings available, as their sleeping apartment was not wholly private; and Mrs.

Nicholson soon went home for a while to her father's.
but Mr. Nicholson, having elsewhere "endured hardness
as a good soldier of Jesus Christ," put "a cheerful courage on," and entered heartily into his work, leaning on
the arm of Omnipotence. Early in the year he entered
upon a new experience and a new relationship. On Sabbath 1st July, a daughter was born to him; and none will
be surprised to learn that the happy father reckoned that
day as one of great blessing, and that he was early upon
the scene on the next day. His mental condition may be
inferred from the fact, that his mother-in-law found him
at night out in the moonlight, with the baby in his arms,
giving it a first lesson in astronomy, bidding it look up at
the moon. The good lady, however, quickly gave him a
lesson on quite a different subject. The Rev. William
McClure baptized the baby, naming her Elizabeth Mary,*
after Mr. Nicholson's mother, and Aunt Mary Carson,
With a heart brimful of gratitude to God, Mr. Nicholson
soon returned to his loved labour. There remained a debt
upon the new chapel, and to wipe it off he went to work,
his wife's brother helping him in the effort. On their way
they called upon Lady Annesley and Lord Roden, each of
whom subscribed a pound. A servant of the latter,
having slighted our friends, said, "I gave them a snub
which will prevent them from returning." But his lord-
ship had them brought back, and during the interview, by
his request, Mr. Nicholson prayed for the young nobleman,
who, with his friends, knelt during prayer. The debt was
cleared off, and a soiree held to rejoice over the event.
Mr. John Hall Nicholson (now a Belfast merchant), presided, and made his maiden speech. Mrs. Nicholson was

* She is now Mrs. E. M. Mackinlay, her husband being pastor of
a Church in Cork.

present, also Mr. Nicholson's kind friends, the Misses Crawford, of Belfast, and Mr. L. Brown. The Rev. G. Goodall and others made speeches. And a Family Bible was presented by the Ballyclare friends to their minister. Mr. Nicholson visited the homes of the people in every direction and soon became a general favourite, and his congregation grew apace. The poor, away in back streets, the sick, and especially the dying commanded his particular attention, and to these his visits were much blessed, as the following case from the pages of the *Monitor* shows :

MEMOIR OF JANE IRWIN.

"Jane Irwin, wife of John Irwin, of Ballynure, Co. Antrim, died on July 29th, 1843, aged 38 years. For many years she was a stranger to the sweets of true religion, though a person of good moral character. The affliction which summoned her from this mortal state, was a lingering consumption. Both her parents feared the Lord, and were members of our Church at Bangor. When Mrs. Irwin found herself declining in health, she longed to see one of her own ministers, not being aware there was one so near as Ballyclare. My predecessor, Mr. Barker, was found out, and the afflicted woman received him as a messenger from the Lord. He was requested by her and her husband to establish preaching in their house. Soon a class was formed, which is now very promising. For several days previous to her death she suffered much, but was wonderfully supported by Divine grace ; and with patient resignation she calmly waited the coming of her Lord. She had experiened the Lord's mercy early in her affliction, and He was with her to the last. She had no exceeding joy, but it may be truly said of her, that she died in Jesus. She told her husband that the fear of death was taken away ; and a few minutes before her departure urged him to continue in prayer that her spirit might be received by the Saviour she loved. The deceased was interred on the Sabbath, and in accordance with her request the remains were followed by the minister, leaders and friends, with singing of hymns, to the graveyard. And before the body was covered with the clods of the valley, her death was improved by the writer from Rev. xiv. 13.

Aug. 16, 1843.   S. NICHOLSON."

In December, Mr. Nicholson sent to the *Monitor*, a detailed account of his work :

"Soon after last Conference, the ministers and leaders engaged to pray to God for a revival of religion upon this station ; and they have reason to bless the Lord that prayer was not offered up in vain. At the lovefeast, held on the second Sabbath in July, the Lord manifested His presence in a powerful manner.   During the sermon which was preached upon the occasion, the Lord watered many hearts with the dew of His heavenly grace : and at the penitent meeting which was held at the conclusion, many sinners were brought into the glorious liberty of the children of God. The meeting lasted several hours and was most orderly. It was a time which will be long remembered ; often two at once would rise to declare what God had done for their souls.   From this time, an unusual heavenly influence rested upon all our meetings, and our leaders became more anxious for the conversion of sinners.   They visited from house to house, inviting strangers to attend our services, and our congregation, in a short time, greatly increased, especially upon the Sabbath evening. We also reclaimed some from the world, who are now most promising members of our church. We opened prayer meetings in new places, which were owned of God to the salvation of precious souls. The hallowed feeling which existed was not mere excitement, or a momentary impression, but from what we have since witnessed, we believe the blessings received will be lasting as eternity. The means of grace are regularly attended by all the members, and the Word of God is precious to them ; and their liberality in attending to the wants of their minister, and supporting the Gospel is only bounded by their means. On December 10th, I administered to a good number, the dear memorials of the dying Lord. I selected my text for this occasion from 2 Cor., iv., 5. While I preached the word the gracious influences of the Holy Spirit rested upon the congregregation, and many were melted into tears. And the Saviour made Himself known in the breaking of bread. My own soul was unspeakably happy in God. The Rev. G. Goodall preached the Missionary Anniversary Sermons on the 17th inst., the congregations were excellent, the people heard with great attention and a solemn sense of the Divine presence was experienced. The collections exceeded our expectations. The Missionary meeting was a great success. The Rev. G. Goodall presided. Addresses were delivered by the Chairman, the Revs. T. Seymour, W. Sorsby, and S. Nicholson. A delightful missionary spark was kindled amongst the members ; and two females volunteered their services as collectors for the mission. I appointed special services for the fol. lowing week, and in eight days, I had twelve preaching appointments. Our congregations are increasing, and God is owning our work. Not unto us, O Lord! not unto us, but unto thy name we ascribe the praise. Amen."

Thus with *ceaseless* activity, in dependence upon God, Mr. Nicholson continued to prosecute his labours, his steady aim being the salvation of souls. Mrs. Nicholson remembers to this day, the names of persons who, during this year, became members of the Society, and remained steadfast. In 1844, Mr. Nicholson's brothers, James and Thomas, emigrated to America, and his sister Margaret came to reside with her elder brother; and she remained with him for six years, when she followed her brothers, who had gained good positions in New York. It is she to whom we refer, in an earlier part of this memorial, as Mrs. Captain Benson. Benevolence was always a prominent feature in the disposition of our friend, and he was ever ready to encourage and help any godly youth whom he found anxious to work for the Lord. Mrs. Nicholson found him actually sharing his own needed clothing with a poor, but pious young man, whom Mr. Nicholson was afterwards instrumental in introducing into mission work. In addition to his manifold labours our brother had "to give attention to reading," and study, and to prepare for his annual examination at the District Meeting.

The Irish Conference of 1844 assembled in *Salem*, Belfast, on April 15th. English deputation: Rev. Wm.

K

Baggaly (who was chosen president), and B. Fowler, Esq.
Secretaries : Revs. Thos. Seymour, and Wm. McClure.
Sermons were preached at five in the morning. Several of
the brethren preached at the Docks. The Mayor of Belfast occupied the chair at the missionary meeting. In the
address to the English Conference, favourable mention was
made of the retiring superintendent, Rev. G. Goodall. Mr.
Nicholson was continued on probation, and was appointed
to the Portglenone Station. The Rev. Wm Baggaly was
appointed superintendent by the English Conference.

Portglenone consisted of one long street of irregular
houses, divided by the river Bann. The Chapel, a neat
structure, stood at one end of the town. One after
another of the sturdy, intrepid missionaries had travelled
this station and won many souls for Christ, including
Romanists. Extreme poverty prevailed everywhere. In
a letter to the Mission Secretary the Rev. Wm. Cooke says,
"As a specimen of the people inhabiting the country
around Portglenone, I may mention that I saw people
whose garments were so patched and party-coloured that I
could not ascertain which was the original garment. The
Greeks contended about the identity of the Argonautic
vessel; here they would have found many similar subjects
of disputation equally difficult to decide." Mr. Nicholson,
having travelled a part of this station before, knew the
people, and they loved him. But now he has no colleague, the second preacher having been withdrawn. Our
devoted friends found uncomfortable lodgings in the house
of a blacksmith, where they could hear the sounds of the
hammers, often mingled with the oaths of the workmen,
who refused kind invitations to join the preacher and his
family at family worship. Mr. Nicholson found that the
Circuit Steward and the Superintendent of the Sabbath

School was likewise clerk of the Parish Church. There were a few earnest people connected with the cause, including Henry Hamilton, who was "very loyal to the Society." Mrs. and Miss Nicholson took hold of the School, often carrying the baby with them ; and Mr. Nicholson, though doubtful whether his appointment was of the Lord, entered upon his work with true missionary zeal. There were long journeys, some of the monthly preaching places being eight and ten miles distant. On some Sabbaths there were three preaching appointments at as many different places. The friends at Bellaghey highly appreciated their former minister's visits, which were much blessed. Catholic in spirit, "the friend of all and the enemy of none," our brother soon became widely known and respected. He was on the most fraternal terms with the Presbyterian ministers, who helped him in many ways.

Mrs. Nicholson speaks in very grateful terms of a medical doctor, named Madden, as also of a Mrs. Daly, the mother of a priest. It was necessary, however, to guard constantly against giving offence to the Romanists, as they were treacherously revengeful. There were often faction fights amongst the people, in one of which a young man was killed, during Mr. Nicholson's residence at Portglenome.

Returning in winter from a distant appointment, Mr. and Mrs. Nicholson, and Mr. Hamilton experienced an alarming encounter. They heard behind them the sound of horses' hoofs and men's voices. At length a man on horse back rode up alongside the car, and Mrs. Nicholson observed a gun in his hand. She did not speak, and felt fully able to trust in God for protection. Suddenly, as our friends were passing its entrance, a number of men rushed out of a lane, shouting loudly. The horse took

fright, and soon the whole party on the car were thrown
into a ditch. Mrs. Nicholson remembers her exertions to
protect her child from being dashed against a huge stone,
as she was falling. Soon her husband extricated mother
and child from a perilous position. One of the rowdy
men asked Mr. Hamilton who Mr. Nicholson was, and
when informed that he was a " Methodist preacher who
would offend nobody," the men took their departure.
The destruction of a bonnet was the only material damage
experienced. It appeared that they were in quest of a
Presbyterian minister, who had been preaching against
the Papacy. When Mr. Nicholson preached in the open
air many Romanists stood to listen, and did not molest
him.

Amongst the more memorable incidents of this year,
Mr. Nicholson retained a grateful recollection of a house
being saved from destruction by fire through his agency.
It was at Bellaghey, where he preached monthly. He
occupied a bed-room just above the apartment occupied
by his hostess and her children. In the night he smelt
wood burning, and soon found that part of the room
beneath him was in flames. It appears that the wooden
ceiling of the room was low and its boards loose, and
part of these were found to be burning. The mother and
her children would soon have been suffocated in their
sleep had not Mr. Nicholson awoke them. His hostess,
with rare presence of mind and vigour, tore down the
burning timber and threw it out of the window. Thus
were life and property providentially saved.

The extreme poverty of the people involved varied
experiences, some trying and others ludicrous. Mr.
Nicholson visited a house regularly, where in one apartment, a family, including several children, a cow, a goat,

and other animals, eat and slept in strange accord. There attended the Chapel a man whose apparel was of the "party-coloured" type, and his legs were without stockings, but he was truly pious. The Rev. Jno. Lyons had preached in this man's house, and had ridden to it on horseback; but the man complained of having to give the horse fodder. He said "If Mr. Lyons can't come to preach without bringing a horse to feed, let him give up the preaching." The poor man lived in a bog. Mr. Nicholson often told of a cup of tea that was handed him, made of water out of the bog. He found a large water beetle in the cup. He was urged, with sincere hospitality, to "finish his tea," as he had had "a long journey," which was true enough; but the boiled insect was too much for his appetite.

The writer remembers spending a long afternoon at a wedding party, in company with the Revs. D. McAfee and John Lyons; and it was most interesting to hear related by the then aged ministers many reminiscences of their experiences as Irish itinerants. Mr. Lyons told of a man who lived in a bog (likely the one just alluded to), who had been truly converted, but who had hardly any knowledge of the Scriptures. He had heard the account of the slaying of Goliath by David, and was not at all satisfied with it. "What," said he to Mr. Lyons, "do you think of that young fellow, David, throwing stones at the other fellow, and cutting his skull open? It wasn't fair at all, at all! Why didn't David stand up and fight like a man, instead of being a coward, and slinging stones at the man." Archy McMagh lived in this bog; he used to attend the lovefeasts at Portglenone. He was truly pious, but a hasty temper gave him much trouble. He complained of it in very strong terms. But he used to add, "I have the blood of the O'Neill's in my veins, and cannot stand insult." The Rev. Wm. Baggaly wrote a memoir of Archy's father, Daniel McMagh, which appeared in the Methodist New Connexion Magazine for 1846, of which we give an abridgement.

The Lord's Jewels in an Irish Bog.

Burnquarter is situated on a very extensive bog near Ballymoney, Co. Antrim. It is occupied by a number of poor people, who live in small cabins, some of which have actually been cut out of the solid turf. To attempt a delineation of Archy McMagh's cabin would only be to challenge the faith of the most credulous. He rose and offered us the stool on which he had been sitting, but it was scarcely sufficient to accommodate three men, and a lady, as it was not more than twelve inches long. We soon retreated, the best part of Archy's cabin being outside. On the bog at Burnquarter, some of our members and hearers reside. Our indefatigable missionary, Mr. McClune, found them in the year 1842. He crossed their dangerous pits, tracked his way to their cabins, and standing on their worse than earthen floors, preached to them Jesus and the resurrection. A small society was formed, which has been supplied by our worthy brethern, Messrs. W. Barker, S. Nicholson, and J. Baird. In some places the bog is almost impassable, and when the people hear of a fresh preacher being appointed to the Circuit, one of their first inquiries is if he is a good leaper—able to jump over the bog holes. The people are seldom absent from the services. If there is moonlight, well; but if not they provide torches, and crowd the cabin where the meeting is held. Usually, even in winter, the preacher is the only person at the service having his feet shod.

But though poor and simple, they have experienced the quickening and comforting power of the Gospel; and many of them rejoice in the knowledge of salvation by the remission of sins. They left their work at mid-day to hear me preach, and greater attention I have rarely witnessed either in this or any country. A few weeks since, a dreadful fever broke out in this place. Several of our little flock were numbered amongst its victims.

Old Daniel McMagh and his family did not escape. Daniel had his aged partner, his son, daughter-in-law, and several grand-children around him. Daniel and his wife were seized with the fever, and lay upon one bed, not knowing whether would be called away first. In a short time the poor old woman breathed her last. Daniel, in the worst stage of fever, had to be removed from the side of her lifeless clay. No other bed being available, some straw was laid on the damp floor, and there the old man stretched his fevered limbs, and calmly waited his Heavenly Father's will. On the 14th December, 1845, his happy spirit entered into rest, in the 81st year of his age. A few minutes before the vital spark fled, he said, "I have peace; I know I am dying, but *Christ has done it for Dan!*" Daniel had seen himself as the chief of sinners; and often did he look back upon 77 years spent in the service of Satan with the deepest sorrow. But he had peace, arising from an inward conviction that Christ had died for him—*Done it for Dan.*

Surely by the instrumentality of our missions, the poor have the gospel preached unto them."

Salem Manse, Belfast, June, 1846.

Mr. Nicholson's diary contains records covering a part of this year. A few extracts will serve to exhibit the inner workings, experiences and principles of the mind of God's servant. He prays, "Oh, Thou Eternal Jehovah, guide my pen to honour Thee; and enable me to walk closer with Thee; and grant me more of Thy presence, love, and favour. Help me to aim at Thy glory alone." "I have just passed through a severe bilious attack; but it has been sanctified to my good. The assurance— "Underneath are the everlasting arms," was made a great comfort to my mind. I was enabled to exclaim, in the words of the poet :—

"O Love! Thou bottomless abyss!
   My sins are swallowed up in Thee;
Covered is my unrighteousness,
   Nor spot of guilt remains on me,
While Jesu's blood, through earth and skies,
Mercy, free, boundless mercy, cries!"

"I experienced a great elevation and reverence of mind while studying a sermon upon the existence of God.

"O! the glories of Thy mind
Leave all my soaring thoughts behind!"

"Felt a trembling sense of God's presence while preaching upon the Divine existence." "Read with profit a description of 'Jerusalem the city of the Great King,' by *Horne.*" "Studied in Grammar, Rhetoric and Church History." "Visited some families; prayed with a dying penitent; he is now in eternity." I close another day happy in God, filled with His peace and joy. Read part of *Cooke* on the Trinity. A wide field of usefulness opens before me, may I be enabled to cultivate it to the glory of God. Lent our Chapel to the Covenanters, and attended the meetings of their Presbytery. Bigotry is dying! Bless the Lord! Prepared for quarterly examination—Grammar, Rhetoric, and Horne's Divinity. I feel myself but a child in knowledge. O Lord! touch my lips with a live coal from off Thine altar. Preached on the Immortality of the Soul. Received a letter from the Rev. T. Seymour. O how full of marrow and fatness are the letters of this man of God! They do me good. Read *Horne* on Punishment by Crucifixion. 'O Lamb of God! was ever pain, was ever love like Thine!' Preached my farewell sermon; my soul was much blessed.

O my God! how many mercies hast Thou made me prove in the last year. I want to be a man full of the Holy Ghost and wisdom, and thus prepared to enter upon the labours of another year.

Mr. Nicholson, during this year, tried to cultivate the entire ground which had engaged the full strength of two missionaries; but his labours were too widely diffused to be very productive at the central place, or at any point. Hence, though his work was blessed, yet the results did not appear in the accession of members.

Early in his ministerial career, our earnest brother began to excite attention, and make friends, outside the pale of his own Church. Amongst his attached friends was Mr. Bain, who resided in Holywood. Mr. Nicholson's intimacy with this gentleman began about 1844-5. Mr. Nicholson baptized two of the children of Mr. Bain, at the latter's urgent request. To a friend, Mr. Bain said, "Mr. Nicholson's visits are as blessed as an angel's."

A full report of the Conference of 1845 lies under the writer's eye. It commenced on April 13th, the Rev. W. Baggaly being chosen President, and the Rev. W. McClure, Secretary. Three sermons were preached in Salem; and though the day was boisterous, attended with heavy rain and hail, yet two services were held in the open air, conducted by the Revs. J. Seymour, Barker, Harrison, Sorsby, and Nicholson. On April 14th, Rev. J. Baird preached at five o'clock in the morning; and the Conference commenced its sittings at six. The Missionary Meeting was held in the evening, presided over by Andrew Mulholland, Esq, Mayor of Belfast. On the 15th, Brother S. Nicholson preached at five o'clock a.m.; and in the evening in Salem, Messrs. J. Baird and another were ordained for the ministry by the imposition of hands. A day of fasting, humiliation, and prayer was appointed. Petitions to both Houses of Parliament against the proposed grant to Maynooth were resolved upon. The number of members showed an increase in the Circuits retained the former Conference, and the financial affairs were greatly improved."

Mr. Nicholson was continued on probation; and he was removed from Portglenone back to Ballyclare. It should here be noted that the Canadian Mission was commenced in 1837, the Rev. J. Addyman (first missionary), arriving in that country on August 31st, 1837. Now (1845) there were in the Dominion 33 chapels, 37 ministers, 46 local preachers, and 3460 members. Such marked success justified the English Conference in yielding to the demand for more ministers and money, to enable the Canadian Conference to enter upon necessitous and inviting fields of labour opening in every direction. But the result to the Irish Mission was the resolution to withdraw from the more Popish districts, and to leave them to the willing efforts of "the wealthier Protestant Churches."

The change to Ballyclare was most agreeable to Mr. Nicholson and his wife, and the friends received them gladly. This time, comfortable apartments were found in the house of a respectable family. At this time Arianism and ultra-Calvinism prevailed in and around Ballyclare. Mr. Nicholson did not contend with those who differed from him, but just preached, and tried to live the Gospel, leaving the results with God.

From Mr. Nicholson to the Superintendent, Ballyclare, August 8th, 1845.

My Dear Brother,—I feel thankful to God that at the conclusion of another quarter, I have to report a gradual progress of the work of the Lord upon this station. The Most High continues to bless us as a Christian Church, and many of our old members are manifestly growing in grace. There is a growing friendly feeling towards us throughout all classes of the community. At our preaching places all over the Circuit, the good work continues to prosper. Our own people are determined to use their best endeavours to extend the Kingdom of Christ. The congregations in the Chapel are good, and a blessed influence frequently prevails. I have adopted the plan of preaching short and pointed sermons, and afterwards conducting a lively prayer-meeting. This method has been greatly owned of God. On June 1st, I administered the sacrament. While I preached from John xii., 23, both myself and congregation were greatly blessed. The Master made Himself known in the breaking of bread. We had the lovefeast on the first Sabbath in July. On that occasion I preached from Daniel vii, 4. We had about seventy present; and the speaking continued for some hours. I conducted a penitent meeting at the conclusion. Some of the members, being in distress for sanctification, wrestled with God in mighty prayer, that He would apply the atoning blood, and cleanse them from all sin. The meeting continued till nearly six o'clock; and the evening preaching had to be postponed for an hour. Believers that day received a deepening of the work of God in their souls, and sinners were made happy in the Saviour's love.

A few months ago, a man named Keys, left the Presbyterians and joined in church-fellowship with us. His former minister called and told him that he would prove that the doctrines held by Calvin were the only true doctrines of the Word of God. Our friend told the minister that he could not reason much; but this he could declare, that he was never convinced of sin until he came among the Methodists; but now he not only knew his danger and lost condition, but that he had the cheering hope of receiving from Christ the clear evidence that he had redemption through His blood even the forgiveness of all sins. The minister then left him saying that Keys had lost his way, and that *no man could know his sins forgiven.* Keys read Wesley's Sermons; and while in the act of reading, he received power to rely upon Christ as his Saviour, his chains fell off, and the love of God was shed abroad in his heart. He went direct to his wife and told her what God had done for his soul. This took place the week before the love-feast, at which he related his experience with joyous tears.

On July 20th, the Rev. Wm. Baggaly preached our mission sermons ; a solemn sense of the Divine presence was felt at both services. The collections exceeded our expectations. During the summer I appointed field-meetings for different parts of the Circuit. Last Sabbath, we held an open-air service at Hyde Park, about a hundred people were present. I preached from Ezekiel, xxxiii., 11. The power of the Lord rested upon the assembly. We conducted a revival prayer-meeting in a large out-house. Some sinners were greatly broken down, and cried out, " What must we do to be saved?" My Dear Brother, I can truly say that my own soul is alive to God. I am determined to know nothing so much among men as Jesus Christ, and Him crucified. O, may I yet more and more abound in the great and glorious work of striving to evangelize, and mend this bad warld. There is here an open door and a wide field for missionary enterprise to diffuse the simple and saving truths of the glorious Gospel of our common Lord. May the Divine glory more fully rest upon us, and on all the glory may there be a defence. Amen. Amen.

From Mr. Nicholson's diary we learn that on July 26th, he attended Mr. Service's wedding, and visited Shane's Castle, the scenery of which greatly interested him. This Castle is situated near Antrim, and is the seat of the royal O'Neills. The old Castle was destroyed by fire in 1816, and remains in the same condition to which it was then reduced. It is a charming and imposing ruin, standing on the shore of Lough Neagh. Near to this, too, is the Antrim Round Tower, ninety-five feet in height. Its conical top was shattered in 1822, by lightning, as is supposed, and was replaced by a covering of freestone. Who were its builders, and what its use, are questions which continue to baffle the antiquarian. Whatever Mr. Service may have felt, his friend did not much enjoy this wedding day.

From Mr. Nicholson's diary :—

1845, July 28th.—Very unwell; visited Knockstiken, and met Mr. McClure there. He is a holy man of God, full of useful information on all subjects. Mrs. McConnell, of Belfast, joined us at tea. She, my wife and self had a narrow escape from being killed in Belfast lately. A huge horse, attached to a large cart broke away from its driver, and came running furiously down High Street. We took shelter in an entry. Scarcely had we done so when the great beast dashed bodily through a massive plate glass window, at which we had stood an instant before. Praise the Lord for the deliverance!

30th.—This morning at seven o'clock a second daughter* was born to us. May our God endue us with wisdom to train her for Him.

August 10th.—The sudden death of Mrs. Wilson, Mr. Service's mother-in-law, greatly startled me. The sad and unexpected news reached me at Knockstiken. How uncertain is life. I walk on the margin of the grave. 24th.—Preached in the street, and again in the chapel. Had great liberty. Felt unwell, and the Lord sent me a brother who relieved me in the evening. September 10th.— My beloved wife and second babe returned home to-day. May the Lord enable us to strive together for the conversion of sinners. 13th.—Sweet peace reigns in my heart. Have resumed my regular reading and study. *Finney* on Revivals stirs my soul. September: Received a letter from the Missionary Committee, through Mr. Baggaly, suggesting that some one of our missionaries should resign. A copy of the letter has been sent to each of us.

[Canada was urgently in need of more agents.]

Many years ago, I was moved by the Holy Ghost to preach the gospel; and God has given me many souls for my hire, and seals to my ministry. I dare not retire from the work for any man. I have written my mind to Mr. Baggaly. September 24th.—Preached at Mr. Scott's, and baptized his baby. Preached at Thornditch on *The Smitten Rock*. Had a good prayer-meeting in the evening. 29th.—Visited the class for youths, and found a more central place for their meeting. I most sensibly feel my

* She was named Margaret Ann, and was baptized by the Rev. Wm. McClure. She is now the wife of Mr. W. J. Bailey, of Lisburn.

own unworthiness before God. O Lord, fill me with humility and love, and enable me to lean on Jesus as my all in all. October 4th. —T. Jackson spoke in the class this morning, and it was a blessed time.

Mrs. Nicholson supplies particulars about this convert, Jackson. Before his conversion he was a notorious drunkard and blasphemer. He had threatened his wife's life, and she was in terror of him. She asked for a prayer-meeting to be held in their house; and the meeting was announced from the pulpit. The friends went to the swearer's house strong in faith. Jackson thought he would leave his house when the hour for the meeting came, but, ashamed to seem a coward, he remained, but kept in an apartment alone. He, however, heard the mighty prayers that went up to God on his behalf; and soon he was powerfully convinced of sin, and, coming out of his hiding place, he fell down upon his knees and besought the friends to pray for him. Prayer was heard, and the blasphemer was made a new creature in Christ Jesus, and began a life of praise. His conversion made a profound impression. At the next quarterly meeting, he laid on the table £3, as an offering to the Lord, saved, as he said, from drink. He could not read, but Mrs. Nicholson gave him lessons, and soon he was able to spell out the meaning of Scripture. He did not live long. Shortly before his death, he assured Mrs. Nicholson that he was firmly built on the Rock of Ages.

The Sabbath on which Jackson related his conversion was a memorable one in *Bethel;* there was an all-day meeting. On that day Mrs. Nicholson herself bowed amongst the seekers, and the blessed Lord filled her with all the fulness of His love. Zechariah xiii. 1 was divinely applied to her conscience and heart, and she was enabled by faith to wash in the "fountain for sin and uncleanness." The penitent form was filled, and cleared, and filled again and again. Most of the girls in Mrs. Nicholson's Sabbath school class were converted. And Mr. Nicholson received a mighty baptism of the Holy Ghost.

From the Rev. S. Nicholson to the Superintendent, Ballyclare,
January 7th, 1846.

Dear Brother,—During the past month, the work of God has

been prospering on this station. December 10th, 1845.—This evening, I had an appointment at Ballynure; and was engaged visiting for a part of the day. Prayer and visiting do great good. 11th.—I had a meeting at Cloghen; as I was unwell Brother B. held it for me. We withheld the meetings from this place for a time, as the family did not walk according to the Gospel. The leader and myself spol e to Brother McG. He repented, acknowledged his fault, and is meeting regularly in class. The meetings are again resumed. 2th.—We held a meeting in the chapel. I also formed a committee to arrange for the tea party. I was glad to see so many friends offering to provide tables gratuitously. 13th.—I preached at Thornditch. A truly blessed influence pervaded the meeting. God has lately poured out His Spirit in an abundant manner upon this class. Several of the members have been made very happy in God. 14th.—Sabbath—I preached in the morning from Genesis xix. 17. I found great liberty in exhorting all to fly to Zoar—Christ Jesus—for safety. I preached at Cloghen at three p.m., from Galatians vi. 14. The last year I travelled this Circuit, I took this place on the plan, and formed a class, which has increased to fifteen members. It is now the most prosperous part of this mission. At night I preached in Bethel on 'The Judgment Day.' On my way home from Cloghen, I gave the emblems of Christ's broken body and shed blood to a Christian young man, whose life is fast ebbing out in consumption. He served in the army for a few years. 18th.—I preached at Ballynure on Thursday; and conducted a meeting in the chapel this evening. 19th.—I bought drapery for the pulpit this week, and had the crimson cloth put on this day. I studied three sermons for the Sabbath. 21st.—Sabbath.—At the accustomed hour this morning I preached in the chapel to on attentive congregation from 2nd Corinthians iv., 1, 2. And at three o'clock, in a new place in Cogny, from Luke xix., 9. And at night, from Matthew xvi., 28. I trust that sinners were convinced under the word this day. My own soul was very happy, and I felt the power of the Spirit accompanying the word preached. 23rd.—This evening we held our tea party, in the chapel. Near one hundred and forty sat down to tea, which was provided gratuitously by members of the congregation. The meeting was addressed by the Revs. W. Baggaly, Bain (Independent), and Nicholson. 25th.—Christmas Day.

—I preached in the chapel at six this morning, from Luke ii., 14, and at seven in the evening from Isaiah ix., 6. Sabbath, 28th.—I met the town class at eight o'clock. At the morning preaching a good number were present. I selected my text from Galatians iv., 4, 5. In the afternoon I went to Thornditch, where a good congregation was gathered ; and the presence of the Lord was felt. One soul found peace with God. She had been a backslider for years. In Bethel last night I spoke on the "Glad tidings of great joy to all people." O how graciously the Lord assisted me in preaching the word. Bless the Lord, O my soul! 30th.—I met the Sabbath School teachers to instruct them in the Word of God. It was a profitable season. 31st.—I visited and held a prayer meeting in Back Street, at seven o'clock. I also visited a dying female. This night I preached at the watch-night, from Psalm xc., 12, to a good congregation. It was a solemn time. Oh! may we all fulfil our *solemn* vow. Amen. I found my heart much drawn out after God; and formed strong resolutions to be more faithful in my ministerial duties. 1846.—January 1st.—I held a meeting in the chapel, at seven o'clock. It was truly good for us to wait upon God. 2nd.—I was sent for to lecture at the funeral of one of our friends, who died suddenly. When I saw so many present, I improved the solemn occasion by preaching from "It is appointed unto man, once to die." I then sung a few hymns, and set a friend to read the Word of God. This prevented idle conversation at the *wake*. 3rd.—Before the corpse (above mentioned) was removed to its cold house, I preached to a crowd of all denominations from Job xiv. 14. I trust good was done. Sabbath, 4th.—I walked to Thornditch, two miles, and met a large class. We have added five new members in the past quarter. I was humbled in the dust to hear several speak of my *first visit to them* and blessing God for my appointment. I could only weep and exclaim, "What am I, O Thou glorious God, and what my father's house to Thee." In the chapel a goodly number were present at the *lovefeast*. The friends spoke freely and experimentally. I was unable to close it till near dark. I closed with a penitent meeting, at which some souls were enabled to rejoice in the God of Salvation. 7th.—This week, I have three appointments. Last night, I held a meeting in the new place, where we are minded to form a class. In conclusion, I have to praise God for His aid and blessing during the past month. Thank God, I feel it an honour to be thus engaged. May I be kept faithful until death, and then receive the crown of life. Amen.

From Mr. Nicholson's private journal :—

1846. January 8th.—Attended the preacher's meeting; a profitable time. 14th.—Visited ten families, and preached at Mrs. Marshall's. I see more than ever the importance of visiting from house to house. I have preached where we, as a Society, were unknown, and the results have been most blessed. February 4th.—Rev. T. Seymour preached our Anniversary Sermons. May his visit prove a great blessing. I had to supply for him at Whiteabbey. 12th. —Preached in the chapel on Revivals ; the congregation filled the house. I praise God that ever I was born ! O Lord, fill my heart with Thy love ; make me humble; fire my heart with holy zeal. 14th.—This is my birthday. How quickly I am passing on towards eternity. Lord help me to redeem the time, and work while it is day. 18th.—Had a trial with B. Drink ruins souls Lord help me to be faithful. Visited my aged father. O, may he be fully prepared for eternity. March 2nd.—Met a young man who was converted through the instrumentality of Rev. W. Cooke ; he is now a useful member amongst the Wesleyans. Visited a young man at Grange. The Arian Minister was very rude and abusive, and challenged me to a discussion. I accepted the challenge ; but my opponent failed to come forward. The young man died professing faith in Christ as his Saviour and God."

At this time, probationers were required to prepare for examinations, upon a prescribed course of reading and study. Mr. Nicholson, in addition to his manifold circuit labours, had to prepare for these examinations, which were held quarterly. When wearied with hard work, his faithful wife often read aloud to him from the books he was required to read ; and she frequently made such notes as would help him. He had a very retentive memory, but

L

his analytical and logical faculty was not equal to it. Domestically our friends were very happy, but very poor. The widespread failure of the potato crop caused all kinds of food to rise to famine price; and the stipend of our brother was very small. But God honoured the trust of His servants, and "supplied all their *need*." Mr. Nicholson's sister was "patient and loving with his children, and helpful in every way." Theirs was a home of peace and love, because it was "the habitation of the just." True, the little family had their "dark days," but the cloud was always silver-edged. Mrs. Nicholson's father, during one of her visits home, in March, was suddenly stricken with paralysis, and his spirit passed home to God. The reason of her visit was a remarkable dream she had had. To quote further from Mr. Nicholson's journal would be but to repeat records similar to those already given. The collecting of books for a congregational lending library deserves to be specially noted. In addition to the marked growth of spiritual power and fervour in the church, the year was one of numerical and financial increase.

After a Connexional Jubilee Meeting, held at Ballyclare, Mary S. offered *One Pound* to the Jubilee Fund. Her weekly earning was just three shillings, not the price at the time of a stone of oatmeal. The minister and friends thought the sum too much. She earned the money at "flowering," during time saved at the intervals from labour at the public works.

CHAPTER VII.

ORDINATION.

" Good Joseph Cownley, when set apart to the ministry, in 1746, kneeled down, and Mr. Wesley, putting the New Testament into his hand, said, ' Take thou authority to preach the Gospel.' "

" Neglect not the gift that is in thee, which was given thee by prophecy, with the laying on of the hands of the presbytery.— *Paul,*

TO Mr. Nicholson the Conference of 1846 was one of the most memorable. It was held in Salem, Belfast, commencing on April 13th. The Rev. J. H. Robinson (President), and Richard Barlow, Esq., were the English Deputation. We have before us Mr. Nicholson's account of this Conference.

Sabbath, April 12th.—Heard Mr. Sorsby preach early in the morning, and heard Mr. Robinson at 11 a.m., and again at 7 evening. I preached at 5 o'clock at Mrs. Smyth's. A blessed day to my soul. 13th.—I preached at six o'clock this morning upon the Kingdom of God within us. The Conference accepted my certificate as perfect. [It should here be noted that at this time, probationers had to preach before the District Meeting from a text given them a short time before they entered the pulpit.] 14th.—This day I passed a strict examination in view of my approaching ordination. My examiners were the Revs. T. Seymour and W. Barker, and R. Barlow, Esq. I had no difficulty in passing the examination. Conference has received me into full connexion. I praise Thee, O Lord, that Thou has opened my way and blessed me thus far. 15th.—This evening I have been solomnly set apart to the work of the ministry by the imposition of hands. The Rev. J. H. Robinson, of Liverpool, delivered the charge from the words, "Make full proof of thy ministry." O may the preacher's earnest counsels never leave my memory. I felt it to be a momentous undertaking, to engage to spend my whole life in the work of labouring for the salvation of souls. My Master promises that His strength shall be made perfect in my weakness. O may I be kept faithful, and have given me many souls who shall be my crown of rejoicing in the day of the Lord Jesus. We have examined Mr. Nicholson's Ordination Bible. The inscription reads thus, "Presented to the Rev. S. Nicholson, on his ordination, in Salem Chapel, Belfast, on Wednesday evening, April 15th, 1846. *William Baggaly, Superintendent of the Methodist New Connexion Irish Mission.*"

As it is of special interest, we here give an extract from the "Address to the English Conference": "Amongst the triumphant deaths, we cannot omit the name of old Charles Hall, who was one of the thirty-two leaders who formed the Methodist New Connexion in Ireland, in 1798, and continued a faithful and devoted friend till death. He was near 90 years of age, and had heard the Methodist preachers for upwards of 80 years. When a youth he was deeply impressed under the venerable Wesley's preaching. He was a member of Society for over 70 years, and a great part of that time was a class-leader. He was a man of great intelligence and unwearied zeal. He departed this life on January 8th, saying 'Jesus —come.'"

Some of the immediate descendants of Charles Hall are,

at the present moment, amongst the most attached friends of our cause at Broomhedge.

By this Conference Mr. Nicholson was appointed to labour upon the Smithboro' Mission, which embraced parts of the counties Armagh, Monaghan, and Cavan. But this appointment was afterwards altered, and he was located at Broomhedge; and Smithboro' was worked from the other stations, Mr. Nicholson, like the other missionaries, giving a part of his time to it.

The records of the privations, sufferings, and triumphs of the preachers upon the Smithboro' mission are rich in instructive interest. Popery prevailed, which implies that poverty was widespread. Dr. Cooke says, "I rode to Smithboro', and went into a cabin, the most wretched hovel I ever beheld in Ireland. The country abounds with such habitations of wretchedness. It is a common thing to erect a house at the side of a ditch-bank, putting up three walls and carrying a roof from the bank." At this time, about thirty thousand poor people annually visited Lough Dearg, enduring privations, fatigue and suffering to expiate their sins.

Mr. Nicholson and his faithful wife now entered a house of their own for the first time. · Concerning the erection of the Chapel and old Manse, at Broomhedge, the Rev. J. Lyons wrote, in 1830, "We have now a Chapel, 45 feet by 20. Adjoining is a dwelling-house, 24 feet in front. Through the opposition of certain influential characters, the building was kept back till January 12th, *Salem*, Broomhedge, was opened for worship on March 7th, 1830." Salem was afterwards considerably enlarged.

Miss Wright was the first to welcome Mr. and Mrs. Nicholson to Broomhedge. On the day after their arrival, they were carried off, babies and all, to the hospitable home at Moyruck. Miss Wright quietly put two pound notes into the folds of Mrs. Nicholson's shawl, saying, "Ministers after changing circuits are sometimes straitened. Return this when you have plenty." The people, resident in the numerous white cottages, and farmhouses scattered over the district of the Maze, and along the fertile valley of the Lagan, were soon made aware of the preacher's advent amongst them, as the records in his diary testify. He seemed always in haste to accomplish the work given him to do. In his own inferior measure, he could say, "Wist ye not that I must be about my Father's business." He went incessantly amongst the people, and his conversation was "as it becometh the gospel of Christ." He says, "I had a conversation with Miss Wright on Christian perfection. I love this doctrine and will preach it as long as I live." Among the first records in his diary are about services held at Green's, of Darnahome, T Jones's, of Gravehill, Hillsborough, F. Martin's, of Mazetown, and (on the Sabbath) in the chapels at Broomhedge, and Priesthill. At all these places the preacher was heartily welcomed, and for the sensible presence and favour of God, he felt profoundly humble and grateful. He had trying experiences, to which he makes but the briefest reference. He says, "I was greatly tried this day with a letter. I spread it before the Lord, and asked Him to settle it all, and, I am sure, He will do so. Glory be to his Great Name!" "At the Circuit meeting on Monday, some things transpired which grieved me. O my Lord, I belong to Thee."

Mr. Nicholson was called to supply the Smithboro' Mission for a week. The visit, however, was not, even in part, a pleasure trip. He was not insensible to the varied beauties of the landscape as he journeyed; but his whole

heart was intent upon the great purpose of his mission—
to preach Christ, and save souls. Upon his arrival at
Emy Vale (the farm belonging to Rev. J. Lyons), he began
his labours at once, by preaching to the people there
assembled. On Sabbath he preached at three different
places to "good congregations," and "the Lord blessed
the word." He spent eight days visiting, leading classes,
and preaching nearly every day. It greatly distressed
him to come upon a man, a backslider, who had been a
leader, but had fallen through drink. No wonder, Mr.
Nicholson often execrated drink, the instrument of so
much sin and suffering. During this visit our brother
found himself one night in the bed upon which a good
man had died a few days before. No wonder, that the
preacher could not sleep, and that exciting thoughts
stirred his imagination. He was not superstitious, but
questions concerning the sanitary conditions of his surroundings forced themselves upon his attention. At
length, the agitation becoming unbearable, he arose, and
gently awaking the sleepers, made certain enquiries about
the sheets upon his bed. 'Twas true they had not been
washed since the corpse had lain upon them, but then his
hostess had slept in the bed since the death had occurred.
This information did not quiet the preacher. Happily the
light of morning soon came and relieved the situation.
Yet Mr. Nicholson fully sympathised with the bereaved
family, and afterwards wrote a memoir of the departed
one, a brief epitome of which we here subjoin, as it
furnishes another trophy of mission work :

" John Meaklim was born at Drumnail, County Monaghan. His
father, R. Meaklim, was awakened under the preaching of Gideon
Ouseley, and joined the Methodist Society, in 1803. He fell asleep
in Jesus in 1837, aged eighty-four. John, the subject of this

memoir, became a true Christian in spirit and conduct, but was a
man markedly modest and reserved. It was his delight to entertain the ministers in their rounds. During his last affliction he
suffered much, but bore it with Christain submission. He was
anxious about his little children, but was enabled at length to
trust them to the care of the 'Father of the fatherless.' On the
night before he died, a friend, who was praying with him, was so
overcome with a sense of the Divine presence, that he was almost
obliged to cease. At that moment the dying saint's speech returned, and he broke out in prayer in an extraordinary manner,
his ideas and language were quite different from what they had
ever been previously. He continued to wrestle in mighty prayer
for a quarter of an hour. Those present exclaimed, 'Surely God is
in this place!' He died on May 14th, 1846, aged forty-one, leaving
a wife and five little children to mourn their loss."

Often Mr. Nicholson overtaxed his strength, and suffered
in consequence.

In his diary (June 1846) he says, "I preached at Mrs.
Carlisle's, but the effort greatly increased my illness. I
started upon my second visit to Smithboro', thinking my
headache would get better on the way; but at Whitley's
Hill I broke down altogether and could proceed no further.
My sickness increased, and I lay in pain all night. In the
morning my exhaustion was extreme; but I began to call
upon the Lord, in faith, to restore me, and very soon I
began to recover. And the Lord filled my soul so richly
with his love, that I could not refrain from praising Him
aloud. I cried out, Christ has come! I find Him unspeakably precious to my soul! I cannot but speak of His
mighty love. I cannot fully describe the peace and joy
which then filled my soul. I thank God for the affliction,
for it has humbled me, and the glimpse into eternity,
which I had, has solemnized my mind. And I trust my
relatives were blessed likewise, through seeing the hand
of God upon me, and His grace in me." Our brother was

not fully convalescent till he was found at work again, preaching at Priesthill, Hillsboro', Kilwarlin, Clougher, Lisburn, Magheragall, Ballinderry, &c. After his return from a second visit to Smithboro' he says (July 30th), "preached at Mr. Fullerton's* (son-in-law of Rev. J. Lyons), near Lisburn, and felt the Divine presence while speaking from, ' Quench not the Spirit.' "

From Mr. Nicholson to the Mission Secretary : —

Broomhedge, Sept. 3, 1846.

My dear Brother,—I trust the good work of God is advancing both on this station and in my own heart. I was never more at home in the work of the Lord.

July 31.—Called in Belfast on business. Saw the good hand of God upon me in temporal matters. Preached at seven o'clock at Mrs. Topping's, Kilwarlin, from Hebrews iv., 9. Had liberty in pointing out the character of God's people, and the nature of the rest for them.

August 1st.—Engaged this day in study for the Sabbath. Direct me, O Lord, in the choice of appropriate subjects, such as Thou wilt bless in the conviction and conversion of sinners. 2nd.—Met my class at Broomhedge. Preached in the morning in Lisburn from Matt. vi., 10, and at night from 1 Thess. v., 19. Met the preacher's class, attended the Sabbath School, and conducted a prayer-meeting in Mr. McC—.'s at four o'clock. A good day. 3rd. —Visited about eight families. Directed two sick persons to the Lamb of God, and strongly urged them to prepare to meet Him. 4th.—Preached at Brother Dalton's, and visited eighteen families. Prayed with Brother Martin, and read several chapters to him from the Word of God, and some short memoirs from the *Magazine*. He has been an upright Christian, and a steady leader with us for many years. He is now dying of consumption, but his peace abounds. 5th.—Walked to Lisburn. Visited by the way, and called on most of the members in the town. Preached at eight o'clock from Matt. xxiv., 44. 1

---

* Grandfather of Mr. Fullerton, one of Mr. Spurgeon's Evangelists, whose name often occurs in the *Christian Herald* (1888). The seed sown forty years ago is seen to-day.

had unusual liberty in delivering the counsel of God. O may it bring forth fruit after many days. 6th.—Visited the neighbourhood of Moyrusk, and preached in Mr. Dickey's from Rev. 11, 14. I had unusual liberty, O may the message be blessed. 7th.—I am to preach to-night at the Mill-hill. This is a new place where there has been a small class formed lately.

Sabbath, 9th.—Met the class in Miss Wright's; had a truly blessed time. Some wept for joy. Preached in Broomhedge at the usual hour from John iv., 35, 36. The unction of the Spirit rested upon my own mind while I proclaimed, 'Lift up your eyes, for the fields are white unto harvest.' Oh! may the Church and all Christian ministers now put in the sickle and gather many souls to Christ.

16th.—Sabbath.—This was a most happy day to both preacher and people. I preached in Broomhedge, at eleven, from Gal. vi., 14. I was graciously assisted with light and power from on High. The Sacrament after sermon. Christ made Himself known in the breaking of bread. We sat in heavenly places. 21st.—Returned to Broomhedge after spending eight days at the sea-side. I experienced a feeling of discontent, and longed to be again engaged in declaring the glad tidings of great joy. How delightful it is to be constantly employed in the great work of the Redeemer. May I spend all my remaining life and strength in winning souls to Christ. 23rd.—Sabbath.—Preached in the forenoon in Lisburn, from Matt. xvi., 20. Met the minister's class; it was a truly blessed time. One of the members of this class met in my grandfather Nicholson's class, forty years ago. O, how she wept and praised God, when recounting all the mercies of the Lord from that period till the present time. I preached in Zion at night, and baptized a child. Prayed with Brother Martin, who nears the gates of death. He is weak in body, but able to rely upon the merits of Christ for salvation. 25th.—Yesterday and this day visited about twenty-six families. This is a blessed employment and profitable to preacher and people. Visited J. Martin; he is very low; but continues happy in God. I preached near Lisburn last night, to a congregation of attentive hearers. This night I preached at the Milestone to the largest congregation I have ever had in this place. A blessed feeling pervaded the whole service.

26th.—Attended the [Connexional] Jubilee meeting at Belfast; it was a profitable time to me. I was pleased to hear of the great liberality of the English friends. *I am grieved that I cannot give what I could wish to this fund.* 27th.—Preached at Mr. Catney's, Clougher, upon, "What must I do to be saved?" The people, I believe, heard with a desire to obtain salvation. 28th.—I thought J. Martin so ill and weak this night, that he would not be able to bear preaching in his house; but he would not give it up, and asked me not to speak as loudly as usual. On Wednesday I found him in a doubting state. He told me he had lost his hope, and that he felt himself too unworthy to be saved. I read to him, and quoted many precious promises. I also prayed with him, but all in vain. The enemy was now making his last attack before leaving the tried one for ever. Our brother continued in a desponding state for nearly two days. This evening I found that his peace had returned. He joyfully exclaimed, 'Christ has done so much for me through life, and having kept me thus far,.he will not surely leave me now in sorrow to sink.' He then spoke of having a funeral sermon preached, and hymns sung on the way to the graveyard. I remarked that when that would be going on on earth, his redeemed spirit would be among the blood washed throng before the throne "Oh! yes," said he, "that will be the case." 30th.—Sabbath.—Met my class. Preached at Priesthill, morning and evening, from Acts xvi., 33. and Hebrews xii., 1, 2. The Spirit's influence accompanied the word. I bless the Lord for such happy seasons coming from His presence. 31st.—Preached J. Martin's funeral sermon from Rev. xxiv., 13. The house was full of people, and many stood outside for want of room. Hymns were sung on the way to the graveyard. Mr. Argue spoke at the grave. Brother Martin "died in the Lord."

The foregoing represents the character and amount of work accomplished by Mr. Nicholson monthly till the end of the Connexional year. We add but one or two additional extracts from his journal. Cholera was alarmingly prevalent in 1846-7. Mr. Nicholson says, "While preaching at B. Jefferson's, near Lisburn, upon '*the judg-*

ments of the Lord on account of sin," the servant girl was
seized with cholera. It was alarming, but the Lord gave
me peace. May the people learn to fear God, and forsake
sin." In the Magazine for 1847, from the pen of Mr.
Baggaly, appeared a memoir of the Rev. W. Mc. Clune.

"Mr. Mc Clune was born at Whitehouse, in 1817, and
was born of the Spirit when a young man. He became a
minister of the Methodist New Connexion, and was received
into full connexion, in 1843. He died of consumption, in
great peace, on Nov. 11th, 1846. 'His career was short:
but if life is to be measured by the amount of labour performed, and the good that is done, he lived long.' His
zeal was quenchless; his fault was that he attempted too
much.' 'Honest and candid, he was without guile'."

Mr. Nicholson says, "I visited Rev. W. Mc. Clune,
whose health failed in Dublin, and he came to rest a few
days at Mrs. Crook's. Oh! how emaciated the dear man
is! "I (S.N.) preached this day (15th Sept.) friend
Dalton's funeral sermon: endeavoured to describe the
happy death of the righteous. The house was not sufficient
to accommodate all the people who wished to be present.
Sep. 26th.—The Lord sent me a five-pound note, through
my brother-in-law, just at the moment of urgent need.
Hitherto the Lord's promises have not failed—'shall supply
all your need.' My dear wife has gone with her brother
to spend a short time at her father's. May her health be
restored, and she long spared to me."

By the Conference of 1847 (Rev. P. T. Gilton, President),
Mr. Nicholson was removed to the Newtownards station,
where he laboured two years.

The Rev. Jno. Mc Clure visited Newtownards in 1799,
engaged a preaching-room in Movilla St., where he soon
formed a class. In 1801 James Davidson was walking the

streets in great soul-trouble, when he saw the members of the class wending their way to their meeting-place. He followed them, "forced his way in," and that evening found salvation. He afterwards became and remained till death one of the principal office bearers and main supporters of the cause. A lady from Bangor, being on a visit in Newtownards, attended the preaching in Movilla St where she was convinced of sin, and "soundly converted to God." She joined the Methodist New Connexion, was a great friend to its ministers, and at her death, bequeathed a legacy to the Bangor and Newtownards Stations. In 1820. a small chapel was erected in Mary Street, Newtownards, on ground left to the Society by Mrs. Chambers. In 1838, the small chapel, grown uncomfortable, was sold, and through the prodigious exertions of the Rev. Thomas Seymour, sufficient funds were raised, and a new commodious sightly chapel was erected. Dr. Cooke preached "powerful opening sermons."

The years 1846 till 1849 in Ireland were years of famine and disease following upon the "potato blight," when thousands of sufferers perished.

Newtownards suffered from the "famine" more than any other town in the North. In private memoranda left by him, Mr. Nicholson says. "At the Conference of 1847, there was a preacher for whom it was difficult to find an appointment. As he would not have been agreeably received at Newtownards, I was removed to that town, and he was appointed to Broomhedge, where the friends seldom complained of their ministerial appointment. 1847 was one of the years of the great famine. During the entire year I toiled amongst the starving poor, the dying, and even the dead required my attention. I have always been of a nervous temperament, and afraid of infectious

diseases; but, at this time, the Lord strengthened me and
qualified me for the work of mercy and charity. I visited
scores of fever cases throughout the town. I also visited
the Poor's House, and the Fever Hospital, when it and
the temporary sheds contained from six to eight hundred
patients. I visited a family, members of our Society,
regularly, who had fever in their house for twenty weeks.
At this time I suffered from a slight attack of fever, which
rendered me unable to preach for several weeks.
Through it all, however, I was able to visit a little every
day." Mrs. Nicholson adds, " The other ministers of the
town avoided the infected houses and localities as much as
possible; but my husband visited indiscriminately. He
carried with him certificates for the admission of fever
cases into the hospital. He had double work, in finding
out the sufferers, and then getting the doctor to certify.
Oh! the scenes of filth and wretchedness, hunger,
nakedness and disease which my dear husband witnessed
and tried to relieve. Hundreds had no bed-clothes whatever, and but an excuse for a bed or none at all; and they
covered themselves at night with the scant garments
which they wore during the day. I can never forget
many individual cases which came under our special notice.
A poor man came for a 'line' to get his wife into the
hospital. The poor woman was ' down in fever,' and had
a baby just six weeks old. The man said he ' dooted they
wad both d'e, but he added ' a dinna care for 'am caught
mysel'.' They were all admitted to the hospital : the
poor fellow himself was the only one that succumbed. We
had meal to give out to the starving ones ; and of a morning above a hundred poor creatures would be gathered
about our door. One day a poor woman fainted in the
crush. The patients in the hospital were dying daily

An old woman, who had a horse and rough cart, was employed to cart the pauper dead in their miserable coffins to the graveyard. One day she was proceeding with her load of death, the coffins piled one upon another and secured with a rope. Suddenly the rope broke, and her ghastly load fell in a confused heap upon the street. There was established a public soup-kitchen; and several wretched creatures hung about the place, waiting for soup, till they sickened and died on the street. Thank God! many of the people, seeing the judgment of God, fled to Christ for refuge and were saved."

We have just perused the copy of a long letter written in earnest, vigorous terms, which Mr. Nicholson prepared in June, 1847, and addressed to the "Magistrates, and Guardians of the Union of Newtownards." It appeared in the public papers. The letter called attention to the abounding filth of the streets and houses, the unseemliness of the woman undertaker and her cart, the unsanitary condition of the graveyard, &c. The appearance of this letter raised a commotion amongst the "authorities," and aroused the ire of certain official individuals, whose neglect it unintentionally exposed; and counter letters appeared in the public prints. But very soon the graveyard was attended to, a hearse and male driver took the place of the old woman and her cart, scavengers appeared in the streets, and sanitary inspectors paid domiciliary visits. Well done, Brother Nicholson, you were always the friend of the poor, and yours was true Christly benevolence. The friends of the Connexion in England formed a Committee to raise funds for the famine-stricken in Ireland; and to the extent of their means and even beyond, they forwarded monetary and material help through the ministers in Ireland.

A large printed "plan" of the Newtownards Circuit,

covering six months of the year 1847-48, lies before us. It gives the names of seventeen places where preaching services or prayer meetings were held regularly, including Portaferry, Greyabbey, and Kirkcubbin.   Upon the plan also appear the names of J. Mc. Cormick, W. Dobbin, J. Mooney. F. Fowles, D. McMillan, A. Bittle, N. Davidson, J. McKee, and G. Walker.   A few extracts from Mr. Nicholson's diary will give some idea of his evangelistic labours at this time :—

1847.—July 11th.—While I was preaching in the open air, from, "We must all appear before the judgment-seat of Christ," a woman near me dropped down and expired. Oh! how awfully uncertain is this mortal life. 16th.—Addressed about seventy in the open air, in East Street. Street preaching brings the tidings of salvation to many perishing souls who are never inside a place of worship. At night much fatigued, but it is sweet to spend my whole strength for God and souls. 18th.—Sabbath.—Thirteen present at the morning class. Glory be to God, for class-meeting! In addition to the ordinary services, I preached in the open-air in Greyabbey at three o'clock, a large number heard with greatest attention. 24th.—Since the last entry in my journal, visited thirty-seven families, conducted a prayer-meeting, held a leaders' meeting, and attended three preaching appointments To-morrow we are to hold a camp-meeting. Called to see Brother McMillan, who is ill of fever. Found him happy in God. The lives of our members hitherto have been preserved by our dear Lord from the raging fever. 25.—Sabbath.—A grand time at the camp-meeting. In the evening Mr. T. Seymour preached in Zion upon the *General Judgment*. The people were greatly moved and some cried aloud for mercy. Two found peace. 30th.—Held a meeting in Brother W. Dobbin's wareroom.   August 1st.—Sabbath.—Preached to about 140 children from Prov. iv., 1. 5th.—Another daughter born to us this day. Thank God for preserving the life of mother and child. This day was observed by our Society as a day of humiliation, prayer, and thanksgiving. In the time of famine we have been satisfied; in the time of judgment we have only beheld the reward of the wicked; in the time of death the Lord hath held our souls in life. Praise his name. 10th.—Short of cash, but the

Lord will provide. Miss A. Bradbury has been with us upon a visit for some time, and her presence has cheered us. She has rendered us most willing help in our work. After the sermon at Greyabbey (in Presbyterian Church lent for the occasion) took up a handsome collection. There had been no open-air preaching in this place for twenty years. 11th.—Preached on the street at Greyabbey. Mr. Creevy came and stood beside me, and after the service kindly invited me to his house. Mrs. Nicholson adds that "Mr. Creevy was from Moira, and when Mr. Nicholson met with him in Greyabbey he was the teacher of the Church Day School. Mr. Creevy afterwards emigrated to America, where he was received into the ministry of the Methodist E. Church, in which he attained a good position. Mr. Creevy wrote Mr. Nicholson urging him also to emigrate to a "sphere of vaster usefulness," and proffering to introduce the friend of his father to an an appointment at once. Mr. Nicholson wrote thanking Mr. Creevy, but said that he had made his choice for life; and as God was with him he was satisfied. Mr. Nicholson's brothers, prosperous men in New York, united with Mr. Creevy in trying to persuade my husband to go out to America, where they said his children would be much better provided for than in Ireland; but he would not be persuaded as the conviction was strong upon him that God would have him labour on where his work was being so richly blessed." 23rd.—Preached in Mill Street in the open air. Some came to mock, but before the service ended they appeared as solemn as the grave. 27th.—Preached near Kircubbin to a crowded house, and most of the people were anxious for pardon or holiness. Two found peace, one of them was a man above sixty years of age. Tears rolled down his wrinkled face while he spoke of the Saviour's love. 29th.—Sabbath.—Preached on the street in Portaferry to a very attentive congregation. When I had done, a man who attended the meeting last night came to me and stated that a woman, who was in great distress about her soul in that meeting, found pardon after she went home. The Wesleyans lent me their chapel in the afternoon. 7th Sept.—Rev. W. Baggaly preached our anniversary sermons, and baptized our baby, calling her Caroline Matilda after Mrs. Baggaly. I preached in the open air. Two souls found peace at the prayer meeting at

M

night. On Monday evening, at the prayer-meeting in the chapel, another soul found peace. Praise God! 26th.—Preached in Grey, abbey and in Kircubbin on the street. In the latter place a man attempted to pull me down off the chair, but the Sergeant of the police prevented him. October 6th.—Visited Lisburn and preached in friend Anderson's on *Regeneration*.* 13th.—Heard of the death of T— in fever. He heard me preach on the street, asked me to hold a meeting in his house, and attended Zion a few times. How sudden! 16th.—Asked the Lord to go with and preserve me, and then visited the fever hospital. What a sight met my view. Many delirious. One patient, a young man, imagined he was at his usual occupation driving the post car, and was loudly urging his horses to go forward.

Dec. 11th.—I am just recovering from an illness of many weeks. I praise my God for His gracious dealings with me and for His preserving mercy. Of many defects in myself I was made painfully conscious. But in the Atoning Blood I found a peaceful refuge. The God of love manifested Himself to my soul so fully and intimately, that all doubts and fears and misgivings fled away from my mind like mists before the rising sun. Oh, those wonderful manifestations of God to my soul! I shall never forget their glory and blessedness. Yet I feel that I am nothing, Christ is all and in all.

1848, Feb. 21.—Friend Scott informs me that on Sabbath at the Lord's Table he received the sense of pardon. 24th.—Many are dying in cholera. Monday was kept as a day of humiliation and prayer. I preached in Zion on the words, " For death is come up into our windows, and is entered into our palaces to cut off the children from without, and the young men from the streets.'' Mrs. Dixon was to have brought her baby to be baptized, and her

---

*The manuscript of this sermon is before the writer. The penmanship is neat and plain, contrasting greatly with the caligraphy of Mr. Nicholson's later years. Tho sermon is a very full, correct, scriptural, practical discussion of the vital doctrine of which it treats. And if in stylo it is somewhat verbose, it abounds with eloquent sentences, apt figures, and appropriate illustrations and anecdotes. Above all, the sermon supplies internal evidence of being the product of a regenerated mind.

husband (a drunken man) was to have accompanied her ; but on he day for the baptism he was seized with cholera, and in a few thours lay a blackened corpse. He died in Greenwell street, called locally the " Devil's elbow," because of its wickedness. March 18th.—Preached in Comber and baptized a child of friend Conkey's, a man filled with the Spirit. A class meets in his house. March 30th.—Five cases of cholera in the hospital to-day. Lord save the people!

April 5th.—Professor Wilson, of the Royal College, Belfast preached for us in Zion, on Sabbath morning, and the Rev. W. Patterson, of Bangor, in the evening. Collections good considering the times.

The presence of the Rev. Samuel Hulme at the Conference of 1848, as President, rendered it memorable. He was then in his prime, and was a preacher of lofty, chaste, accumulative and persuasive eloquence. The Northern Irish have always shown a high appreciation of great sermons. The report of Mr. Hulme's sermons, on this occasion, ran thus, " At eleven o'clock in the forenoon (April 9th.), the Rev. S. Hulme, from Halifax, delivered a powerful and effective discourse, on 'perfecting holiness in the fear of the Lord.' And at seven in the evening, he preached again, from the words, 'Glorious things are spoken of thee, O city of God.' For clearness of conception, originality of thought, cogency of reasoning, beauty of illustration and force of appeal, this discourse could scarcely be surpassed. It was a masterpeice of thought and eloquence."

By the English Conference of 1848 the Rev. James Stacey was appointed Superintendent of the Irish Mission. For nearly half a century now, Dr. Stacey has occupied a first place amongst the most cultured ministers of Methodism His clear, incisive, philosophic, antithetic, textual sermons have always supplied a rare intellectual

as well as spiritual inspiration. The Rev. T. Seymour,
at a meeting of the Irish ministers, on behalf of himself
and his brethren, presented the Rev. W. Baggaly with
an address and a copy of "Calmet's Dictionary of the
Bible," on the eve of his return to England, as expressions of their esteem and affection. For Mr. Nicholson
Mr. Baggaly conceived a special regard, which was
mutual. To Caroline Matilda Nicholson, his wife's name-
sake, Mr. Baggaly sent the present of a sovereign
annually, during the child's brief life of twelve years.
Out of affection for the memory of Mr. Baggaly, Mrs·
Nicholson wishes the following letter to appear in this
memorial:

"Birmingham, July 11th, 1848.

Dear Brother,

I shall always look back with pleasure on the acquain-
tance formed with you during my residence in Ireland. And
though partially interrupted by my removal to this country, I trust
you will not suffer it to be entirely broken off. You are fond of
your pen, so that I promise myself the pleasure of a letter from
you at least occasionally. And when time will allow, such
favours shall be acknowledged. It rejoices me to know, that you
do labour zealously and faithfully in your Master's service. It is
a privilege to be employed in such a work as this. You labour
under difficulties and many discouragements. But though it may
be yours to sow in tears, I trust you will reap with joy. God has
honoured your pious toils, and I trust He will honour them still
more abundantly. My old friends in this town seem very happy
and very hopeful. My aged mother and sister are not a little
rejoiced to have us in the same town with them. But, like you,
my great anxiety is to be useful; the strength I have shall be
spent in the service of my Lord . . . You would have been
delighted had you been with us here on the 2nd inst. Oxford street
Chapel was a busy scene indeed. Forms were brought into the
aisles. Many went away not being able to get in. I hope the
school. and indeed the whole circuit under your care, will do well.

My wife desires her Christian love to you, Mrs. N., and family, to whom I also send a similar message.

And believe me,

Dear Mr. Nicholson,

Yours affectionately,

WM. BAGGALY."

The Conference (1848) adjourned on April 12th, and within a week thereafter, Mr. Nicholson had preached six times. To the superintendent he writes :—

"Newtonards, August 4th, 1848.

" My dear Brother,—

"It will afford you pleasure to learn that God is still with us ; and that, since Conference, our congregations have been very good. And we are labouring, and praying, and believing for a revival of God's work on this station. April 18th.—I had to attend six preaching appointments this week; met a class ; assisted at a revival prayer-meeting ; and took part in the Primitive Methodist missionary meeting. May 2nd.—Preached in Bowtown. I enjoyed an unusual baptism of the Spirit. From fifty to seventy attend preaching in this place. 3rd.—Preached in John Street, in the open air. A young man, a Roman Catholic, was deeply affected, and has since attended the preaching. 17th.—At the class on the Sabbath, God watered our hearts, and lifted our minds to things above. At 11 o'clock I preached from 1 John i. 7. Blessed, glorious subject! The congregation was large, and the power of God came down upon the audience. At 4 o'clock I addressed about two hundred in the open air. When we commenced to sing, the poor people came running from adjoining streets to hear the Word of Life. Many of them have not clothing to attend God's house, and they hail with grateful hearts a sermon in the open air. At night I preached from Hebrews xi. 6. 27th.— Preached seven times this week, once in the open air. Sabbath, June 4th.—Preached at Low Ards, from Rev. xiv. 6. Sabbath, 11th —This was a day of the Son of Man upon this station. In the morning, preached in the chapel from Mark xiii., 33; and at the camp meeting, Bowtown, from 2 Cor. x., 5, 6, to about two hundred persons. Brothers Dobbin and McCormick assisted, and other brethren engaged in prayer. At night, after the evening sermon, conducted a prayer-meeting in the chapel. About thirty poor sinners came forward, deeply in earnest for the pardon of their sins. Sabbath, 25th.—Preached at Priesthill, and held the love-feast after sermon. Met with some of my old friends with whom I spent some of my happiest days, when I was first called out to preach the Gospel. I find that some of them who used to receive me gladly into their houses, are now no more. They died happy, and I shall soon find them again in heaven, when all our toils are over. I preached at night in Lisburn. Much good was done at the prayer meeting after preaching. Sabbath, July 2nd.— Preached twice, met my class, and addressed about one hundred and fifty children in the school. 6th.—Visited from house to house, and preached at night in Mill-street to a congregation of poor, but attentive worshippers. I tried to show them the torments of hell, and the joys of heaven, to alarm or allure them to seek salvation before it be too late. Sabbath, 9th.—Blessed love-feast. 16th.—Large and respectable congregations in the chapel. O, how easy to preach, when the Lord gives the word. 17th.—I heard the Rev. James Stacey preach in Ballymacaret. It was a good sermon, and the Lord made it a blessing to my soul. I trust the Lord will support our dear brother, and crown his labours with success. And now I have laid before you part of my labours since Conference. This has been one of the happiest quarters to me since I came to this station. I visit a great deal among the people. God makes this a great blessing to my own soul. The brethren have entered into a covenant to pray for a mighty revival.

In another letter to the Superintendent, written early in 1849, Mr. Nicholson says, " This is a fine field for Missionary labour; there are open doors for the Gospel at every turn. We have six prayer meetings held every Sabbath, in different parts of the town and country, and several new preaching places that I have not been able to take upon the plan. The school is doing well. This, I have found from experience, should be closely connected with the church. A few Sabbaths ago, I preached to the teachers and scholars, from ' Feed my lambs.' God made the service a blessing to them. I believe, with the Rev. J. A. James, ' Where so many precious souls are gathered, capable of eternal blessedness, the minister cannot speak to them too frequently . . . No part of ministerial labour yields a quicker and larger return.'" In another communication Mr. Nicholson adds, 'On April 1st, I preached a Missionary sermon in Greyabbey. The Rev. D. Jeffery (Presbyterian) kindly gave me the use of his church, attended and concluded the service, and contributed to the collection. Two years ago I was warned not to preach in the open air in this town, lest I should be stoned. I, however, tried it in the name of the Lord, and good was done, and at present there exists a very blessed feeling towards Methodism and our cause in particular. While I am writing, J. Andrews, Esq., J.P., Comber, has forwarded me a donation of ten shillings to assist the cause."

The above extracts refer mainly to the routine of circuit work, but hardly touch the continuous, benevolent and merciful domiciliary, and philanthrophic labours prosecuted by this true friend of his kind. The dire famine was slow to abate, and cholera for some time continued its appalling ravages. We cull the following from Mr. Nicholson's private memoranda:—" During my second year at Newtownards, cholera prevailed to an alarming extent. It was reckoned at one period, that about two hundred persons were swept off in this dread plague inside three weeks. No town in the North suffered so much from it as Newtownards. Poor half-starved creatures were daily cut off by it. I and another minister (Rev. J. M'Cullough) went from house to house, taking medicine with us, and not one to whom we gave the medicine died. We took every known precaution to avoid the infection, and the Lord preserved us. Trusting in Him, I lost all dread of the plague."

Mr. Nicholson early acquired a high estimate of the value of open-air preaching, and pursued the practice till old age. Those who remember his earlier years say, that as a preacher, he was highly effective when he stood in Nature's Temple canopied with her azure dome. The

following quotations are from an article by Mr. Nicholson,
which appeared in the Magazine for 1849. They alike
exhibit his views upon the subject treated and reveal the
earnest spirit and evangelistic zeal of the writer. The
article is entitled,

" *The Duty and the Fruits of open-air Preaching, Illustrated
by Facts.*"

"The Lord Jesus, when upon earth, set us the example
of out-door preaching, and the first ministers had their
commission from Him to go and preach the gospel throughout the world to every creature. Those men of God
erected the standard of the cross in the ship, on the shore,
by the highways and hedges ; everywhere, they stood and
proclaimed Jesus Christ and Him crucified. Wesley,
Whitfield, and others, of the first race of Methodist
preachers, revived this apostolic plan, and opened their
commission under the broad canopy of heaven to listening
thousands, many of whom were by the power of truth
thus illuminated and turned to God. The good effected
in this way cannot be estimated until that day when the
Lord will come to make up His jewels.

[Here Mr. Nicholson introduces the cases of his grandfather and Magorian as fruits of the practice advocated.]

In the summer of 1838, the Methodist New Connexion
held a camp meeting near to Lurgan, and four of our
ministers officiated on the occasion. A few years after
one of those preachers visited that town and preached in
Providence chapel. After sermon, a man came to the
minister and asked him if he remembered preaching at
the camp meeting above referred to. The man was
answered in the affirmative. 'Well,' said he, 'at that
time I was a stranger to the love of God and to the power
of true religion ; but under the sermon you preached on

that occasion I was enlightened and brought to Christ, and now I am a leader in your Society.' When Mr, Lyons in his turn came to Newtownards, it was the summer season; and as his favourite employment was open-air preaching, he took his stand near the court-house, on the fair green, under the shade of some large trees, and there to a large assembly proclaimed the free salvation of the world by the death of the Redeemer. Under that sermon D. McMillen was convinced of sin, and in a short time was savingly converted to God. He has been a useful leader in our church for some years; and is at present one of the stewards of our Society. During the years of 1840 and 1843, the writer was stationed on the Portglenone station with Mr. Lyons. Often we travelled through rough and unfrequented parts of the counties of Antrim and Derry; and wherever we could collect a few together, either in the market places, fields, or highways, we proclaimed the glorious Gospel of the blessed God. In Portglenone, Innisrush, Maghera, Gullyduffy, Castle-dawson, Bellaghey, Randalstown, Gow, and other places we preached to thousands of attentive hearers in the open-air. Many poor, illiterate, superstitious people heard the Gospel in this way who never heard a plain gospel sermon before. They listened to the melting story of the agony and sufferings of the Son of God, and many were affected to tears while they listened. In the summer of 1847 we held a camp meeting in the town of Newtownards and four ministers addressed the meeting; and the cloud of the Divine presence rested upon us. Many of those naked, famine-stricken creatures who attended that service were, in a few weeks, hurried into eternity by want and disease. Our hope is that some sought and found mercy from God, and may be our crown of rejoicing in the day of the Lord

Jesus. And while we rejoice to see our chapels filled, yet we have seen and known of a greater amount of good being done by open-air preaching under one sermon, than has been effected by ten in-doors. Why not, then, revive this old apostolic, primitive plan that God owned and does own? Is our work done? Have we reaped enough of the golden harvest, so that we can allow Satan to gather the remainder? O shame upon us! I fear, that the fields, and towns, and villages may be swift witnesses against us at the *bar of God*. I feel that I am guilty as well as others, and that I ought to have preached more to the profligate, and destitute, and the outcast, who never enter the house of God. May we have more of the spirit of our Master, who went about doing good! May we have more love for souls! Many, about our doors, are dropping into the grave, perhaps into hell, and numbers of others are not prepared to meet God. Will they blame us from amid the flames in the burning world forever, that we made no special effort for their salvation? The fields are white to the harvest; let us have the bowels of Jesus Christ, and go forth to work, using the Spirit's two-edged sword, and the shield of faith, being instant in season and out of season. ' He that goeth forth and weepeth, bearing precious seed, shall doubtless come again with rejoicing, bearing his sheaves with him.' "

CHAPTER VIII.

POWER WITH GOD.

"I have known a good man to pray as if he would do violence
to Heaven, and then seen the blessing come as plainly in answer
to his prayer as if it were revealed, so that no person would doubt
it, any more than if God had spoken from heaven."—*Finney.*

A PROMINENT and respected name amongst the
ministers of the Methodist New Connexion in
England was that of the Rev. P. J. Wright. He
visited the Irish Conference of 1849 as Representative; and
the Irish brethren elected him as their President. His sermons and addresses were highly appreciated and much
blessed. Mr. Nicholson's first impressions of Mr. Wright
are thus expressed, " He is a little man, but seems clever."
The " address to the English Conference said, ' Our people
still continue to suffer from the calamity that visited our land
three years ago. During no year of the past three have their
sufferings been greater than during the one just terminated.
Some of our most worthy members have been called away
by death." Mr. Nicholson was removed to Broomhedge,
where he laboured the lengthened period of five successive
years; and they proved years of unusual blessing, as we
shall see presently. " Miss Jane Crawford accompanied

Mr. Nicholson and his family to Broomhedge " : her kindness then and afterwards is had in grateful remembrance
by Mrs. Nicholson. Upon Mr. Nicholson's arrival at
Broomhedge the first entry made in his diary says, " One
of the brethren who welcomed us here three years ago
died of cholera the other day." The following extracts
from Mr. Nicholson's journal are a fair sample of his
labours throughout the year :—

June 1st.—Preached in J. Topping's, Kilwarlin. Mrs. Topping
died in the Lord about two years ago. I could hardly reach home
to-night from fatigue. But, O, how sweet, to be tired for Jesus.
July 2nd.—Spoke at J. Donaldson's.* He was enlightened a few
years ago through our ministry, and is now a leader, having a
class in his house. The Maze Course passes near this friend's door.
July 22nd. (Sabbath).—Held a camp meeting at Mrs. Carlisle's,
Maze. Revs. T. Seymour, A. Mackey, and S. Nicholson conducted
the service. It was the Sabbath before the Maze races. At 6 p.m.
in Zion, we had a truly blessed and melting season. Aug. 24th.—I
took my stand at Mazetown, in the open air, and spoke with unusual liberty for about an hour. I had many to hear, who never
enter our chapels. Sept. 1st.—We had a tea-party at Broomhedge,
to clear off the chapel debt. A. Crawford, Esq. raised seven pounds
towards the object, and since Conference, has expended five pounds
additional upon the interior of the chapel. Oct. 7th (Sabbath)
—Held our love-feast and the members from Priesthill joined us.
Some came forward to the penitent form in earnest about salvation·
Oct. 27th.—Sunday School tea party—one hundred present. After
the children's examination, rewards were distributed.—Messrs.
Carlisle, Jones, Walsh, Brady, Gorman and Shields delivered
addresses. Oct. 28th (Sabbath)—I spoke in Lisburn from ' Why
should the work cease." Mr. Seymour and his partner are labouring (in Lisburn) for the salvation of souls, and God is crowning
their labours with success. At Priesthill in the evening we had
the drops of a shower. 30th.—Mr. P. Thornton and I were out

---

* Six children of J. Donaldson's are at present (1889) members of the Methodist
New Connexion. One son is a leader, and two daughters are married to leaders.

collecting. We have expended about £9 on Priesthill chapel. A few days ago Mr. T. M'Connell, sen., accompanied me on a collecting tour on behalf of Broomhedge chapel-debt. On our way we called at Portadown. The Rev. J. Ballard (Wesleyan) showed us great kindness. J. Shillington and J. A. Shillington, Esqrs., most cheerfully gave us subscriptions. The proprietor of the hotel would not accept payment for our night's lodging, &c. Nov. 16th.—Sunday School tea-party at Priesthill. About one hundred and fifty sat down to tea. This school is as old as our mission in this land. Five ministers have been raised up from its classes. The scholars number about 130. Oct. 20th.—Preached at night in a new place, Brother P. Gorman's. He is one of our leaders, a promising young man. Nov. 28th.—Attended Newtonards Sunday School tea-party, and was glad to find the School and Bible classes in a flourishing condition."

The name of Jones,* for many decades of years, held an honoured place in the society at Priesthill, and branches of the family are still found, in different places, amongst the attached friends of the Mission. One of this worthy name was John Jones, whose memoir was written by Mr. Nicholson, who was much beloved by the family. A few extracts from the memoir will here be acceptable to many friends.

"Our aged brother, John Jones, died in the Lord, on Feb. 11th, 1849. He was an exemplary member of our community for about twenty years. It was through the example and persuasion of his devoted partner that he was led to unite with our society. She died happy in the Lord about two years ago. Ruth Jones was a woman of great industry, strong Christian principle, great simplicity, and most ardently attached to our ministers. I have often been delighted to hear her speak of their zeal, usefulness and humility. When I heard of Brother Jones's illness I visited him, and found him depending on Jesus for mercy and eternal life. He

---

* S. Jones was for many years a leader, and one of the Superintendents of Zion Sunday School. He was spared till old age. On the morning of the day he quitted earth for Heaven he was able to lead in prayer, and his daughter was greatly struck with the unusual earnestness of his petitions.

told me that he was ' on the Rock,' that Christ was ' precious,' and
that he had 'no fear of death.' He continued in a happy, peaceful
state of mind till Sabbath morning, when his redeemed spirit
quitted the earthly tabernacle to dwell for ever in that house not
made with hands, eternal in the heavens. May all his children
follow him as he followed Christ."

The Conference of 1850 had for President, the Rev. W.
Mills, and the Rev. J. Stacey discharged the duties of Secretary.   The Conference recorded its thanks to Almighty
God for the return of temporal prosperity throughout the
land.   It likewise devoutly expressed its gratitude to the
Divine Head of the Church for the large measure of spiritual prosperity and increase upon the Mission.   The English
Conference appointed the Rev. Thos. Mills as Superintendent.   It is noticeable, that Mr. Nicholson sought personal
spiritual profit at every meeting he attended in connection
with the Lord's work.   No Church meeting was to him a
mere business committee.   His journal abounds with records of thanks for baptisms of the Spirit received at
leaders' quarterly meetings, and Conference.   All were
means of grace to him.   His routine circuit work at
Broomhedge need not be further minutely traced.   Activity
was emphatically a law of our brother's nature : there was
no standing still either in his personal religion or his work
for Christ and souls.   Two obituary notices from his pen
appeared in the Magazine for 1850 and 1851.   We introduce the memoirs written by Mr. Nicholson as they serve
a variety of valuable ends.   Surviving friends are gratified
impressed and edified through reading the biographies of
their pious ancestors.   The triumphant deaths of Christians
illustrate the power of the Gospel's hopes to support at the
most trying moment of existence.   The memoirs, to which
we immediately refer, exhibit in a tested form the quality
of the fruit resulting from the labours of God's servants.

They likewise serve to reveal the spirit of the writer. Mr. Nicholson felt true commisseration for the suffering, and full of Christian charity, he sought out the afflicted, and delighted to minister comfort to the dying.

" On August 15th, 1850, our dear Brother, Joseph Thompson, died in the Lord, in the twenty-fifth year of his age. About six years ago, he united in a youth's class at Priesthill, composed of James Carlisle,* J. Dalton, P. Thornton,† J. Watson,‡ and a few others. He had met only a few times with the class till he was convinced of sin, and led to cry for mercy. The Lord set his soul at liberty while one of the members was engaged in fervent supplication for him. In a short time he began to teach in *Zion* Sunday school, and was made a class-leader. He was earnest and diligent in his work for God, and was a young man of considerable power in prayer. Alas! consumption soon marked him as its victim. One day, during his illness, his wife found him bathed in tears, and anxiously asked him what was the matter. His reply was, that in Christ he had the fulness of joy, had acceptance with God, and a clear evidence he was His child. To Miss Wright he said, ' I never knew the power of religion until I was afflicted; and at night, when all are asleep in the family, I have many happy hours of sweet communion with my God.' To his wife he said, 'Trust in God; He is a kind husband to the widow, a Father to the fatherless, and He will be a rich Provider. Do not forget also to serve Him, and train up our child for God.' The night before he died, I asked him if he enjoyed the comforts of religion. His reply was, ' I have been very unwell during the past two days ; but when I was at the worst, I was most happy in God.' On the next evening his liberated spirit was borne on angels' wings, to the regions of immortality." "S. N."

Who could not envy the young brother who was calling

---

* James Carlisle still lives, and for about half a century has laboured in various offices, in connection with Zion, Priesthill. He bears the highest character, as an humble, transparent, upright follower of the Lamb.

† P. Thornton, during a long life, was a devoted leader of the Priesthill Society. He died in the Lord a few years ago.

‡ Lived a useful life, and died in Christ, many years ago.

upon God on behalf of Joseph Thompson when the Lord spoke peace to his distressed conscience. At present (1889), the practice, in many quarters, is to induce anxious souls to assent to certain gospel propositions, and then to assure them that they have "a right to be satisfied." Whereas, like the penitent publican, we must go personally to God through Christ, and seek, by faith, mercy and salvation, and the conscience should not be satisfied until the Spirit immediately imparts the knowledge of salvation by the remission of sins. The biographer of M'Cheyne rightly says, "It will be observed that he (McC.) never reckoned his soul saved, notwithstanding all his convictions and views of sin, until he really went into the Holiest of all on the warrant of the Redeemer's work; for assuredly a sinner is still under wrath, until he has actually availed himself of the way to the Father opened up by Jesus. It is 'he that comes to Christ' that is saved."

"It is recorded in Holy Scripture that 'the memory of the just is blessed; but the name of the wicked shall rot. Mr. Rob. Anderson, the subject of this memoir, was born at Magheragall, near Broomhedge, in the year 1821. His mother was a cousin to the late Mr. Hugh Murray, of Moira, one of the expelled thirty-two leaders, &c., who founded the Methodist New Connexion in Ireland. Robert became a member of Miss Wright's class in 1840. He said, "It was in the time of a severe illness, that I first sought the Lord Jesus with all my heart. My life was despaired of, and I found I was not prepared to die. Oh, what awful distress and anguish of spirit I then endured! I sought the Lord with a sorrowful and broken spirit. When I reflect the cup of misery I then drank, it makes me tremble. I did not desire to converse much with any one; and my mind was full of doubts and alarming fears. The distress I endured banished sleep from me. At times I durst not open the Bible, lest my eyes should meet some awful threatening of God against me, and that would remind me of the flames of hell prepared to consume a guilty rebel. I continued in this wretched state of mind for a length of time; and I did not recover strength of body until I received power with God through faith in the Lord Jesus Christ. Some time after his conversion Brother Anderson lost the fervour of his first love, through mingling with light and trifling company. He said, 'I remained some time in a state of gloom, and distance from my Saviour, till I read Wesley's sermon on ' Forsaking the World,' which was made a blessing to me. The Rev. Wm. McClure, about this time preached a sermon on the same subject, which was also made a great blessing to me.' After this he had some sore conflicts with the enemy; but he made the Cross his refuge, and by prayer applied to the Redeemer, his pleading Advocate, and would not rest till ' his peace was restored.' To the writer he remarked, ' I have all along looked too much to my own heart, and too little to the fulness in the Redeemer. Since you last visited me I had a conversation with my brother-in-law, James Carlisle. He told me of the late James Dalton, of Moss, who did not experience the joys of salvation till he began to praise God for His mercy.' Brother Anderson's last sickness commenced about April, 1850, and it was very severe, but he praised God for it, as it drove him nearer to his Saviour. He was of a retiring disposition; but rendered such service to the Church as he was able. Brother Edward McClune,* his leader attended him during his last illness, and his visits were much blessed to the dying one and the afflicted family. Before his departure brother Anderson triumphed over the enemy, bade us all farewell, and then quietly passed away. His last words were— ' Come Lord Jesus, come quickly.' 'S. N.''

In his journal (1850) Mr. Nicholson gives an account of visits which he paid to Mr. D. of the Nursery, Hillsboro', who was suffering from cancer. He had enjoyed religion, but Mr. Nicholson found him a backslider. Very soon, however, the " prodigal child came home;" and Mr.

---

* Edward McClune was somewhat peculiar, but a man of earnest piety, punctual habits and sterling worth. He lived a bachelor life, devoting his best thoughts and energies to the cause of God till old age. His memory is still fragrant at Broomhedge. He died in great peace. The Rev. T. Seymour preached at his *wake*, and Mr. J. Carlisle, inspired by the sermon, addressed the people, when the power of God descended, and three persons, members of the same family, were converted.

Nicholson had the joy again and again, of hearing from his lips ejaculations of praise and thanksgiving for restoring grace. "My love increases every day," "I can now thank God for sending this affliction upon me," were some of the sufferers exclamations. Shortly before his death, he had a severe and protracted encounter with the enemy: but during a visit from God's servant the tempted one gained the victory. To Mr. Nicholson the grateful sufferer said, "While you were praying, I got a fresh hold of the Saviour." He died in great peace soon after. The foregoing illustrates one valuable class of Mr. Nicholson's work; but he was equally zealous and successful in his labours in the pulpit, the school, the cottage, &c. In a letter of the Rev. T. Seymour's (Superintendent of the circuit), which appeared in the Missionary notice of the year under review, he says, " During the past summer some matured persons, even heads of families, sought admission into the school (Priesthill), and were found with their children, learning to read the Bible. A Roman catholic, who, with his wife and family, was on his way from Connaught to the English harvest, being in great distress for the want of bread, called at the house of one of our friends and obtained not only food, but also employment. He was induced to attend the preaching. Divine light penetrated through the mists of superstition in which his mind had been long enveloped. He began to read his Bible, and soon perceived that Popery and the Bible could not be both true. In a short time he totally renounced Romanism, joined the church at Priesthill, and is now an active teacher in the Sabbath school. The Sabbath schools at Broomhedge and Priesthill have been much increased of late."

We now approach a period in our narrative of unprecedented blessing. Mr. Nicholson had witnessed many revivals, but none of them had been big enough to meet the full desires of his heart. He was ever striving after and praying for a revival of pentecostal power and extent. The voice of his audible and importunate pleadings for the salvation of souls, issuing from his study, was quite familiar to his family. His surviving children are easily able to quote many of the petitions which they overheard their revered father repeat again and again in his private pleadings. He used to get the leaders and others to join him in a covenant to plead with God, thrice daily, for a special outpouring of the Spirit. A paper of his, on the power of united prayer, written about the time under review, lies before us: it is an essay most impassioned and sanguine in terms.

"Bangor, August 27th, 1850.

My dear Brother,

      I am anxious to see the work of God prospering more fully upon the stations. I have been speaking to the leaders at Priesthill and Broomhedge to begin to pray more to God for a revival of His work. For myself, I deeply feel on this subject, and am resolved to urge all the leaders to pray and labour more earnestly for the salvation of immortal souls which are perishing. I would feel it most helpful and encouraging to know that you were engaged in this heavenly exercise. It is my daily practice at present, to devote to prayer for a great revival the hours of nine and twelve o'clock forenoon, and six evening. Dear Brother, meet me at the Throne of Grace, and God will hear and grant us abundant blessing. . . . These remarks spring from love.

I am,
Yours very affectionately, in Christ,

S. NICHOLSON."

' To Mr. JNO. CARLISLE.' "

The expectation of a mighty revival grew and extended all over the circuit, ministers and leaders sharing in it.

Some saw the cloud of a hand-breadth arising, and in it the promise of a saving shower of plenary extent.

The Conference of 1851 met at the usual time and place, the Rev. Thos. Addyman being, by the suffrages of his brethren, President. The most noteworthy statement made at this Conference was that of a brother from Priesthill, who said, "that God had given him an assurance that, during the year, there would be such a revival of religion at Priesthill as never had been known by any of the people." The revival came; and, had we the power, we should record the fact in letters that would flash with coruscations of light, that *it came in answer to united, believing, importunate prayer*. During its progress, individuals were singled out as the subjects for intercessory prayer, and the suppliants received the assurance, that God would grant their requests, and on their way to the meetings, they were sometimes able to name some of the individuals who should find salvation. The ministers on the Lisburn circuit were the Revs. T. Seymour (Lisburn), J. Shuttleworth (Priesthill), and S. Nicholson (Broomhedge). We shall give the thrilling account of this gracious visitation, as nearly as possible, in the words of the brethren whose joy it was to gather in the sheaves. While the civilized world had its attention centred on the Great Exhibition of 1851, as the harbinger of peace amongst the nations, in the quiet, rural seclusion of the Maze, God was giving His servants to witness the power of that Gospel which alone pacifies and regenerates individuals and nations. The following extracts are from the Missionary notices for 1851.—

" For some time past, a blessed work of God has been going forward here (Broomhedge). On Sabbath, July 20th, we had a revival prayer-meeting at seven a.m., when about forty attended. At eleven o'clock, I preached; the Lord gave me unusual liberty, and the Holy Ghost rested on the people. At two o'clock we held a camp meeting about two miles from the chapel. About three hundred persons were present; three sermons were preached on the occasion. I spoke from, 'These shall go away into everlasting punishment.' I did my best to show the wicked the very torments of the damned, and that place of punishment prepared for the devil and his angels. One young man was cut to the heart, and shortly afterwards found peace with God. At night, Brother Gordon preached an admirable sermon. We afterwards held a prayer-meeting, and God poured down His Spirit upon the people. On Sabbath, July 27th, we commenced a week of special services, and had a good prayer-meeting in the morning. At eleven o'clock Brother Shuttleworth preached from 'Why sit we here until we die.' The Spirit of God applied the Word to many hearts. At the evening meeting, several penitents came forward and found mercy. On Monday evening, Mr. Seymour addressed the people on the Gospel plan of salvation, and a sense of the Divine presence was experienced. The meetings on Tuesday and Wednesday nights were most precious. On Thursday, Brother James Carlisle addressed the people, and the presence of the Lord was powerfully felt. Several came forward in distress, and some found mercy, and testified that God, for Christ's sake, had pardoned their sins. On Friday, the chapel was crowded We continued in prayer with the penitents till eleven o'clock, and several entered into the liberty of God's children. Here, the week-night services ceased at Broomhedge. But the next week the work broke out still more gloriously at Priesthill; and many, who did not find peace at the former, have been set at liberty at the latter place. I cannot state the precise number that have been converted to God during these services; but I trust that fifty souls will be added to the Broomhedge Society." *

"We betook ourselves to prayer and renewed exertions. The leaders had one night for prayer and spiritual counsel. For many weeks we had a great struggle with the enemy. One Sabbath evening, as I returned home much depressed, the devil said, 'It's no use; the Lord will not revive His work.' I had not, however,

* Rev. S. Nicholson.

been long at home, when Brother James Carlisle came in and said
' Good news, good news, God has saved a soul to-night ! ' I replied
' Brother, that is the best news you ever brought me.' On August
3rd, at the Lord's Supper, God set another soul at liberty. In the
evening many were brought into great distress, a few came forward
as penitents seeking mercy, and some obtained peace with God. On
my way home, I called at Mrs. Carlisle's, and there I found a
number of persons, who had been at the meeting, in great anxiety
about their spiritual state. We went to prayer, and before we
parted, God spoke peace to their souls. At the same time, Brother
Larmour was engaged in prayer with a number who had called at
his house in distress. The next night was the regular monthly
meeting of the temperance society. The meeting was large, and
soon resolved itself into a meeting for penitents. The form for the
anxious was soon crowded. Before the meeting broke up, to many
the Spirit said, ' Go in peace and sin no more." From that night,
the revival continued to increase in extent and power. God seemed
to have touched the hearts of the people in almost every house·
They flocked in hundreds every night to the house of prayer·
About the hour for commencing the service, the people would be
seen running from all directions that they might be in time to get
inside. It is calculated that often there were from six to seven
hundred inside and around the chapel. But how shall we describe
the effects of the power of God which fell upon the people? There
were no mockers. The proud unbelievers trembled in the presence
of the Lord of Hosts. The groans and agonizing cries of many
anxious ones no pen or tongue could describe. Some struggled in
agony for hours, and would not give up. When God lifted the
light of His countenance on these souls the effects were overwhelming. Brothers and sisters and friends would embrace them,
and praise God aloud. This glorious work has not been confined
to any age or class. The educated and the illiterate, the moralist
and the notorious sinner, the strong man and the delicate maiden,
were all bowed down before God. We were compelled to continue
the meetings till a late hour, as the penitents were unwilling to
leave without comfort. There is found in almost every house in
the neighbourhood of Priesthill one or more converts. Our greatest difficulty now is, the want of accommodation for the people.

Our walls have become too strait for us, and the cry has gone forth *Arise and build.*" *

" In Lisburn, there is a good work going on. In ordinary times it would have been a *great* work. Many have sought the Lord with strong cries and tears, and between twenty and thirty have been converted to God." †

" This is the twentieth night we have had special revival services in Broomhedge Chapel and Priesthill. Many souls are brought to God—even *children, old sinners* and *profligates!* The work commenced in Broomhedge, and is extending to every part of the Circuit. I have had some blessed times of revival in every place where I have travelled, and such a mighty display of God's power *I never witnessed before.* We formed a Total Abstinence Society, and about 500 united in this cause. Many were then led to hear the Word, and conviction rested on their minds. God shall have all the praise." ‡

" Such a revival has taken place (at Broomhedge, &c.) as was never known on this Mission. Night after night there have been twenty and upwards converted to God. In the day-time two groups of people have assembled in the different fields around, to seek the Lord. The business of the district has been half suspended, during the last fortnight. A camp meeting was arranged to be held on Sabbath last, in the open ground around Priesthill Chapel, but nearly half the congregation appeared to consist of penitents, so that no one could preach, but all the people joined in prayer. The earnestness and agony of the awakened were extraordinary. One whole family, notorious for wickedness, and for fighting amongst themselves, have been converted. Many wicked people have come with the crowds, from curiosity, who have been convinced of sin, broken down in godly sorrow, and professed to have received peace with God. To describe the thrilling scenes, the intense excitement, the many affecting incidents and wonderful conversions which mark this revival, would be difficult indeed. The work appears to be all of God, in answer to prayer. Three brethren made a covenant together to meet on each Thursday evening at the chapel (Priesthill), to pray for a revival ; and for

---

* Rev. Jno. Shuttleworth.   † Rev, T. Seymour.
‡ Rev. S. Nicholson.

several months they met and prayed accordingly. God has heard prayer; and the work is now going on." *

"There are now at [least one hundred members added to the three societies. The good work is still going on. At Broomhedge the revival is now (September) nearly equal to what it was at Priesthill, when at the highest. In Lisburn, nearly thirty profess to have found peace. On Sabbath week, I spoke in Smithfield market place, and one man, an entire stranger, was converted. He immediately went home and brought his wife to the penitent form." †

"The good work began at Booomhedge in July, continued and progressed in September with still greater power. Our chapel, which was closed for years on Sabbath evenings, had to be opened for evening services, which was conducted by the leaders. Crowds attended; souls were deeply convicted of sin, bowed at the penitent form, and found redemption in Christ's blood. When we resumed the revival services on August 29th, it was the middle of harvest; but the hardy sons of toil attended week after week at these meetings. Our Broomhedge Chapel was open for five weeks, and nearly every night we had a meeting. On Sabbath, Aug. 31st we had about sixty at the early morning prayer-meeting; and at night, fifteen souls found peace. On this day I opened a class of about thirty-five young converts, and Mrs. Nicholson met about twenty females in the parlour. To give you anything like a full description of the manifestation of saving power, which we have had from the presence of Jehovah, would be out of my power. One old man, hardly able to walk, came to the meetings, was deeply convicted, and attended night after night till he found peace. At the fellowship meeting on September 14th, he was the first to declare his sins forgiven, through the blood of the Lamb. At this meeting about one hundred were present During these meetings, not less than *eighty* persons professed to find mercy, or purity of heart. I thank God, the work has not ceased. Last night (November 16th) we had eight penitents. One man, who stood out through all the revival, was brought into deep distress for pardon, and at near ten o'clock, he was enabled to lay hold

* Rev. Thos. Mills, Superintendent of the Mission.
† Rev. T. Seymour.

on Christ.   Eternal glory to God, Father, Son, and Holy
Spirit!!"* .

Individual cases of conversion of extraordinary interest
occurred during this revival, one of which was that of
a Roman Catholic.   His anxiety was intense, and his
search after the knowledge of salvation through the remission of his sins importunate and agonising.   He
attended the meetings nightly ; and indifferent to appearance, he would press forward, fall down upon his knees
at the minister's feet and look up in his face imploringly.
He was pointed away from *man* to the Great High Priest
of our profession, by faith in whose blood the poor fellow
at length found the blessing he sought.

We cannot forbear recording the names of a few of the
converts of 1851, and adding a sentence or two about
some of them :—Thos. Moore and Thos. Carlyle were
amongst the boy-converts.   They, with other youths of
like spirit, began a juvenile prayer meeting in Samuel
McLatchy's, and out of that meeting there went a " band
of men, whose hearts God had touched."   Thomas Moore
is at present a clergyman of the Established Church in
England.   Thos. Carlyle was but twelve years of age
when he was converted, and soon was known as " the
boy preacher."   He had flaxen hair, a fair complexion, a
bright countenance, and a soft, gentle voice.   There was
offered to him a lucrative situation, but to Mr. Nicholson
he said, " I should not care, if the firm proposed to make
me proprietor of all their business, I would not accept it,
if there be any hope of my being called to the ministry of
of the Lord Jesus Christ."   When Mr. Nicholson took
young Carlisle with him to the Conference (1856) as a
candidate for the probationary ministry, the Rev. Wm.

---

* Rev. S. Nicholson

Baggally said, "Brother Nicholson, what induced you to bring that boy here?" Very soon, Thos. Carlisle was found amongst the most beloved and popular young ministers in England; and God blessed his labours abundantly. Alas! his ministry continued but fourteen years, when he passed to the higher service above. Wm. Jno. Robinson has been for decades of years a leader and local preacher; and is at present a successful business man and an earnest, liberal supporter of *Salem*, Lisburn. Robert McLatchy has long been one of the main pillars of a Primitive Methodist Church in Glasgow. Sarah Bradbury, now Mrs. D. Carlisle, is at this moment a faithful worker for Christ in Lisburn. James Robinson has been chiefly instrumental in forming a Wesleyan Society and erecting a Chapel at Bessbrook.

Mary and Agnes Gorman, the former of whom is now the devoted wife of W. J. Robinson. We can but mention the names of Wm. and A. Bell, Wm. Gordon, James Larmour, Jane and John Donaldson, and Thos. Dornan. Wm. Jno. Anderson's name merits special notice. For many years he was one of the steadiest, most loyal, earnest, self-sacrificing office-bearer's Broomhedge Circuit ever had. Under sermons preached by Mr. Nicholson and Mr. J. Gordon, in the open air, he decided for Christ.

A memoir of Mr. Anderson, from the pen of Rev. T. G. Seymour, appeared in the Magazine for Nov. 1869.

Another notable case was that of Robert Boyd, who came to the Maze a drivelling drunkard, often suffering from *delirium tremens*. He was convinced of sin under a a sermon in James Carlisle's field. He had acquired ultra-Calvinistic views, but Jno. iii., 16 was applied by the Holy Ghost to his distressed conscience, and the word "whosoever" dispelled his fears, while God's mighty love, seen in the gift of His Son, broke the penitent's heart for sin and from sin, and his soul was set at liberty. He became an ardent total abstainer, a Sunday School teacher, a leader, etc., and was instrumental in the conversion of souls. He remained steady till death, which occurred a few weeks ago. The writer knew him for over twenty years; on his death-bed Brother Boyd left the request that we should preach his funeral sermon from Jno. iii., 16, which we had pleasure in doing to a crowded congregation in Zion, Priesthill. Shortly after his conversion friend Boyd heard Mr. Nicholson preach on the duty of restitution. Boyd remembered that he owed a publican one shilling. He would not sleep till the debt was paid; he reached Crumlin about midnight, awoke the astonished publican, paid her the debt and immediately started for his distant home.

The Conference of 1852 had for President the Rev. Jno. Hudston, a very amiable and highly cultured man, and a good minister of Jesus Christ. It was found that two hundred and twenty-six members had been added to the Mission during the previous year, but sixty had removed. The Rev. Jno. Taylor was appointed Superintendent by the English Conference. In the *Missionary Report* for 1852 it is stated that, "our Chapel* at Priesthill has been enlarged by the erection of an additional wing, which is more than half the size of the original building; and it is so crowded, that it will likely have to be enlarged again soon. At Broomhedge we had three classes which met

---

* The first place of worship at Priesthill was not as now, a structure of stone but was built of mud and thatched with straw. The congregation was systematically arranged into a complete separation of the men and women, who sat on humble forms ranged on opposite sides of "the house." The singing was slow and solemn . . . The worship was earnest, the piety sincere and the morality pure."
—*Memoir of Rev. T. Carlyle.*

regularly, and a fourth which met occasionally, now we have eight good classes meeting regularly. Since the returns were made to the Irish Conference, we learn that the revival has not ceased, but has broken forth again with undiminished power, the meetings being crowded at the three principal chapels, and sinners being cut to the heart and crying to God for mercy." Mr. Nicholson was fully alive to the importance of inducing the young, especially the juvenile converts, to seek after general, as well as Biblical knowledge. Hence, he established Sunday School Libraries; and he was in frequent communication with the great Tract Depots. In his journal he says, " I obtained a grant of tracts, value two pounds, from the *London Tract Society.* We have a good library for the young at Broomhedge, containing one hundred prime religious works." Peter Drummond appreciated our indefatigable friend's labours, and generally favoured his application for tracts. Here is a first letter from the pen of this celebrated publisher:—

"Stirling, April 28th, 1852.

My Dear Sir,

I had the pleasure of receiving your refreshing letter of the 22nd inst., and we are putting up for you a small grant of our tracts—say 1246, chiefly short ones. I see from your letter and enclosures, that you have had and still have a wide field for all such efforts. Please see what sort you would prefer After you get acquainted with the tracts, and if spared and able, I shall always send you what you want. O let us be earnest that the Lord would give us grace for *our* day. It will not be long. Souls are precious and ETERNITY is at hand. Rouse up to prayer on behalf of our Tract Work.

Yours,

PETER DRUMMOND."

Mr. Nicholson had never reason to exclaim, "They

made me the keeper of the vineyards; but mine own
vineyard have I not kept." The revival was in him as
well as around him ; in his own experience he verified the
truth of the proverb—"He that watereth shall be watered
also himself." His work for God and souls powerfully
reacted upon his own mind, aroused into activity and increased in strength every sanctified faculty and holy
principle within him. The Spirit who spoke peace to the
conscience of the believing penitent at his side, at the
same instant, shed richer light upon our brother's understanding and deepened his conviction in the Divinity and
power of the Gospel. His principal knowledge of Divine
things was acquired in the school of experience and
Christian labour. A sentence or two, from many of like
sentiment occurring in his diary, will exhibit the reverence,
and adoring gratitude and love which often swelled his
breast:—"Oh! how my soul was melted, blessed and
comforted ; my eyes filled with tears ; I bowed down and
sobbed out my adoring thanksgivings and praises to my
God. The eternal Spirit has assured my heart, that the
vision of approaching blessing which I have had, will
surely come to pass. Hallelujah to God and the Lamb!"
In the *Magazine* for June, 1852, appeared another obituary
notice, contributed by Mr. Nicholson, of a woman who had
been brought to God through his instrumentality. He says,

"On January 14th, 1852, our dear sister Collins departed this
life. Her father, Mr. Wm. Green, received our ministers into his
house about twenty years ago. In the year 1836, Mrs. Collins was
born of the Spirit at a revival prayer-meeting, whilst the writer
was engaged in prayer. She was early left a widow. Her leader,
Mr. Dickey, admired her growing piety, and devotion to God. She
suffered much during her last illness, which was protracted. I
visited her often and found her happy in Jesus. On the night
before she died, she gathered her sisters and friends around her,

and in the most fervent and feeling manner, exhorted them each and all to dedicate themselves unreservedly to the Lord. Just before she expired, she said, 'I bless the Lord! I praise the Lord! Victory!'"

Meanwhile the revival continued and "broke out" again and again in increased strength. Life begat life. Youths who had caught the holy fire, banded together in prayer and Christian effort for others; thus the work spread. In a lettter to the Superintendent, dated September, 1852, Mr. Nicholson says, "Instead of a falling off last quarter, as was feared, we had an increase on the conference returns at Broomhedge. Our congregations are large, and a few only of the converts are unsteady. I attended a new prayer meeting lately, where three brothers all led in prayer during the proceedings. A short time since, the whole family were unconverted; now, as the fruit of our revival, six of them are saved by the blood of Christ; to God be all the praise! We are about to hold revival meetings again at Broomhedge. I find that my strength is in the Word of God, prayer and faith."

Our earnest friend's revivalistic efforts did not lessen his pastoral and domiciliary labours; he lived amongst the people, and his visits were not perfunctory, he felt a real interest in the welfare of the people. Often he passed from the bed-side of the dying straight to a revival prayer meeting. It was only occasionally that he published accounts of the triumphant death-bed scenes which it was his joy to witness frequently. Mrs. Dornan of Moyruck, commanded much of his attention and sympathy during her last illness. In an obituary notice, dated December 1852, he says:

"I have been highly favoured of the Lord in being called to witness about a dozen happy deaths on this Circuit. We have bright evidence amidst the gloom that surrounds us, that there are some children of light who have not defiled their garments. and they shall walk with Christ because they are worthy. Their presence strengthens our faith. It was the privilege of Mrs. Dornan to hear the Gospel preached in her father's house by our first missionaries : the Revs. Scott, Lyons, Donaldson, Livingstone, Brothers, &c., who opened their commission in the north of Ireland. Their unwieldy Circuit then took in about six counties. Her son has shown me some of his dear mother's quarterly tickets bearing the date of 1810. Mrs. Dornan lost her husband very suddenly, his fatal illness lasting but a few hours. After long continued prayer on their behalf, she had the joy of seeing all her children converted to God during the recent revival. During her last illness a class met in her house. To Brother Robinson, her leader, she said : ' When this affliction kept me at home, the Lord was so kind as to meet my case, and send His servants to my house.' Her whole experience is summed up in the following statement from her lips :—' I have no fear of death, nor of falling away from God. I feel prepared to die; all slavish fear is removed. I was very ill last night, but I had mighty comfort, and I was so happy, I should have been glad to depart to be with Jesus in heaven.' Her last words were—' *Dear Saviour.*' "

God's servants were allowed to retain as members but a proportion of their converts, and many of these were soon thinned off by emigration, etc., as time advanced ; yet, with rare fortitude, the good men toiled bravely on. In the Missionary notice for December 1852, it is stated, "Four of our most promising young men (at Priesthill) have been taken out by the Church of England, as scripture-readers ; some others have left the home of their childhood, to seek rest in a strange land Though these things have somewhat depressed us, yet our cry is 'Onward,' our faith and hope are in God."

"On October 28th, we had a whole day of thanksgiving to Almighty God, for what He has wrought in this Circuit. At Broomhedge, God is still magnifying the power of his grace in the conversion of sinners." Yes, God was still working, and His servant, being a partaker of the divine nature, was a co-worker with God. Catholic in spirit, Mr. Nicholson willingly co-operated with Christians of various denominations in work for God; and men, of varying ecclesiastical sentiments, were sometimes found at his meetings. His diary (1852) contains an account of a total-abstinence meeting, held in Broomhedge chapel, at which sixty persons signed the pledge; and on the platform were two clergymen of the Established Church, one of whom was the Rev. H. Hudson (afterwards a Canon), a man well known for his kindness of heart. A man named "Bunnel" Green, who had been a notorious drunkard, signed the pledge at this meeting and became a changed man; he often afterwards said to our friend, "Mr. Nicholson, if it had not been for you under God, I would have been in hell long ago."

It was a great joy to our brothers's heart to find his own eldest child amongst the converts during the revival; and his emotions of gratitude were irrepressible when she presented herself as a communicant at the Lord's Table, and received from her father's hand, the memorials of her Saviour's broken body and shed blood.

As schools were scarce, and children growing up around him in ignorance and idleness, Mr. Nicholson, early in 1853, rented a house in Magheragall, and gathered a Sunday School, which began with fifty children. The effort cost much labour, as he had to collect funds to meet all liabilities, including clothes for some of the poorer children. He likewise held special services at Miss Wright's, Mr. W. Bennett's, and at Mogabbery, the fruit of which is seen to this day. About this time, in mid-winter, Mr. Nicholson and Mr. Edward McClune nearly perished in a

snowstorm near the River Lagan on their way home from
Priesthill; it was midnight ere they reached home, utterly
exhausted.

No wonder, that his health broke down, under labours
so prodigious, requiring him to take rest for a time. In
his diary he makes favourable mention of Messrs. W. J.
Anderson, R. Richey, R. Jefferson, J. Turtle and other
christian workers, who assisted him in his meetings.
He likewise records help rendered him by Mr. W. Smyth,
and Mr. Jas. Megarry. In those days, Mrs. Nicholson had
a baby to nurse, and she tells of how she used to rock the
cradle and pray for the meeting proceeding in the chapel
adjoining the Manse; she would leave her sleeping infant,
go to the chapel door for a little while, speak to some careless or anxious ones near, and then return to her charge.

In its address to the English Conference, the Irish
Conference, of 1853 (Rev. L. Stoney, President), says,
" The spirit of revival is still in operation, particularly at
Priesthill and Broomhedge." Returning from Conference,
his heart aglow with fervent gratitude for past success,
and inspired with high hopes for the future, Mr.
Nicholson entered on a fifth year's labours at Broomhedge,
and the wave of revival flowed with him throughout the year.

It will be appropriate here to notice the mutual sympathy and brotherly love which prevailed amongst the
Irish Missionaries of those days, as numerous letters, found
amongst Mr. Nicholson's papers, testify. Here is one from
the pen of a minister, who for many years was the con-
temporary of our friend, and often his colleague in labour:

"11, Aungier St., Dublin,
June 25th, 1853.

" Dear Brother,
I received your very kind letter this morning,
enclosing me half-a-pound note (a subscription), which you ought

o

not to have done as, no doubt, you have your own pecuniary difficulties. We all felt for your kind brother*—I mean all the Connexion, for he was a firm friend. When I was in England, some of our brethren, who have been Superintendents, asked most anxiously and affectionately after him. Well, perhaps these heavy calamities may be sanctified to his future, yea, to his eternal welfare. I am glad to know that Mr. Taylor has received even a temporary assistant in the person of Mr. Henn; and also that the glorious work of revival is returning to your circuit.

Poor Dublin has been the most murdered place I ever knew...... We have a regular battle. On our side, it is plain preaching, faith and prayer: on the other side, misrepresentation, falsehood, envy, malice, &c., &c. God will stand by the right. It is adding a few gray hairs to my head, but I doubt not as to the issue.

Dear Brother, eternity is at hand: I almost hear the trumpet sounding, and see the Saviour coming. Oh how will unfaithful, time-serving shepherds appear before Him! O Brother, let men say what they will, clear your skirts of the blood of souls. May God help you. With kind regards to Mrs. Nicholson, from Mrs. Seymour and myself,

Yours most affectionately, in the Lord Jesus,

T. SEYMOUR.

Rev. S. Nicholson."

Labouring, as he did, in the South, Mr. Seymour acquired a deep insight into Popery, the chief instrument of Ireland's woes. The Magazine for March, 1854, which lies before us, contains an article by Mr. Seymour on, "The Cause of Ireland's Degradation and the Means of Her Recovery." In this paper he says:—

"We could show, by a comparison of the last census with the Poor Law Report, and Criminal statistics, that, just in proportion as Romanism prevails in any country or district, in the same ratio are ignorance, destitution and crime found: and that, on the contrary, education, morality, and social happiness keep pace

---

* Mr. J. H. Nicholson, who had suffered ruinous losses in business. He was however, able to meet all his liabilities.

with the prevalence of Protestantism in Ireland. Popery, like a millstone, lies heavy on the heart of the nation. All other systems of error have been laid under contribution to make Popery a masterpiece of Satanic ingenuity for the ruin of souls. 'Here, for instance, you have Pharisaism contributing its outward purifications and traditions. Here you have celibacy and monastic austerities, borrowed from the Gnostics, who thought matter the source of evil, and the flesh the source of sin. And here, above all, you have Paganism baptized in the name of Jesus, with Peter for Jupiter; Mary, the Papists' queen of Heaven, for Juno, the Pagan's, and saints and angels for gods and demigods. Aye, and so shameless has been the plagiarism, that purgatory is accurately described in Virgil's Æneid; the present statue of Peter at Rome is the identical statue of Jupiter Capitolinus: even the Pope's chair is said to have been pilfered from the Mussulman; and Romulus and Remus are worshipped as the two holy bishops, under the names of Romulo and Remigio,' It is a mistake to regard Popery as merely a corrupt form of Christianity; it is not Christianity at all, it is against Christ. Heaven's own remedy for Ireland's chief woe is the Gospel of the Son of God."

Writing to the Superintendent, on March 1st, 1854, Mr. Nicholson says :—

" I have good news to send you. The Lord is with us on this station, and has been through the year. In July last, we had our Field Meeting, at which the attendance was large. At night several found peace. A backslider was reclaimed. One who had been prejudiced against penitent meetings, and who stood out against them through all the revival of 1851, came forward in great agony. Two of us had to hold him at times. After the meeting in the chapel he came into my house, and while Mrs. Nicholson, myself and a leader were engaged in prayer, his soul was set at liberty, and filled with love. In Magheragall district before the revival, I have preached to six persons, but last summer we had a hundred. Sixty children attend the new Sunday School here. We have now worship in the School room every Lord's day at three o'clock. The immense labour I have gone through the last few years has greatly impaired my health. I have been on this station now nearly five years, and what have I seen? Not less than twenty happy death-beds! The congregations have increased threefold; and our Sabbath collections have more than doubled. Our classes have increased from three to eleven. Our annual income has more than doubled. In my first year we had only forty members who met in class, but at our last October quarter we stood 110 and 13 on trial. What hath God wrought! Another of our friends died happy yesterday. Mrs. Nicholson is just out visiting a little girl of thirteen, who is departing happy in Christ. May the Lord find me a place next year where I shall see sinners brought to Christ. Yea, He will—I have faith."

To the Conference of 1854, the Rev. P. T. Gilton was the English Deputation, and according to custom, was chosen President by the Irish brethren. At this Conference the venerable John Lyons retired wholly from mission work, and his parting words were deeply affecting. When in his prime, he bore some resemblance to the lion in physical strength and courage.

One morning, when performing his ablutions outside the farm house, in which he had preached the night before, he saw a furious man, whom two men were trying to hold back, coming, as the man said, to "thrash the preacher for exposing his character before all the people, in the sermon the night previous." Mr. Lyons, taking in the situation, began to roll up his shirt sleeves, and shouted to the men, " Let him come forward." At the sight of the big strong man, in the attitude of self-defence, the angry man altered his mind as to the purpose of his visit, and after mutual explanations, Lyons and he became quite friendly. On another occasion, a threatening mob was approaching the Rev. T. Seymour, who was preaching on the street; Mr. Lyons took his stand beside his weaker brother, cautioned the rowdies, and assumed an attitude of defence. The preacher was not molested.

While the "Third Readings" of Conference were being prepared, Mr. Nicholson, as was his wont, put the question of his circuit appointment into the Master's hand, and when he found himself "down for Lisburn," he accepted the appointment as from the Lord.

The Rev. John Taylor had established "Ragged Schools," in Belfast, into which hundreds of poor children were gathered, some of whom had to receive food and clothing as well as a free education.

Mr. Taylor raised the funds, paid the teachers, and superintended the schools. He held public examinations of the pupils, and his work attracted general attention, and was favourably noticed by the press. This new departure antedated those greater educational schemes, which, ere long, brought a possible education within reach of every Irish child. Very soon "Ragged Schools" were started all over the Mission. Mr. Nicholson started the *first Ragged School in Lisburn*. From old circulars before us we learn, that the Messrs. Richardson, and W. Cordner, J. Bolton, and W. Gregg, Esqs., Miss Stuart, Mrs. Nicholson, and others of the wealthier class, were amongst the subscribers. In certain quarters, however, jealousy arose, as the following from the Missionary notice (Oct., 1854) shews:—"Lisburn is reviving. Mr. Nicholson has commenced a ragged school, with about 70 children. It is the first in Lisburn. The friends of another denomination have offered him £10 to give it up to them, and because he refuses, are about to open an opposition one within twelve yards of his. The congregation in Lisburn is much improved."

Early in this year Mr. Nicholson received very welcome visitors from New York—his brother, James Whitla Nicholson, who, with his wife, had come home on a visit principally in quest of health. Cholera was very rife iu Lisburn at the time. This good brother set to work immediately, with the view of relieving the suffering. He bought medicine, and, with his clerical brother, visited every case of cholera of which they heard, and all to whom they gave the medicine got better. It was a great joy to Mr. Nicholson and his family to have the daily society, for a time, of wealthy friends so nearly related to them· And it was a cause of mutual gratification to the visitors and visited, and praise to the Lord, that the brothers were enabled to carry relief to many who otherwise might have perished. The favourite steamer, by which these kind friends from New York purposed re-crossing the Atlantic, they found, upon reaching her starting place, could not supply them with berths. That steamer perished, and when Mr. Nicholson and his wife reached New York, they found the churches draped in black for many loved ones in their watery graves.

Mr. Nicholson reports effort and success thus :—

"This Circuit was in a very low condition last Conference. I began to preach in the open air both on the Sabbath and on the week nights. We also established a Tract Society, and by some ten distributors had several hundred tracts changed every Sabbath. The cholera was made a blessing to many in arousing them to seek the Lord. We have had seven weeks of special protracted meet‑ ings, which were well attended, and some came to the penitent form, and found mercy through the blood of Christ. We had also several temperance meetings in the chapel, which did good in making some sober who had never attended the sanctuary of the Lord. So many of our people were ill we had fears about our missionary meeting. Early on that evening I preached in the open air, to a weeping congregation, who seemed to feel the power of God while I proclaimed, 'Come, for all things are now ready.' Oh ! how the people thanked me for bringing the message of mercy to them in the day of their calamity. Cholera had been raging in a lane near where I stood, and a corpse was removed a few minutes before I began my sermon. At the conclusion of the service I hastened to the chapel to hold the missionary meeting, which proved a great success. We have realized above £10 this quarter for the mission. Our congregations are double. Our day school has 100 scholars. To God alone be all praise and glory! Amen !"

Mrs. Nicholson made soup daily for the poor children of the School, and supplemented the labours of the day school teacher, by holding an evening school for girls in her own kitchen, which met twice weekly, and at which sewing and knitting, as well as reading, etc., were taught. Our friends were occasionally made familiar with domestic affliction. In March, 1855, their eldest child was seized with a fever, having taken the infection, it was believed, from some of the ragged children, that came daily for soup. Thus, they who would lift up the fallen must, in a sense, bear their sickness.

CHAPTER IX.

"Oh, Lord, I must get nearer to thee. Bring me, Oh! I beseech
Thee, bring me into closer fellowship with Thee, and if it be needful to this end, that I pass through fiery tribulations, Lord, let
them come without delay."—*Rev. W. N. Hall.*

THE Conference of 1855 met as usual in Belfast,
in April. The Rev. T. W. Ridley and Dr. Teale
were the English Deputation, and the former was
called to the Presidential chair. The Address to the
English Conference says :—"The past year will long be
remembered, as the annals of Europe do not present a record
of events more important to the church and the world, than
those that have been recently transpiring. The [Russian]
war has attracted every eye, and its present influence is
painful and disastrous. The poor of this country have in
many ways felt its direful effects. Thousands have been
unable to obtain employment. In Autumn, the cholera
raged terrifically in some of the localities where your
missionaries are stationed."

Mr. Nicholson was removed to the Priesthill circuit,
whose minister had to give part of his labours to Lurgan
and Saintfield. At the latter place Mr. Nicholson called

to see a Mr. Mc D., who had not lived very agreeably with his wife. He had sent for Mr. Nicholson, who found him seriously ill, and professing to enjoy the peace of the Gospel, but yet joyless, and uncertain as to his acceptance with God. Mr. Nicholson spent a few days with the sick man, whose fears did not subside. "Is there anything on your conscience, anything wrong between you and God, that you are unwilling to put right?" asked the preacher. It appeared that though Mr. Mc D. had received a fortune with his wife, he had made a will leaving her but a trifle of what was justly hers. "It won't do," said the honest preacher, who believed that, while "God would save penitent sinners, he would not whitewash scoundrels." Mr. Mc D. made another, an honest will; and soon after found true peace, and died happy. In the Missionary report, Mr Nicholson says :—

"I have not witnessed all the good effected during the past year my soul could have desired, but, blessed be God, we have not been left without some fruit. We have conducted some protracted meetings that were greatly owned of God in the salvation of immortal souls. During the summer, we held seven field meetings. We have commenced three new classes, and opened several new preaching places. The congregations have been larger, the night congregations crowded to overflowing; and we have added forty-one new members, with twenty-six on trial. The Sabbath School is doing well, and the committee have resolved, if possible, to establish a lending library for the young. We have held monthly temperance meetings, and have distributed about six thousand tracts. The circuit is about twenty miles in length. I never felt more the weight of immortal souls."

As elsewhere, so here, Mrs. Nicholson gave unwearied help to the various interests of the church.

Mr. Arthur Stansfield, of Hillsboro, tells of a very remarkable answer to prayer, which Mr. Nicholson ha about this period. He called at the house near Hillsboro, of a gentleman who lay seriously ill. Mr. Nicholson was told that he could not be allowed to speak to the sufferer, as the doctors had given strict orders that no stranger should be allowed to enter the sick chamber. He, however, asked liberty just to look at the sick man, in silence, from a distance, which request was granted. The patient asked his wife who the visitor was, and being informed, he said, "Mr. Nicholson, come in." Mr. Nicholson softly approached the bedside, whispered words of comfort and help to the sufferer, and read and prayed with him, in tones calculated to soothe and quiet, rather than excite or hurt. After this visit, as they walked along together, the friend who accompanied Mr. Nicholson noticed, that he seemed absorbed in deep thought, and did not speak for some time. Suddenly he stood still, his face beamed. with the expression of joyous satisfaction, and in tones of strongest confidence he exclaimed. " As sure as there is a God in heaven, that man (just visited) shall not die, for God has heard my prayer just now, and given me the assurance that he will recover." To the surprise of the doctors the sick man did recover, and for many years thereafter, lived a godly consistent life. And he always attributed his recovery to Mr. Nicholson's prayers. As our narrative advances, the evidence accumulates to shew that prayer was the chief force in Mr. Nicholson's life. About this time, Mr. Nicholson took part in services, held in Dr. Munro's Barn, which were much blessed, the Doctor's own daughter being one of a large number who found peace in Christ.

The Conference of 1856 met at the usual time and place, and had for President the Rev. W. Baggally, who was accompanied by Benjamin Fowler, Esq., the Lay Repre-

sentative, from England. We learn from the "Minutes"
of this Conference that Mr. Nicholson was appointed to
take charge of the Lisburn and Broomhedge Stations, as
successor to Mr. Silas Henn, who had laboured acceptably
as a Supply on these Stations, the previous year. Our
sanguine brother entered upon his arduous labours,
trusting in God for strength. Of the year's labours he
had just discharged, he wrote, "If I had any laziness in
my bones I have surely lost it the past year. I feel that
if I have to work as hard for the next few years, I shall
not be long an inhabitant of this world." In November
of this year, he received intelligence of his aged father's
death. Some time after his sons left him, Mr. Nicholson,
Senior, had to dispose of his farm; and he was thankful
to be able to discharge to the last farthing every claim
against him. He found a comfortable home for the remainder of life under the kind care of Mr. Turtle of
Aghalee.

"Lisburn, Nov. 17, 1856.

"My Dear Brother,

My aged father died at 2 o'clock p.m. on Thursday last. The tidings reached me at Mr. Bennet's, where I was
preaching. He died in Christ. The last time I visited him was
about a fortnight since, when I found him happy in God. He said,
'Tears of joy mine eyes o'erflow that I have any hope of Heaven.
Amongst other verses of hymns, he repeated the first verse of one
of Watt's—

'I'll praise my Maker while I've breath;
And when my voice is lost in death,
Praise shall employ my nobler powers,' &c.

The Wesleyan Preacher visited him, also Rev. Mr. Hill (Episcopalian), who said that he had never met a person so clear in his
experience of the love of Christ. I mourn the loss of my father,
but to him it is infinite gain. . . He had left the request that
the Rev. Jno. Armstrong should preach his funeral sermon, which

request was complied with on Saturday. Mr. Armstrong preached a most feeling and appropriate discourse.

'O may we triumph so when all our warfare's past.'

The Lord is blessing us here, we had a number of penitents forward on Sabbath week. On the same Sabbath they had a glorious time at Broomhedge, almost equal to the great revival. Glory be to God! We unite in love to all.

Yours affectionately,
S. NICHOLSON.

To Rev. T. Seymour."

The Missionary Report makes favourable mention of Mr. Nicholson's labours of this year. But he had much exceeded his strength, and laid the foundation of a severe illness.

After careful deliberation, the English Conference, of 1857, recorded the following resolutions :

"That the Irish Conference be discontinued, and that an Annual Meeting of the representatives of the stations comprising the Irish Mission shall be held . . . to be constituted after the model of the English District Meetings. That the Chairman of the Annual Meeting shall be appointed by the English Conference ; [and] shall represent [the Irish Mission] at the English Conference, and that another person be appointed [by the Irish District Meeting] to attend the Conference, to represent the Irish Mission, viz., a preacher and layman alternately, when practicable."

The Galway Mission was Mr. Nicholson's next appointment ; and here we give, in substance, Mrs. Nicholson's account. She writes, "At the Conference of 1857 it was said that Mr. Nicholson was just the man for Galway, as he would conciliate the people, and not offend their prejudices. We were not prepared for such a journey, as our funds, never high, were exceptionally low at this time, and we had just been defrauded of six pounds by a man in whom Mr. Nicholson had unwisely confided. We had an aged woman as servant who persisted in going with us, and it was a mercy she did, as the sequel will show. On our way to the 5 p.m. train for Dublin, Mr. D. providentially put into my hand two pounds as a loan. On our arrival at the hotel in Dublin, my first care was to examine the sleeping accommodation. Such beds I never had seen, old carpets for quilts, etc. Our bill next morning was fourteen shillings. Fifty-five shillings were required to pay for our tickets to Galway, including half a ticket for our youngest child. My poor dear husband was unutterably distressed when he found our stock of cash, ten shillings short of this amount. He decided to send five of us on by the train then about to start, while he and our eldest daughter remained and went in search of our minister in Dublin. The ticket collector demanded full fare for our youngest girl, as he insisted she was over six years old, whereas she was under that age. We were all turned out upon the platform. But two gentlemen interposed threatening to report the ticket collector if he did not allow us to proceed. Their threat prevailed.

The morning was bright, many objects of interest came quickly into view, including the Bog of Allen, which stretched its vast expanse away out to the distant horizon, and the children were delighted with what they saw ; but I was unable to share their pleasure. In my confusion and distress, I had neglected to get the address of the person who had charge of the key of Galway Manse. It occurred to me to enquire upon our arrival, for a man whose name appeared on a bill in the railway carriage. The Manse was half a mile from the station, and we had no money to pay a cab, but a porter helped us to carry the luggage. I left my old woman and the children seated on the door step of the Manse, and, silently asking the Lord to protect them, I went in search of the key. I found the gentleman whose name I had seen on the bill, and he was able to instruct me where I should find the key. A young man, a Catholic, helped me, and engaged to meet Mr. Nicholson upon his arrival at midnight.

A man in Dublin proposed to accompany my dear husband and daughter to Mr. Shuttleworth's. When they had gone a long distance, Mr. Nicholson, under a sudden impulse, asked a gentlemen who was passing for the address he sought, and then found, that their guide, doubtless from some ill design, was leading them in the wrong direction. The gentleman called a cab, put them in it, and they soon reached a brother minister's hospitable home.

Our first morning in Galway found us without food or money to procure it. There was no steward ready to help us, and we did not know the members. We bowed together and spread our wants before our Heavenly Father, feeling confident that He would supply them all. We had the names of the people with whom Mr. Nicholson's predecessor had done business, and I resolved to apply to one of these for a loan, but Oh! how hard I felt it to do so! It was a baker,—a Catholic,—to whom I applied. He said, such a request was unusual, yet he seemed to take a real pleasure in complying. Afterwards, we found very kind people amongst the members. From the beginning, our cause had suffered continuous opposition from the low Romanists, all manner of petty insult and persecution had been offered, with the view to drive us out of the town; and on our first Sabbath, during worship, a lot of dirty things were tied to the knocker of our door.

Alas! in a few days, my dear husband was seized with a dangerous fever. He and I were out in search of members who lived at a distance. When we came to a bridge, he felt so weak, that he had to sit down. A policeman noticed him, and proposed to call a cab ; but after resting a little, he was able to walk home. That was the last journey he took for a long time. The truth is, he had overworked himself before he left for Galway, and a burning fever was the result. Dr. Cologlin was very kind ; he said, " My dear, good woman, I fear, it is a bad fever he has ; but don't be distressed, we will do all we can for him." He said a nurse was absolutely necessary. " Doctor," said I, " we are unable to pay one, and with God's help, I will nurse him myself." He said, I could not do it, and added that he would pay ten shillings per week of her cost. He warned me not to go near my husband, as the fever was one of the worst kind, and had carried off thousands.

I prostrated myself before God, and besought Him to take charge of us all, and I felt persuaded that He would ; I do not remember ever having such a nearness to God in prayer as then. He seemed to say, "Ask, and receive, that your joy may be full." I refused to supply the nurse with whisky, but she used over a pound and half of tea weekly. A gentleman not far from us had had fever, and one night, whilst his two nurses lay drunk, he arose in his delirium, climbed through the window, and his dead body was soon after found lying on the street pavement. This case made me so anxious about my dear sufferer, that I could hardly sleep. One night, he did get out of bed and was proceeding towards the window, but we soon got him back to bed. The doctor was very attentive, visiting him three and four times daily. In his delirium, my dear husband's mind was full of the truth so dear to his heart. He preached and prayed, and instructed imaginary penitents. He talked about the river that proceeds from the throne of God and of the Lamb, the tree of life, and the Lamb slain from the foun-

dation of the world.   The Catholic nurse had to hear it
all, and often tears started to her eyes.   She said that she
had nursed her own clergy, but never had heard so much
about God and Jesus, and heaven, before.   The doctor was
a highly skilled physician, who usually was paid two
guineas for his advice; but he charged us but a small sum.
I trust the Lord rewarded him.

Friends far and near, hearing of our affliction, were very
kind. The Rev. Mr. Baggally and his wife (Wesleyans)
called several times to sympathise and pray with us, but
wisely did not enter the sick room.   One Sabbath, the
Wesleyan congregation prayed specially for the recovery
of the dear sufferer, and one of the members called the
next day, to tell me he was sure God had heard prayer,
and that my husband would be spared. Letters from the
North reached me nearly every day, some of which contained much needed cash, of the latter was one from Miss
Wright.   One day a gentleman from near Hillsboro'
accompanied by a friend, called, and put in my hand three
pounds, sent by Mr. Hart,* of Hillsboro'. I praised the
Lord for the timely help, as just then our need had
reached a point of extremity. One day a genteel servant
brought me six chicken, a bottle of wine, and some tea
and sugar, but I never knew whence she came. Of course,
our Heavenly Father had put it into the sender's heart to
help us.

It was a great pain to me to witness the struggle with
disease of my dear husband, who lay unconscious for a
long time. I found relief in crying continually to Him,
whose eyes are ever over the righteous and His ears always
open to their cry. One day, Mr. Nicholson called for cold
water, but our water was bad.   I applied to a gentleman

* Father of Sir Robert Hart, who gave us £50 toward the erection of Priestbill
Schoolroom.—E.T.

near to us, who had a well of good spring water, but he roughly refused to give me any of it. There was a well of good water outside the town, which three of our children found, and from which they carried supplies daily.

At length, the unconscious sufferer's delirium began to abate. It was a glad sound to my ears to hear him ask in his natural tone of voice, 'Margaret, what is my watch hung up there for?' He saw the watch suspended out of its usual place. Now the doctor ordered him every possible nourishment, including a glass of wine every third hour, but, I believe, the wine injured him and retarded his recovery. If it did him no harm, the nurse one night got hold of the bottle, and soon lay incapable. Mary McConnell our old servant's help was invaluable. But she began to feel unwell, and the nurse said it was the fever she was taking, and that she would have to go to the hospital, which greatly distressed the old lady. I assured her that she should never leave my house for the hospital. She had a slight attack, which passed off soon and safely. I should mention the kindness of the Rev. Mr. Lewis (Independent), and the Rev. Mr. Adair (Presbyterian). The latter had had the fever, having caught the infection by contagion. His two sisters were specially kind in sending us fresh eggs. They were natives of Kilbride, Co. Antrim. On the twenty-fifth day, when my husband reached the crisis, we thought he was dying, and I raised the children from their beds, to bid him farewell and receive his parting counsel, should he be able to speak. And Oh! with what agony of entreaty we called upon God for help. Praise the Lord! the crisis was passed safely, and the sufferer began to amend slowly. I soon found that the wine and the nurse could not get on well together in the same house, so I parted with the latter. It was at the time when there

P

was most danger from contagion; but I trusted in the Lord and he preserved us.   Truly God hears prayer.

Mrs. Daly, whose husband was a Church clergyman in a high position, called to see us, and made me a present of wine and money, saying we were but stewards of God's good gifts and that she felt it a privilege to assist the Lord's people.   She was not afraid to enter the sick chamber as she had put herself, she said, in God's hands ere she left her home.   The Catholic lady, who resided next door to us, enquired for Mr. Nicholson every morning, and sent him many delicacies, such as jellies.   She asked for a Bible instead of the book we offered her as a present, when we were leaving Galway.   On June 24th, early in my husband's convalescence, I noticed men collecting fuel opposite our door which, I was told, was for a great bonfire.   I was alarmed, and applied to the police to have the fire prevented.   The Sergeant said it would be difficult to prevent the demonstration, but promised to see what could be done.   He succeeded in having the fuel removed.   And he sent two of his men to pace up and down before our house till midnight.   A few friends raised as much as paid our part of what the professional nurse cost us, and sent it by Rev. Mr. Baggaly.

When my husband was able we went, by the doctor's orders, to the seaside, where we dropped tracts on the sand: we saw a lady picking one up and tearing it to pieces. The fever had made great ravages in Galway.   We were told, that houses in which the bodies of people who had died in fever lay, whom no one dared to carry to the graveyard, were burned to the ground, the dead being consumed in them.   During Mr. Nicholson's illness it was decided to abandon the Galway mission, and that he should return as soon as able, and occupy the Manse at Broomhedge.   It was a most expensive time, and though we had received much help, yet when about to leave, we found it necessary to sell a part of our books and what furniture we had, that we might pay all claims against us, and have sufficient to pay our travelling expenses. We felt it a great hardship to have to sacrifice the books at a fraction of their cost. The journey to Lisburn was almost too much for Mr. Nicholson. The doctor said it would be years before he fully recovered his former strength. Oh ! with what gratitude, and praises, and thanksgivings, we acknowledged the kindness and care of our Heavenly Father in providing for us, and checking the fever, preventing it from spreading amongst us, and bringing us safely to our friends again.

Mr. Nicholson's visit to Galway seemed fruitless ; but the God of our life had His own gracious purpose in His dealings with us at that sad time. One thing we know, Mr. Nicholson would not have received equal medical skilled attention at like cost,* in any other place known to us. And our love to God, and faith in Him, received an increase of strength, which remained with us ever after. Glory be to the Father, and to the Son, and to the Holy Ghost ! Amen."

As Broomhedge, at this time, was but a part of the Lisburn Circuit, it had no resident minister ; Mr. Nicholson, therefore, was requested to take up his residence in the vacant Manse. He had now to learn that, "They also serve who only stand and wait." The District Meeting of 1858 placed him as a supernumerary for that year, with a small allowance. His financial condition was trying, and his family felt the pinch. But soon, we find him at Newtonards, that station having been "left without a preacher,"

* The Doctor accepted a part of his bill afterward.—E.T.

but his family remained at Broomhedge. At the end of the ecclesiastical year he wrote :

"On my arrival here about June last, I found the church in the lowest state of depression ; no Sabbath evening preaching in the chapel, and the Sunday school had been closed for a year. I first tried to engage the friends to unite in prayer to God for the descent of the Holy Spirit. I circulated 4,000 tracts, opened new prayer-meetings, etc., and preached in the open air as often as my strength would allow. The Sunday school soon numbered 170 children. In July we issued 1,000 bills announcing special services. One night 17 came forward to be prayed for. The work rolled on gloriously for twelve weeks, and the number of penitents rose to a hundred. The Sunday collections have doubled. I have had over two hundred of a congregation in the chapel. Sometimes there are 200 children in the Sabbath School. Two nights in the week we have a free night school; about forty attend. A young man who was taught in our school, sent us one pound for our funds from India. He sent £20 for his widowed mother and sisters. The friends promise to raise £50 next year."

In a meeting held by Mr. Nicholson at the close of this year, a young man named Wm. Dobbin was converted, who should have special notice here. He was the son of Mr. Wm. Dobbin, who had long been a devoted lea

Wm. Dobbin, Jun., lived only a few years after conversion ; but if the length of his life be measured by the magnitude and extent of its holy influence, then he lived long. A memoir of him was issued, in pamphlet form, written by the Rev. Thos. Hill. Wm. Dobbin, Jun., was born on October 2nd, 1842, born of the Spirit on the first Sabbath in [June, 1859, and died in the Lord, July 2nd, 1864. His zeal resembled, and was fully equal to, that of Thos. Carlisle. He superintended the Sabbath School ; and he went like a flame of holy fire through the prayer and other meetings. In him the Rev. J. Chadwick had an efficient helper in open-air work, and the youth's words of exhortation were tipped with fire. He and Mr. Chadwick went into a room, where a number of godless young people were dancing, and God's servants transformed the ball into a prayer-meeting. Young Dobbin was much respected in and around his native town, and persons of all classes visited him during his last lingering illness. Amongst the visitors came an officer of the Army, who in the sick-room began to talk about a splendid estate that was then in litigation. The dying saint interrupted the conversation by saying, " I have no estate in this world ; I don't need any. If I had one, I should now have to leave it. But I have an estate, yes ! ' Blessed be the God and Father of our Lord Jesus Christ, which, according to his abundant mercy, hath begotten me again unto a lively hope by the re-surrection of Jesus Christ from the dead, to an inheritance incorruptible, undefiled, and that fadeth not away!' Yes, I have an estate, the lease of which will not expire with the lives of two or three individuals, but the tenure of which will last as long as eternity." Mr. Chadwick writes, "Occasionally the picture may be overdrawn, but in our dear brother Dobbin's case, the fear is of our saying too little. In this instance, it would tax the most skilful limner to do justice to the original." Surely the preacher, under whose ministry Wm. Dobbin caught the holy fire, merits a lasting memorial.

From a letter to Mr. Nicholson from his wife, dated September, 1858, we learn, that a youth named John Bailey, was drowned in the Canal, whilst his parents were at worship in Broomhedge Chapel. With companions in sin, he had gone out upon a raft to fish, and through the raft overturning, was drowned.

The Revival of 1859 furnishes a stirring chapter in the

history of God's work in Ulster.   Dr. Lynn is correct
when he says : "The majority of the ministers of that day
(prior to the revival) did not believe in sudden conversions,
and much less in the assurance of salvation previous to the
hour of death."*   But the dead churches, in 1859, received
a quickening which has deepened and increased ever since.
Mr. Nicholson had long been a student of Finney and his
passion for saving souls grew with his years, so that 1859
found him ready for the work.   The District Meeting of
1859 appointed him to Bangor, but ere he entered upon this
new sphere of labour, he had the joy of seeing the revival
in full operation at Broomhedge.   At the invitation of
Brother W. J. Robinson, Mr. Alex. Magee visited Broomhedge, and stood up in the chapel to tell a crowd of
earnest hearers about the revival in Ballymacoy.   But soon
a boy gave a piercing shriek, and fell upon the floor
"stricken," and immediately about thirty others fell in
like manner.   W. J. Robinson exhorted the crowd outside
from the door of the chapel, till his voice utterly failed.
The work soon spread in every direction.   Mr. Nicholson
wrote : "Within seven nights, before I came to Bangor,
I witnessed three hundred turned to Jesus, in Broomhedge."
Many of the converts of this period, at Broomhedge, were
known to us.   There were William Mooney and his
earnest family.   William, a short time before his death,
said to the writer: "If it be the Lord's will, I should not
like to suffer long at the last."   He was in his usual
health on the morning of the day he quitted earth for
heaven.   Francis Bailey is working for God to-day, and
rearing a godly family.   Samuel Buchanan is preaching
amongst the Wesleyans in New Zealand, and his brother
William is in Canada.   Robert Tinsley still lives, and

often tells us of "the work in 59." Thomas McClune, a few years ago, died in the Lord. During his last illness, he said to his doctor, "You need not be afraid to let me know if I am going to die, for I am prepared, thank the Lord." There also still live, Wm. H. Totten, a leader, Thos. McCarthy, and Elizabeth A. Dickey. If space allowed, a host of others might be named. It should here be stated, that the Rev. B. Turnock, was Superintendent of the Mission, during the years of the great revival. He took full advantage of the general awakening, and reaped a glorious harvest of souls for the Master. Under his earnest leadership, the Mission acquired a great increase of strength. His son, the Rev. B. B. Turnock, M.A., studied in Q. C., and in Belfast was converted to God. He went as a missionary to China, but returned in a few years utterly broken down in health. After a few years feeble labour at home, he was called to his eternal rest. He was a young man of humble mind, amiable disposition, scholarly tastes and habits, and high Christian culture. Had he lived and regained strength, he would have proved a polished shaft in the Divine quiver.

Mr. Nicholson carried the revival with him to Bangor, coming out of a fire he was aflame with zeal, and inspired with faith for an unprecedented awakening. The people were nearly as hard as the cold rocks of Bangor's coast, but our brother smote the rocks, in the name of Lord, and tears of repentance began to flow. A man who heard him pray in a house where was a *wake*, said: "Mr. Nicholson has stirred up the whole of Bangor." Mr. Nicholson reported his work thus:

"I came to Bangor with fear and trembling. On my arrival, I prepared, and preached in the chapel in the evening, and one soul was led to Christ, who has since united with us in class. I held

open-air services every Sabbath, in various parts of the town.   On
Saturday, Aug. 6th, I visited Mrs. Oliver, who had been striken
down in her own house, and found her full of peace, through faith
in the blood of Christ.   Also visited about seventeen other like
cases.   Aug. 7th.—Preached in Newtonards, and was delighted
to see a large number of young converts, many of whom I had
met at the penitent form, last year.   Preached in the open-air in
Bangor, in the afternoon.   Mr. Hamilton, Primitive, also preached.
Just as we had finished, a womam was stricken down, and carried
into her own house under deep conviction.   After the service in
the chapel at night, I went to visit penitents in Church Street.
J. Wright Crawford, Esq., accompanied me.   His grandfather was
James Wright, of Moyrusk, one of the old pillars of our Church at
Broomhedge.   God is making young Mr. Crawford a great blessing
to the converts.   He is the worthy son of a worthy father, Mr. A.
Crawford, Mount Prospect, Belfast.   Visitation went on half the
night.   Aug. 11th.—As I was closing my sermon a young woman
tried to get out of the chapel, but fell stricken down near the door.
Two Presbyterian ministers gave out psalms outside, and began to
sing, thus attracting the people.   The ministers preached for an
hour.   Aug. 19th.—We had a service outside, and immediately
after, a prayer-meeting inside the chapel.   Three were stricken.
It was one o'clock when I retired to rest.   Sabbath, Aug. 20th.—
Preached on the street; some were afraid to approach me lest they
should be stricken down.   We have, at this date, of those brought
to the Lord at Bangor or its vicinity, about one hundred persons.
Sabbath, 28th.—Had only spoken a few words in the morning,
when a man sunk down in the pew.   I saw him after; he is happy
in Christ.   This day we had some cases that were painful to look
upon.   They wrought convulsed for hours.   They were, at times,
deaf, dumb, and blind.   Mr. M—— and Miss J—— would, at
times, have destroyed themselves, had they not been prevented.
The holy deportment, and manifest joy of the young converts
prove the work to be of God.   This is the fifth week of services in
the chapel, and the interest is deepening and widening every day.
A Roman Catholic, from Armagh, related her experience at one of
our meetings.   Her cousin is a priest.   We have opened the Temperance
Hall for daily mid-day meetings.   The working people come in for
one hour.   I am assisted in this service by the Rev. Mr. M'Cullough,

Presbyterian. One. poor woman was convinced of sin at the midday prayer meeting to-day. We hardly pass one day without hearing of conversions. Thus, God is working, and who shall let Him."

Amongst the phenomena of the revival of 1859 were the "visions," which some of the converts had. They sank into a state of somnolency, in which they saw or thought they saw, the spiritual world—heaven, hell, saints, angels, but above all, Jesus. But a fraction of the number converted at Bangor through Mr. Nicholson's agency joined the Society. The revivalistic work of our earnest brother did not lessen his pastoral labours. Nine members died during the year, and these had had his unwearied attention during their last illness. Under the writer's eye lies in manuscript, a memoir of Robert Patterson, one of the nine deceased. Mr. Nicholson says that this aged pilgrim had joined the Society at Bangor in 1817, and held in turn nearly every office in the Church. He was loyal to the principles of the Connexion; and was held in esteem by all classes. He had a brother in the Wesleyan ministry. Robert Patterson, died in great peace, on February 13th, 1861. During his second year at Bangor, sickness invaded Mr. Nicholson's home, and four of his children were taken from him. One died at the very hour her father was commencing the service on the Sabbath, and another passed away on the Saturday following.

A friend at Bangor, who remembers the particulars of this sad bereavement says, that a feeling of great sympathy moved the congregation when they saw Mr. Nicholson in the pulpit whilst one of his children lay at home a corpse, and another was at the point of death.

Yet he would persist in his work. Mrs. Nicholson wrote a memoir of one of these dear children which we here insert.

CAROLINE MATILDA BAGGALY NICHOLSON.

She was the eldest of four children, who were carried to an early grave by scarlet fever. She was born in Newtonards, Co. Down, on 5th Aug., 1847, and was dedicated to God at her birth by her parents. She was baptized by the Rev. Wm. Baggaly, when we presented her afresh to the Lord.   At an early age she learned to read ; her first reading lesson was from the sacred page—the birth of Jesus Christ. A dear friend from Downpatrick visited us, who was in the habit of praying over the open Bible. After she left us, I went into the bed-room, and found the child on her knees, and the Bible open before her.   I said, "My dear, why have you the Bible, and you cannot read it properly ?" She said, "This is what Miss H. does, and, Oh! it is so nice to feel God will love me, mamma." Being early taught to read, a Testament was given her as a reward for her progress. It was her constant companion. It might be said of her, as of Timothy, that from a child she knew the Scriptures, which, I trust, made her wise unto salvation. One trait in her character worth noticing was truth. In all cases I could depend on her word, even when it implicated herself in a fault.

Many were the questions she asked, and pointed out difficult passages of Scripture she wished explained. It gave me great pleasure to try to sow the seed of the Divine word upon the soil of a tender heart uncontaminated by the things of the world. Thus she grew up, adding each day to her stock of Bible knowledge.

She had premiums for merit from the superintendents of the Broomhedge Sabbath School, when only seven and eight years old; also in Lisburn, she had a handsome Bible given her at an examination there in January, 1857, which she prized highly, and which was her companion in her bedroom every day. When at school her companions were select.

After we removed to Bangor, I sent her and her sister to what I thought a select school, as I was careful about their morals. She often said, " Indeed, mamma, I wish I had not to go, for the girls are so rude; will you allow me to lend them some good books? it might make them better." She became, however, fond of dress ; that was the only thing on which I had to put a restraint. She was backward in speaking in the class, and in course of time she became lukewarm, and lost the ardour of her first love.

During the revival of July, 1859, at Broomhedge, for seven nights before we left it, the mighty power of the Holy Spirit's influence was felt by old and young ; it was estimated that nearly 400 found peace with God through believing. I had the happiness of seeing nearly all my Bible-class made happy in God ; she, too, on 3rd July, while her sister talked with her, saw her need of a Saviour ; and when her father gave an invitation to the anxious to come to be prayed for, she went forward, and for three hours she wrestled with God, until she found peace. She was so weakened that she became unconscious, and was laid on my bed. Her countenance was so changed that her sister did not know her ; when she heard her voice, she clasped her arms round her neck, saying, " Lizzy, dear, I saw my crown, and I will be very sure no one shall wear it but myself." She told all around her what a dear Saviour she had found, and invited another sister to come and love Jesus now.

During the summer of 1860, we had revival services in our chapel at Bangor. Many of our dear friends from Lisburn, Broomhedge, and the Maze visited us, and assisted in the above services. Messrs. J. and D. Carlisle spoke often on the necessity and advantages of serving the Lord in youth. On the last Sabbath in September her father spoke on Luke xv. 7, and the Lord sent the word home to her heart, so that she cried out to me, " Oh, mamma, pray for me." The arrow of conviction had come home to the hearts of two more—a sea captain's wife, and an old sailor. The prayer-meeting was resumed at half-past nine o'clock ; my dear Caroline Matilda received the witness of the Holy Spirit that she was a child of God. The other two were able to testify that Jesus Christ had power on earth to forgive sins. Often did my dear child say that work was light, and her mind happy, since the Lord healed her backslidings.

A friend asked her to come and stop in his house for a time. She was there for a month ; she made herself useful in his shop, and she lamented over the shop girl, that she would not give her heart to God. She had sold an article at a fraction less than the price, and she asked me if a mistake would be counted sin with God. I explained, that sin was the transgression of a known law. She pitied the poor, and would part with her pence to procure comforts for the sick. Never had a mother more comfort with a child than I had with her from the time she found the Saviour.

Grace overcame her naturally hasty temper. She accompanied her father to most of his preaching appointments, and could have repeated the substance of his sermons. It was her joy to make her father and me happy, and to sit by me in God's house. On Sabbath nights she would take care of the other children, to let me go to meeting. She could not sleep at night without a token of love. On two occasions when I said she had forfeited her kiss, she retired to bed, but came down again weeping, saying, ' Do forgive me, mamma, as I cannot sleep; and I will never vex you again.'

"On Feb. 19th, she was quite prostrate in scarlatina; she asked me to pray with her, as her mind had become clouded. While I read Isa. liii. and prayed, she experienced faith, and felt that Jesus was still her Saviour. The fever was so severe she began to wander on the third day, but talked of the love of Christ. When I remarked to her she might die, she said, ' Oh, mamma, I cannot leave you yet, for I have not been as good to you as I might have been, and I have done nothing for Jesus. In twelve days another sister was taken ill, and carried to the bosom of Jesus. Matilda seemed better. She went into the room where two more sisters lay ill. I said we should have prayer together, for the Lord had spared her, though he had taken her two sisters. We prayed together, that was her last day on her feet. The swelling increased round her heart. A second doctor was called in; but dropsy set in, and so rapid was its progress, that on March 25th, both medical men had given her up. On that day our third child and only son passed away to Him who gave him, in the short space of twenty-two days. We thought our cup was full to running over, and while my dear husband, having just commended her to God in prayer, stood by Matilda's bedside weeping, her head being supported by the nurse, the dying child said ' Don't weep for me, papa; I am going to Jesus.' After a pause she added, ' Will you all meet me in heaven?' But God, who is full of compassion, and lays on us no more than we can bear, gave her back from the grave for a month longer, for which we will ever praise Him, When she saw me grieving for the dear little ones who were gone. she would cheer me by saying, 'Sure, mamma, you often prayed that we might be a whole family in heaven; God is answering your prayers, and you should not fret.'

"Several times she said to me, 'It would be better for her to die now, when she was prepared, than to live and perhaps forget God and lose her soul.' She loved prayer so much, that her father prayed two or three times a day with her; and if I did not, she reminded me.

"One of her school companions came to visit her. She said, 'Fanny, I am going to die, I know I am; will you meet me in heaven? Love God, and get your sins pardoned. I am not afraid to die, because Jesus died to save me.' An old woman who came to wash, she often asked to sit by her, pleading with her to forsake sin and love the Saviour. Oft did the poor old woman leave her in tears, and promising to follow her advice. Having some money of her own, she asked to be allowed to give a piece of silver to the old woman; that was her last gift, and only two hours before she departed.

"For six weeks she was not able to lay her head down on the pillow, yet no murmur ever escaped her lips. Six blisters in succession were put on her heart and side, which were very painful. Her sister said, 'How do you bear them, Matilda?' 'I pray to Jesus,' said she, 'and He helps me; you know He suffered more for me.'

"I went into her room, and her tears were falling; I inquired the cause, with alarm. She said, 'I only want Lizzy to live, to love Jesus more, and be kind to father and you when I am gone, and to meet me in heaven.' Once when I thought she was asleep, she said, 'Oh, mamma, that is a beautiful description of the New Jerusalem, in Rev. xxi.; won't it be delightful to be there, and all the little children, too?' It seemed to loosen all the affection that bound her to earth. Two nights before her death she played two tunes on the concertina, and sang to them. She loved music.

> "Rock of ages, cleft for me,
> Let me hide myself in thee."

was a favourite with her; and—

> " There is a fountain filled with blood,
>   Drawn from Immanuel's veins," &c.

She could see from her window the church and cemetery where
her two sisters and brother were laid ; and she contemplated their
rising first and flying up to meet the Lord in the air, to be for ever
with the Lord. The last night was a restless one. She suffered
much, and told her sister she was near her latter end, but did not
wish to talk of it, as it grieved father and me. She urged her to
live near to God, that they might be re-united in heaven. She
slept little, but dreamed she had recovered, and that I was dead ;
and she felt disappointed at her recovery, as she had purposed
being in heaven first, and being able to meet me on my arrival
there, to welcome me. At eleven o'clock she sent for me, saying
she felt weak, and she asked me to talk to her of Jesus. I asked
her if she was still able to hold the promise. " Yes," she said ;
Jesus will be with me in the valley." I pointed her again to the
Lamb of God. She had often said she would like to be a witness
for Jesus, and be able to speak of Him to the last. God gave her
the desire of her heart, and she said aloud—

> " Jesus, my Lord, I know his name ;
>   His name is all my boast :
> Nor will He put my soul to shame,
>   Nor let my hope be lost."

Bless the Lord ! her pain was gone ; she laid her head on my
bosom, and passed away ; without a sigh she fell asleep in Jesus,
aged thirteen years and a half. April 25th, 1861.

During Mr. Nicholson's term in Bangor, a wealthy lady
from Cork, attracted by his earnestness, became one of his
regular hearers while she remained in Bangor. She found
peace through his instrumentality. For many years after,
she sent him subscriptions annually for the poor and other
benevolent objects.

The Summer of 1861 found Mr. Nicholson stationed
again at his loved Broomhedge, where he continued another
period of two years. Though keenly feeling the anguish
of bereavement, yet he entered with all his might into the

Lord's work; and at the end of the first year twenty-one new names were added to the roll of members. Throughout the second year (1862-3), the "cotton famine" cast its dark shadow over the weaving district of the Maze and Broomhedge. The American Campaign began in the spring of 1861, and very soon the five million acres of American Sail, that were under the cotton crop, were isolated from Europe. Hundreds of cotton weavers, scattered over Mr. Nicholson's area of labour, were thrown out of employment, and reduced to the point of starvation. Benevolence was one of our brother's most prominent characteristics, and he often indulged it at the expense of his own and his family's needs. On his way to the railway station he was known to give his last shilling to a needy case, leaving himself without a penny to purchase his ticket. During the cotton famine his benevolence found the fullest active expression. An influential "Relief Committee," to raise funds for the relief of the sufferers of the whole district, composed of gentlemen in and around Lisburn, was formed, and thousands of pounds were raised and carefully disbursed. A. T. Steward, one of New York's millionaires, was a native of the Maze; he did not forget his countrymen in their time of need. In addition to large monetary help, he chartered a ship, and sent a cargo of corn, flour, and bacon.

In addition to disbursing regularly the supplies from the Committee, which involved enormous labour, Mr. Nicholson raised funds and got help from various other sources. Mrs. Nicholson, too, toiled unceasingly amongst the poor, going from house to house and preparing detailed lists for the information of the Committee. She likewise got ladies to help her with their needles, whilst she cut

out garments for the naked. Here is a clipping from
the public press :

"The Rev. S. Nicholson, Broomhedge, has received 63 yards of
broadcloth, value for about £12, from F. M Fox, Esq., Mirfield,
England, through the Rev. J. Livingstone,* Brighouse. The cloth
is being made up for the poor of the district." Also amongst Mr.
Nicholson's memoranda we find a note of thirty blankets received
for the poor."

Referring to this work the Rev. B. Turnock wrote, "I
can bear my testimony to the zeal and energy displayed
by Mr. Nicho'son in relieving the poor; his labours are
very praiseworthy." Over thirty members left Broomhedge station this year in quest of employment, ten of
whom were leaders.

About this time, the Irish Beneficent Society ceased,
and its balance of cash was divided amongst the remaining
annuitants, Mr. Nicholson, being the junior member,
receiving the smallest share. The offer to incorporate
their society with the wealthy English one had been refused by all the Irish brethren, except Mr. Nicholson,
and he was ineligible, being alone.

As another proof that our brother and his family were
in the care of a special Providence, it should be recorded,
that during these years of scarcity, their felt wants were
often supplied in a wonderful manner. One day, Mrs.
Nicholson was in tearful need of fifteen shillings ; Miss
Wright, without being aware of the need, called and left
just this sum. An incident of this period, illustrating the
effect of Mr. Nicholson's pointed preaching, should here
be noted. Bro. R. Tinsley purposed, after morning
preaching, spending the remainder of the Sabbath
amongst worldly friends at a distance. But Mr.

---

* An Irishman.

Nicholson's sermon stopped the devoted man and sent him home again.

Lisburn was Mr. Nicholson's next appointment, where he had laboured so successfully in previous years. This time his incumbency continued six years, till 1869. We shall here give extracts from his published reports of those years, and shall add facts from other sources. "In last June (1863), we had only two places for week-night preaching ;*, now we have seven, besides two weekly prayer-meetings and a Bible class for young men. We have also raised one new class. In these labours God has greatly blessed my own soul. We have had several conversions. A women was led to Christ through reading our tracts, and has since died in peace. One young man was brought to God, and has been made a great blessing since. Providence has blessed him with means, enabling him to devote his whole time to study and the visitation of the poor, etc. We have effected improvements upon the chapel at a cost of £15."

The "cotton famine" still prevailed in Lishurn, and bundles of printed circulars, before us, show that our benevolent brother's labours to relieve the unemployed were prodigious.

" For nine months past (1864-5) this town has suffered much from fever. Several of our families have been broken up by affliction and death. One and another of our old members have been taken from us by death, but our loss is their infinite gain. We held services for seven weeks, every night but Saturday. One of the converts is now in the consumptive hospital. We have 1,200 tracts in circulation." "In the autumn (1865), we held six weeks of revival services. The Rev. D. Round, superintendent, preached for us at one of these services. A young man one night was attracted by the singing, came in, and was converted to God. Soon after he sickened and died, but his end was peace. We return an increase of four members, and fifteen on trial. Glory, glory be to God! One of the little ones (scholars) who often sung 'I want to be angel,' has gone, through the merits of the Saviour, to the angels' home. Not unto us, O Lord, but unto Thy name be the glory !"

Q

On 17th January, 1866, the Rev. Thos. Seymour entered into his eternal rest. He was a man of a very superior mind, an orderly, impressive preacher and a very faithful pastor; and was much beloved and esteemed all over the Mission.

"During the past year (1866-7) two families have left us, one for Belfast, the other for Canada. Mr. B. Jefferson, the head of the latter family, was for twenty years a leader here, and our ministers preached monthly in his house, and that of his father, for more than fifty years. Three of our members have died during the year. Mr. McCoy was ninety-five years of age. He had our ministers to preach in his house for above forty years. Mrs. McConnell also had received quarterly tickets for more than fifty years. Brother Samuel Atkinson, a promising young man, an exhorter and leader, also died. His illness was short, but his anchor was cast within the vail. In January, I was laid aside by severe illness, which continued six weeks. The Lord raised me up from the borders of the grave. May it be to show forth His glory more and more."

We remember Mr. B. Jefferson mentioned in the foregoing extract. He was a quiet brother till 1859, when he received a mighty baptism of the Holy Ghost, and ever after he spoke and prayed with marvellous power. When praying he would sometimes unconsciously move upon his knees along the floor, and his fellow-suppliants would have to shift out of their place to allow him to pass. A few years ago, from Danville, Knox County, Ohio, U.S.A., he wrote a letter to Brother James Carlisle, or rather began the letter, for he was "called home" on 7th December, 1883, before he had finished it: it was concluded by his daughter. We give an extract from it:—"My eldest son died of typhoid fever. Thomas, the youngest, has just completed his medical studies and obtained his Diploma. My daughter, S. J., is the wife of Dr. Balmer, who has a fine practice and acquired a rich property. They are both members of the M.E.C.; they teach in the Sabbath School, and my daughter presides at the organ." In the Magazine, March, 1868, from the pen of Mr. Nicholson, appeared a memoir of Samuel Atkinson, to whom reference is made in the above extract; also by the same writer, in the Magazine for October of the same year, a memoir is given of James Atkinson, a brother of Samuel's. In the latter touching biography, Mr. Nicholson says, "It was a painful scene to visit the family. The father trying to make himself strong for duties he was not able to perform; the elder brother passing away in consumption, and poor James as weak as a child." The father alluded to produced oil paintings of high artistic merit. He was an humble, devoted man of God. Mrs. Hunter, his daughter, who had been bereaved of her husband, resided with the afflicted ones. In a brief space the four of them passed away in consumption. Mr. Nicholson was to the dying ones like a ministering angel, yea more, for there flowed from his heart human sympathy and a Christian brother's love and condolence.

Mr. Nicholson attended the Huddersfield Conference of 1867 as Irish Representative, and his devoted wife accompanied him to England. High Street Chapel, where the Conference held its sittings, for capacity, cheerfulness, and richness of architectural design, stood unrivalled amongst the sanctuaries of Huddersfield. Upwards of eighty religious services had been arranged for, in connection with this Conference. The Rev. John Taylor was President. A new costly chapel, very little inferior to the one just described, had recently been opened at Lindley. Here Mr. Nicholson preached on the first Sabbath of Conference, and the large congregation gave ample proof that they greatly enjoyed the earnest, fluent, eloquent sermon of the Irish missionary.   They acknowledged that God was in the preacher, and the Holy Ghost in his word.   At the Conference Missionary Meeting our brother had the privilege of relating some of his experiences as an Irish missionary, and his narrative was well received by the vast assembly.   The Rev. John Stokoe, who spoke immediately before him, humorously referred to Mr. Nicholson as 'the wild Irishman;' but his words met with marked disfavour generally.   Upon his return Mr. Nicholson took delight in describing to his Irish friends the wealth, liberality, earnest piety and ungrudging hospitality of Huddersfield Methodism.

" We have this year (1867-8), as usual, to report several removals. One of our young women, an earnest worker, emigrated to New York, where she is at present employed as a Bible-reader in the Methodist Episcopal Church.   We held special services in the chapel, also open-air services in different places." Mr. Nicholson's last year (1868-9) at Lisburn was one of excessive toil.   A scheme to renovate and reconstruct the Chapel was entered upon, at a cost of about £150, and the labour of raising the money fell principally upon the minister.   He was no stranger to this kind of work, and feeling it was for the Lord, he pursued it as prayerfully as he did the most spiritual labour, and he always attributed his great success in raising funds to the immediate help of God.   He succeeded in effecting the improvements, and in raising nearly the whole of the money.   He continued to preach occasionally at Broomhedge. One day on his way thither, he took a seat in a cart, at the request of the driver.   Soon the horse ran off, and the cart was overturned, covering Mr. Nicholson in a ditch.   The Lord preserved his servant from injury."

About this time, with their father's sanction, and under the wise oversight of their mother, two of Mr. Nicholson's daughters opened a business at Lisburn, which they diligently pursued for a few years.   Miss Nicholson from

1861 till her marriage was teacher of a Day School at
Lissue. J. N. Richordson, Esq., supported the school.
He and his amiable daughter were most kind to Miss
Nicholson, whose labours were highly appreciated.

CHAPTER X.

MEET FOR THE INHERITANCE.

" Less, less of self each day, less of the world and sin :
More of Thy Son I pray, more of Thyself within.
More moulded to Thy will in all things I would be :
Higher and higher still, liker and liker Thee.
Riper and riper now, each hour let me become,
More fit to serve below, more meet for heaven above."

Bonar.

WE are able to speak of the subject of these memorials from personal knowledge, having had fraternal intercourse with him from 1865 onward. The terms "peculiar" and "eccentric" were applied to him; and, no doubt. in some respects, he was not as other men are. It would seem that his nervous system was not in a state of normal strength ; and perhaps on this account he had not always a due measure of control over his mental states and general deportment. He was liable, too, to act upon sudden impulses; and he was easily imposed upon. His nervous, restless, temperament made him impatient of the self-restraint which close attention to the details of any business required. Mathematical problems to him would have been an agony. At the Annual District Meeting, he was required to read a schedule, giving a statistical account of members and of his Circuit's financial transactions during the year, and the effort seemed always to excite his brain unduly. The bare enumeration of so many members deceased or removed or added to the Church did not satisfy him. As he read, revival scenes would rise before his mind, painful partings, or triumphant deaths would recur to his memory; and he would lay aside the "dry figures," and describe he visions of his mind and the emotions of his heart. Indeed, we have seen him lay aside his schedule half read and deliver a stirring address on the work of God generally.

But if in some respects he was weak, in all virtue and goodness and purity of aim he was eminenly strong. He was "an Israelite indeed, in whom was no guide;" and he was, all through life, the simple child of a special Providence. The hand of God was specially seen in giving our brother a wife who was fully able and willing to help her husband, just where he specially needed human help. As God gave him one of the wisest and best of mothers, so He gave him one of the most suitable and devoted of wives.

> "A guardian angel o'er his life presiding,
> Doubling his pleasures, and his cares dividing."

Mrs. Nicholson says that she, and her husband too, noticed that immediately before any special trial came upon them, God seemed to prepare His servant for it, by giving him a special manifestation of His favour and Spirit. For example, before their great bereavement in Bangor, Mr. Nicholson had a vision of his Saviour's glory, which filled him with wonder, love, and praise. Under the weight of glory he fell prostrate before God, and seemed

for a time in a trance. The glory of this visitation remained with him, supporting his mind throughout the
terrible affliction.

Our brother was one of Nature's most ardent lovers.

> "'Tis born with all: the love of Nature's works
> Is an ingredient in the compound Man,
> Infused at the creation of the kind."

We have seen him rejoicing in the sun, and gazing with
rapture upon the summer landscape. We have heard
him describe with delight the peaceful seasons of rest and
enjoyment he had had in the seclusion of his own garden,
amongst the bees and butterflies and flowers. Gentle
Nature often threw her rich mantle o'er him, quieting his
agitation, and reminding him of the rest in the Eden
above. In his Diary, his allusions to the seasons are
frequent. He noted the appearance of the flowers of
spring, and of the swallow. He recorded the date of the
cookoo's advent.

> "Thrice welcome, darling of the Spring!
>   Even yet thou art to me,
> No bird: but an invisible thing,
>   A voice, a mystery."

It was his delight to gather his children around him,
and tell them of Nature's works and wonders. In this
way, he found agreeable lessons for them upon the
character of the Creator.

> " Receive
> Thanks, blessings, love, for these, Thy lavish boons,
> And most of all, their heavenward influences,
> O Thou that gav'st us flowers ! "

The briefest sketch of our brother would be defective
which failed to mention his cheerfulness and humour.
On a soiree platform he was a favourite, as he generally

had a cheerful word for all, and a healthy humorous allusion for the young. Amongst his children, he could be as mirthful as they. Indeed the more sedate mamma, who sometimes took a more sombre view as to Christian propriety, felt it her duty, at times, to remonstrate with father and children with reference to their excessive mirthfulness.

Dr. Clarke said that with him it was an axiom, that the sermon which did good was a good sermon. Judged by this test, Mr. Nicholson preached good sermons. The preacher himself was an influential part of the sermon. His matter was severely evangelical; of the "down grade" Theology, he had a perfect horror. Like Gideon Ouseley, he knew the "Disease and the Remedy;" and his sermons were mainly an exposure of the disease and an exposition and recommendation of the remedy. A certain erratic newspaper correspondent wrote, that Mr. Nicholson dwelt much upon "the blue blazes of dark damnation." This was as false as it was offensive and profane. He never used the language quoted. Sad to relate, he who wrote the scurrilous criticism died intoxicated in a public house a short time since. Mr. Nicholson, believing that an endless hell was no myth, warned his hearers with tearful earnestness to flee from the wrath to come. But the burden of his sermons was the love of God in the redemption of the world by our Lord and Saviour, Jesus Christ. We have heard him preach with glowing fervour from John iii. 16, his own heart all aflame with the love he was eloquently describing.

He loved his Bible and knew it well. To us he once said, "I never use a concordance." He did not suffer "atrophy" of either brain or heart. To him the whole Bible was God's Word. Of this he had the witness in

himself. His faith begat faith in his hearers. On the
wings of faith, he soared aloft quite beyond the region of
human philosophies. To his faith's interior eye, "the in-
visible appeared in sight, and God was seen by mortal
eye." He loved the pulpit, and greatly enjoyed his own
sermons. To him the holy excitement of the sacred desk
was an exhilaration and inspiration. He loved the souls
of men, and while striving to attract them to the cross, he
was himself drawn nearer to Christ ; and all his sanctified
faculties were stimulated and strengthened in the exercise.

We have him at this moment before our mental vision.
It is the occasion of a united love-feast, representing the
three circuits—Lisburn, Priesthill, and Broomhedge, the
service being at the last place. The people nearly fill
the chapel, and still they come. Mr. Nicholson stands
erect in the pulpit ; he was born of the Spirit in a love-
feast, and now his whole being is in full sympathy with
the occasion ; his chin rests calmly enough on the full
folds of his white cravat ; he seems calm and self-possessed,
but looking more closely, we detect in the preacher, strong
indications of deep emotion. He has been on his knees
many times since the dawn of the hallowed day, and there
rests upon him a divine unction, but he expects a yet
richer induement. He knows every individual before him;
and as the later comers from a distance enter the sacred
edifice, his heart goes out to them in fraternal greeting.
We detect a nervous huskiness in his voice, as he reads
out the words of the hymn,—" And are we yet alive," &c.
His eye kindles. About his features, there is a perceptible
muscular excitement. His inspirations deepen ; his breast
heaves with emotion. Now the whole congregation
prostrate themselves on their knees before God, and the

pent up emotions of the preacher find vent in fervent prayer. Many a hearty "Amen!" is heard all around.

"Heaven comes down their souls to greet,
And glory crowns the mercy-seat."

Prayer has strengthened the preacher, and now he announces his text. The sermon has cost him much prayerful thought, and the voice within has said to him— "Surely I will be with thee." It is a true prophet that now speaks, moved and enlightened by the Holy Ghost. The preacher "begins low, proceeds slow, rises higher, strikes fire;" but the fire is from off the Divine altar. The Gospel from his lips comes not "in word only, but also in power, and in the Holy Ghost, and in much assurance." If the sermon is not constructed strictly after any distinct homiletic standard, or if the illustrations are not all relevant to the subject, the preacher's appeals to the conscience and heart are none the less powerful and persuasive on that account. And the people enjoy the Word, and in the love-feast gratefully testify to the help and comfort derived from it. It may here be appropriate to say, that to us Mr. Nicholson once said, alluding to himself, "You know, Brother Thomas, God is able to strike a straight blow with a crooked stick."

In 1869, Mr. Nicholson was again appointed to Newtonards, where he laboured till 1874. He found the Chapel in need of extensive repairs, and with a heavy and increasing debt upon it. He never was the man to shirk a duty because it was difficult and unpleasant; and so, trusting in God, he resolved that the repairs should be effected and the debt removed. Both objects were accomplished, but the effort nearly cost him his life. The ordinary annual income of the Society had reached the low figure of about forty-five pounds, under our friend's incumbency it reached the average of over sixty-nine. He received eighty-five members; but soon his returns showed one hundred and twenty, with over twenty on trial. In the five years, he raised towards repairs and debt about £200. The Rev. J. Innocent visited Newton-ards in 1869, and lectured on China, in the Town Hall; Mr. Nicholson, of course, attended to all details, including the collection for the China Mission. His financial efforts did not arrest his direct, spiritual, and philanthropic labours. He kept two thousand tracts in constant circulation, held special services regularly, in the open air as well as indoors. He likewise laboured incessantly in the interests of total abstinence, allying himself with the Temperance League, and the Good Templars in the crusade against liquordom. In 1871, application was made for a spirit licence for a shop near the Methodist New Connexion Church. Mr. Nicholson was mainly instrumental in getting up two petitions to the magistrates, who presided at the Quarter Sessions, against the granting of the licence. One of the petitions measured about three yards in length. He was cautioned that he would be in danger of bodily hurt if he persisted in this work, but our intrepid brother feared God only; and he succeeded with the magistrates, they refusing the licence.

About this time another striking evidence of the Divine care was experienced by Mr. Nicholson. He left home for the District Meeting, but unexpectedly missed the train. Soon after the tidings reached him, that the train, which he regretted missing had run off the rails, and two passengers lost their lives.

The writer, being unable for full work, resided a year (1872-3) in Newtownards, and saw his zealous friend at

work. It was evident to all that Mr. Nicholson's supreme
aim was the salvation of souls.

> Give souls to me, dear Lord, 1 cry,
>   Souls redeemed at greatest cost.
> See lowly at Thy feet I lie;
>   Send *me* to seek and save the lost.

He often had the joy of seeing souls saved at the
prayer meeting, after the service on Sabbath evenings.
It was necessary to remonstrate with him about the undue
extent of his benevolence. He lived not for himself : his
was

> "A heart at leisure from itself
>   To soothe and sympathise."

He laboured beyond his strength, and thus brought on
serious attacks of sickness. For many weeks, in 1874, he
lay on a sick bed, his life trembling in the balance, the
cause of his illness being exhaustion from over-work.
But he said the affliction was to him a special means of
grace. If he did not " learn in suffering what he taught
in song," he ranked with those who did so learn, but in a
lower degree, and in a different department of service.

Ballyclare, where he had been stationed twice before,
was Mr. Nicholson's final appointment, in 1874. The
records of his labours here till 1886 are before us. They
exhibit, in increased measure, the chief features which all
along characterised this life-long worker for God : his
loyalty to truth, unbounded benevolence, unwearied
industry, evangelistic zeal, ingenuity and versatility of
methods plainly appear. The expansion of his Temperance creed kept pace with the increase of knowledge
upon the injurious effects of alcohol. He came to see
that the use of inebriating drinks finds no favour in the
Word of God. He likewise learned that a beverage

which was unfit for his own table was out of place upon
the Lord's Table. And his confidence in the medicinal
use of intoxicants broke down altogether. Ballyclare
abounded in public houses, and our earnest Temperance
reformer laboured incessantly to correct their baneful
influence. We shall here transcribe extracts from Mr.
Nicholson's published reports and private journal, giving
the year in brackets:—

(1874-5) "We formed a Band of Hope, which has been a
success. The Chapel has been made comfortable, and an old debt
of over ten pounds paid off. Mrs. Connelly suddenly fell asleep in
Jesus; her life was one grand testimony of her intense love to
God. (1875-6) "A spirit of controversy was promoted by an
Antinomian on the subject of immersion. I feel it a duty to note
the more than brotherly kindness of the Rev. R. C. Turner in helping us in the Chapel and Manse affairs," (1876-7) "We have to
record the happy death of a young man, who passed away rejoicing in a knowledge of his acceptance with God. Open-air services
were held. The Sabbath School continues to prosper." (1877-8)
"We have had deaths, one of whom was Wm. Connelly, one of the
founders of our church here. He exercised a holy influence, and
was much beloved. As a local preacher he was intelligent and
acceptable. He lived to a good old age." (1878-9) Trade has
been much depressed. The out-door services and special meetings
held in the chapel have been owned of God. We have improved
the chapel at a cost of about £12." (1879-80) "We have spent £6
in new lamps, &c., for the chapel. We have lost two members by
death, one of whom was Miss Logan, who attended our services
regularly, although she resided two-and-half miles from the
chapel. Amongst her last words were, 'Christ is near, Christ is
precious." A memoir of Miss J. A. Logan from Mr. Nicholson's
pen, appeared in the *Magazine* for July, 1880. She was an earnest
Christian worker. (1880-1) "During the winter we held special
services for three weeks, and the Church experienced a great
quickening. The training of the young has been attended with
good results. Our open-air and cottage services have been well
attended." "Our eldest daughter is with us on a visit for health

I prayed much to the Lord for her recovery, during her recent dangerous illness, and, bless His name, He heard the distressed father's cry. To preach the Gospel has always been to me a delight, yet God could easily do without me. He has hitherto supplied all our temporal need. £10 have just come to us from New Zealand. I am often unwell now, but the Lord supports me and often fills me with Himself, and gives me to taste the sweetness of His Word. I am now sixty-nine years of age, and have been preaching the Gospel forty-four years. Oh! the goodness of God to me." (1881-2) "Our oldest member, Nancy McVeigh, has passed on to her home in the skies, aged 92. Six new windows have been put in the chapel. I beg to record the uniform kindness of Rev. J. W. Williams, in helping us in many ways. I earnestly desire that the few remaining days of my life may be spent in seeking to save my beloved countrymen." (1882-3) "We circulated about five thousand Temperance tracts. Large numbers enrolled themselves as members of the Total Abstinence Army. A few earnest Christians united in daily supplication for an outpouring of the Spirit. On Nov. 5, the Rev. J. W. Williams preached three sermons, when several young people were deeply impressed. At the close of the third service, and before all the people had retired, a dear girl suddenly knelt upon the mat at the door of the chapel, unable to leave the place till consciously forgiven. The cottage meetings became too crowded, and the chapel had to be opened, and meetings were held nightly for about five months, God's power was richly experienced, and the conversions were numerous. To give an adequate description of the meetings would be impossible. The work seemed like a repetition of the revival of '59. About forty were gathered out of the world. Some of the conversions are specially interesting." One was that of Andrew McL—, a drunkard. He was seen early on Sunday morning mad in drink, with an axe over his shoulder, threatening his wife. Mrs. Nicholson courageously faced the furious man, and induced him to return to his bed. By service time, he was nearly sober and out again, when Mr. Nicholson warned him in terms which increased the miserable man's horror of mind from a dream he had had during the interval from the scene of early morning. He found his way to the chapel, where prayer was being made for him, and there became a new creature in Christ Jesus. He has remained steady ever since. This glorious revival extended to the Wesleyan chapel, and it was reckoned that about three hundred persons in all professed conversion.

(1883-4) "Thank God, the work of last year has proved its genuineness by its permanence. Two of our old members and leaders died during the year, one suddenly, and the other, Mr. Jas. Scott, was ill for some weeks, but was very happy and died in the Lord. Mr. Jas. Williams preached for me occasionally. May the Lord make him a useful, if not a brilliant man. [Mr. J. W. is now in the ministry.] It greatly rejoices my spirit to see the steadiness of Mr. Logan's three sons who were converted in the recent revival. I am now in my seventy-third year. Oh! how short is life. How feeble seem all my past efforts; yet for fifty years my aim has been to exalt Christ." (1884-5) "The fruit of the Revival of '83 appears at the present in town and country. John Millar, one of the converts, is now a local preacher. This young man a few years since, became an agent of the Blue Ribbon Army, and his labours have been much blessed. (1885-6) "About the end of October I caught a severe cold, which brought me near to the gates of death. The Rev. E. Hall visited us and preached to our people. He also sent good supplies to fill the pulpit during my illness. James Dixon, a retired soldier, who was converted at Aldershot, and who lost an arm at the battle of Tel-el-keber, returned to Ballyclare, his native place, and began to work for the Lord. He conducted meetings amongst our people, and through his instrumentality souls have been converted to God."

Mr. Nicholson took a deep, practical interest in this Dixon. He was taken up by the Wesleyans, and has been now, for some years, a successful agent in connection with their Tent Mission over the country. About this year a man opened a new shop in Ballyclare, for the sale of spirits as well as groceries. He attended *Bethel* one night and heard Mr. Nicholson preach from Exodus xii., 30. The preacher denounced intoxicants as having injured nearly every family in the land; and his words against the liquor traffic were most scathing. A cautious " friend " complained that the liquor seller would "never enter Bethel again." But the man abandoned the immoral traffic, gave his heart to God, and settled down as a worshipper at Bethel.

A scrap from our venerable brother's occasional memoranda will serve to exhibit the rigour with which he examined his heart and life in the presence of a holy God. It is dated November 15th, 1885, and is in part a summary of inditements against himself. He writes, "(1) I have read other books to the neglect of the Bible. (2) I have often talked to no good purpose, and thus grieved the Spirit. (3) I fear I have been worldly in little things, which have engaged too much of my thoughts and time. (4) I have grieved the Spirit by neglecting my health. (5) My will, at times, has not been wholly the Lord's. (6) To the newspaper I have given too much precious time. (7) I should have devoted more time to prayer and praise." Here our conscientious brother turns to the brighter side and adds, "(1) Yet, I can say, "The blood of Jesus Christ his Son cleanseth *me* from all sin." And I have had glorious manifestations of God to my soul all through my life. (2) It has been my highest joy for fifty years to hold up Jesus Christ and Him crucified before perishing men; and while doing so I have felt the power of the Holy Ghost. (3) At this moment Jesus to me is all and in all. 'Fixed on this ground will I remain,' etc."

"Father Nicholson's" last sermon in the open air was delivered in the summer of 1885, in a field, to a large audience. The sermon exhibited much of the fervour and power of former days, and the preacher's voice seemed as strong as ever. But afterwards exhaustion ensued; and soon followed feebleness, depression and disease. For

R

many months of the year he was a great sufferer; agonising pain wrecked his body, and it was thought at times he could not survive. In the Spring of 1886, he partially recovered; but he had to write to the District Meeting, asking to be relieved from the regular work.

Resolution of the Methodist New Connexion Conference of 1886:—

"That this Conference cannot allow our esteemed and venerable brother, the Rev. Samuel Nicholson, to retire from the active service of the Ministry without taking fraternal recognition of the same, and testifying its high regard and Christian affection for our brother. It devoutly recognises the goodness of God in sparing him to the advanced age of seventy-five, forty-six years having been spent, but with few short intermissions, in laborious circuit work in different parts of Ireland. Amidst many privations and much personal inconvience, our brother has held on his way, being in labours more abundant, preaching, visiting, collecting everywhere as opportunity afforded for the Church's material benefit and spiritual edification. Nor has he laboured in vain, nor spent his strength for nought, as many souls have been won to Christ by his instrumentality, and now, that through advancing years and enfeebled health he is compelled to retire and become a Supernumery, it prays that the consolation of Divine grace and the comfort of the Gospel of Jesus which he has ministered to others may stay and strengthen his own soul till that day when the Lord shall give to him and all who love His appearing a crown of rejoicing saying 'Well done, good and faithful servant, enter thou into the joy of Thy Lord.'"

Father Nicholson's final residence was Ashfield, Lisburn. Here he could have daily correspondence with his loved daughter, Mrs. Bailey, and her children, whose society was a great comfort to him. His children and grandchildren seemed to grow dearer to our venerable friend as age and feebleness extreme increased upon him. Upon his retirement to Lisburn, he wrote to his eldest daughter, Mrs.

Mackinlay, "You never knew how much I loved you." Imposed inaction was to our brother his greatest trial. Soon he established a prayer meeting in his own house for "the aged and infirm" around him, whom he visited as his strength would allow. Surely his Master will say to him at the last. "I was sick and ye visited me." Mr. Neill says "Mr. Nicholson's visits were frequent, and as he passed through, he spoke words of warning and love to the people whom he found in our place of business. Often, too, on the Sunday he would address the congregation in his loved *Salem* for about fifteen minutes; and he seemed greatly to enjoy the class after the service."

It was Mr. Nicholson's delight to the last to disseminate wholesome literature. He highly valued Dr. Cooke's works, and was the means of introducing them into many families. He occasionally attended the mid-week meetings of the Society of Friends and spoke as the Spirit inclined him, and his visits were well received. Early in the year, he published an earnest tract on "The Revival of Religion." The following is transcribed from *The Northern Whig* : —

ADDRESS AND PRESENTATION
TO THE
REV. SAMUEL NICHOLSON, LISBURN.

Dear Sir,—A few friends, having learned that you had retired from the active work of the ministry, consider the present a most suitable time to mark in some way the high esteem in which you are held, and the endearing relationship you sustain to the Church of the Lord Jesus. Fifty years of faithful and earnest toil have given to your labours an almost Apostolic character, and, now that you are no longer able to engage in the arduous duties of ministerial life, we pray the great Head of the Church to spare you long, and to bestow upon you and your worthy helpmate, " a mother in Israel," all the blessings needful for the present life, and finally may an abundant entrance be ministered unto you into the everlasting kingdom. We beg your acceptance of this small sum of money for present needs, and, on behalf of the Subscribers, we are yours faithfully,

SAMUEL M'CONNELL.
THOS. A. FULLERTON.

8th December, 1886.

REPLY.

MR. CHAIRMAN AND DEAR FRIENDS,—It is hard for me to find words to express my gratitude to you on this occasion. When I at first entered upon the work of the ministry I did not expect such honour would be conferred upon me when I should retire from active service in the Church of Christ. I was early dedicated to Christ by a pious mother, and converted to God when only eleven years old. I have now been sustained for nearly fifty years in this great work of preaching Christ and Him crucified.

In hearing of your kind testimonial to me I felt under a sense of very great unworthiness. I desire to give the Lord all the glory of His grace in me.

You speak of my labours for Christ. Well, we had toil at the first in the Mission work that few have to endure now. Often we were out every night in the month from house to house, never at home for weeks, as at that time we lived much amongst the people, and many young preachers had not any settled lodgings. We travelled many miles in the week in all kinds of weather, and in barns and private houses we proclaimed the unsearchable riches of Christ, and hitherto hath the Lord helped us. I do feel grateful in my heart of hearts for the kind expressions of your respects for us, and for your valuable cheque to me, handed to me by our worthy friend, Mr. M'Connell, in the chair. It also cheers me much to learn from you that the members of other Christian Churches have lent their willing aid, and also did this with expressions of goodwill to me and respect and love.

It is also most gratifying to find Mr. Thomas Fullerton, who is first in every good cause, as one of the leading men on the committee, acting with energy and zeal to get up this Testimonial to me, although a local preacher in the Wesleyan Church. All the above facts point, to the signs of the times, when Ephraim shall not vex Judah, nor Judah, Ephraim, but names and sects and parties fall, and Thou, O Christ, be all in all.

I must again thank you from the [bottom of my heart for this kindness, and it surely must lead me closer to the people of the Lord and to Jesus, the great Master; I must still work for IIis glory as ability will enable me to the end of life.

S. NICHOLSON.

The following account of our venerable brother's last hours is in substance that of his faithful wife. She says, " On the Saturday prior to his death, my dear husband took seriously ill at our daughter's, Mrs. Bailey's. She sent him home in a carriage. He suffered intensely from acute pain, but slept a few hours during the night, and in the morning was somewhat better. Mr. Robinson held the prayer meeting in our house. His visit was much enjoyed by the afflicted one. Mrs. Bailey visited her father in the evening, which proved her last visit. He asked her who had spoken at the meeting (Friends) that day, and what had been the subject of Mr. Pim's address. " Well, my dear," he enquired, " do *you* ever speak for God?" " I do," she replied, " privately, but not publicly." " You should," he added, " embrace every suitable opportunity to testify of God's goodness to you. You are the child of many prayers, and God has done great things for you." He then asked her to pray with him, and as the child poured out her heart in intercession for the dying father, Heaven seemed to fill the chamber. On Monday, the dear sufferer seemed no worse, and was able to lead in prayer at family worship, our daughter, Isabella, reading the 91st Psalm at his request.

On Tuesday morning, being the day before the Queen's Jubilee Day, he prayed earnestly for Her

Majesty's highest well-being In the evening, the doctor, whom I called in, thought my husband would be better in a day or two. But during the night, the pain from which he suffered increased in severity. On Wednesday, at 7 a.m., Mr. Neill, at my request by a messenger, hurried out to see the dear, and as it proved, the dying sufferer, whose whispered testimonies were, "Christ is precious," "I shall soon be at home," "Jesus will never leave me or forsake me." During Mr. Neill's earnest prayer, he whispered hearty responses. Mr. Neill noticed that the hand which grasped his was as " cold as death." I too was struck with the coldness of my dear one's hands, and I wrapped them in a warm shawl. Up to this time, I did not know he was dying, but now the truth flashed upon me. I said, "Father, you have comforted many a one in death." He said, " Jesus is mine and I am his; He will never leave me nor forsake me." I repeated to him the words of the hymn:—"Jesus, lover of my soul," etc, and he seemed mentally to repeat them with me. At length, he cast a last look at me and then closed his eyes, and immediately there reposed on his countenance the stillness of death; suddenly, a ray of light beamed through the window and shone upon the departed one's placid face. Oh! it was beautiful! His face shone with the brightness.

Mr. Nicholson's earthly life thus closed on June 22nd, 1887. The funeral took place on June 25th. A short service was held in the house before the coffin was removed, when the Rev. J. Shone read a suitable chapter, and the Rev. E. Thomas delivered a short address. As the coffin passed to the hearse, the Rev. Canon Pounden, of the Cathedral, Lisburn, placed a wreath upon the coffin lid. Several clergymen and ministers formed part of the funeral cortege, as it passed through the town. J. N. Richardson, Esq. (Society of Friends) was also at the funeral, likewise Lawson Brown, Esq., of Belfast. Mr. Nicholson's remains were interred in Bangor Churchyard, beside those of his four children. The Rev. S. Black (Episcopalian), of Ballyclare, was present at the grave. The Revs. E. Hall, T. Porteus, and M. M. Todd, officiated at the interment. Mrs. Bailey also spoke at her father's grave.

> " Marble will moulder, monuments decay,
> Time sweep memorials from the earth away ;
> But lasting records are of good men given ;
> The date, eternity ; the archives, heaven.
> There living tablets, with their worth engraved,
> Stand forth for ever, in the souls they saved."

Ann Lutton.

www.ingramcontent.com/pod-product-compliance
Lightning Source LLC
Chambersburg PA
CBHW020847270326
41928CB00006B/582